CHRISTIANITY
in CANADA

CHRISTIANITY *in* CANADA

HISTORICAL ESSAYS

by

JOHN S. MOIR

edited by
PAUL LAVERDURE

with a foreword by
MARK G. McGOWAN

Redeemer's Voice Press

Printed and bound in Canada

Text Design: Redeemer's Voice Press
Cover Design: Duncan Campbell
Printing: Peerless Printers '96 Ltd.

National Library of Canada Cataloguing in Publication Data

Moir, John S., 1926 -
    Christianity in Canada

    Published in association with: Redeemer's Voice Press.
    Includes bibliographical references.
    ISBN 0-9688813-0-0

    1. Canada — Church history.   2. Christianity—Canada.
I. Laverdure, Paul.   II. Title
BR570.M58 2001   277.1   C2001-911380-3

The Ukrainian Catholic Mission of the Most Holy Redeemer, Redeemer's Voice Press, and Laverdure & Associates gratefully acknowledge the Jackman Foundation of Toronto for its sponsorship of this book.

Redeemer's Voice Press   Laverdure & Associates
165 Catherine Street   Box 246
Yorkton, SK   Gravelbourg, SK
S3N OB9   SOH 1XO

Table of Contents

Editor's Preface

This is a selection from John Moir's essays written over a period of nearly half a century. Some have already been published but often they appeared in small journals that were only found in the largest research libraries. The rest had been given as speeches and were never available to a wider audience. I had read some of them and heard others even before meeting Professor Moir in 1984 and I remember thinking how they were examples of solid scholarship. I travelled to the University of Toronto and began a doctorate in history with John Moir as my thesis supervisor.

Over the years I collected the articles, discussed them with the author, and decided on the following articles as the best of Moir. Others are still in print and were thus left out of this collection. It is time to share these essays with people interested in the history of Christianity in Canada.

John Moir often called himself, "an average, garden-variety historian." In the fifty years since John Moir began writing about Canadian religious history, what was then an uncultivated field of research has blossomed into a vibrant and challenging garden thanks to his work and to the solid work of later generations of scholars. There has been no attempt to add information here about more recent publications in this field because that would duplicate several excellent bibliographies already available.

Each essay is preceded by a short account of the occasion for which that essay was prepared. Original typographical errors have been corrected. Very occasionally it seemed desirable to make minor changes in sentence structure and paragraphing, and in one case to remove material repeated by a later essay. The notes have been converted to a single style.

I wish to thank John's son Ian and Ian's wife Marta for transcribing the texts into electronic form. Jacqueline Moir, John's wife, helped at every step of the way, as she has done in many other projects that have John as author. The Jackman Foundation and a number of Professor Moir's former students have helped to make this volume financially possible.

Paul Laverdure

Foreword

John Sargent Moir was born in Toronto on February 14, 1926. The elder of Hazel and Richard Moir's two children, John attended Queen Victoria Public School and Parkdale Collegiate. Perhaps a greater influence on him than his formal education was his paternal grandfather, Richard Moir, a retired "country schoolteacher" (sometimes called "the dominie"), who resided with the Moirs on Cowan Avenue in Parkdale. Many years later, John recalled that his grandfather's funeral, in 1948, left a lasting impression on him. John was struck by the number of people from the rural areas of Simcoe County who came to pay their last respects to "the teacher." Whether he knew it or not at the time, John's grandfather, and the sense of importance attached to "the teacher," would lead John into the same profession.

Just prior to the end of the Second World War, John entered Victoria College at the University of Toronto, where he spent four years studying in that institution's honours history program. Upon graduation in June 1948, he was encouraged by his professors to continue his studies at the graduate level. In 1949, under the supervision of constitutional historian Chester Martin, John earned his Master of Arts degree, writing a thesis on the evolution of the political ideas of the *Christian Guardian*, the principal organ of the Methodists in Upper Canada.[1] He then embarked on a Ph.D. under the supervision of the eminent Canadian historian Donald Grant Creighton.

Both Moir and his supervisor had differing visions of what topic would be selected for the doctoral dissertation. The student was determined to write a thesis on the Rebellion of 1837 in Upper Canada—a topic very much in keeping with the contemporary historiographical emphasis on politics, nation building, and the struggle for responsible government in the United Canadas. (Decades later John would delight in asking doctoral candidates questions on the Union period during their oral examinations, knowing full-well that many young historians tended to gloss over the 1840s and 1850s in their preparation of the Canadian field—a sign of historiographical changes in the 1970s and 1980s). John never wrote the definitive work on the Rebellion, although he did publish a selection of rhymes and verses from the conflict in later years.[2] In the end, "the supervisor" prevailed; Creighton convinced John to continue exploring some of the themes from his M.A. on the *Guardian*. In 1954, John earned his doctorate, having produced an impressive study on Church-State relations in Upper Canada that would effectively thrust him into the forefront of the "new" religious history in Canada.[3]

Five years later, the dissertation was published by the University of Toronto Press under the title *Church and State in Canada West: Three Studies in the Relation of Denominationalism and Nationalism, 1841-1867* and was the inaugural volume in the press's Canadian Studies in History and Government Series. John used three episodes in the Union period—the Clergy Reserves, the university question, and separate schools—as foci for his discussion of the competing forces of "centrifugal denominationalism" and "centripetal nationalism." While the volume tended to see the advance of the latter at the expense of the former in each of the three cases, John explored in detail the compromises that were effected between Church and State. Such compromises included the creation of a secular University, but with federated religious colleges and a Common Public school system with an optional separate system for Catholics or Protestants. In toto, the book traced the rise of voluntarism in Canada West and the decline of an Erastian system (that is, state control of the church) originally intended by the British creators of the Constitution of 1791. John's open challenge to the historical profession, however, may have been the book's most interesting feature. As one reviewer observed:

> In an *obiter dictum* Professor Moir charges the Canadian churches with ignoring their pasts. In another he states flatly, and all too accurately, that 'Church histories in Canada are few in number and generally inferior in scholarship.'[4]

In issuing such comments the book became a gauntlet cast down to dare scholars to pose serious questions about the role of religious groups and churches in the development of Canada's history.

Throughout his career John Moir would reiterate this challenge to his professional colleagues, students, and himself. As he continued to mine the rarely tapped veins of the

Canadian religious experience, John's historical work began to focus on three principal interests: the relationship of religion and Canadian identity; the development and character of Canadian Christian denominations; and the craft of history itself. In many ways, his doctoral work and subsequent *Church and State in Canada West* provided the source for each of these three interests in his academic career.

Relations between the Christian churches and the British North American colonies frequently engendered questions relating to one's "identity." As John Moir revealed in *The Church in the British Era* (1972) colonial churches still had ties to the old world, existing European episcopacies, European missionary societies, British and Continental theological thought, and their debates over polity and governance. Nevertheless, these churches also had to address the basic challenges of the colonial environment—limited funds, difficult communications, the rise of political oligarchies, the rigours of frontier life, and the distinctive "Canadian climate." In addition, British North American Christians encountered a denominational, cultural and linguistic pluralism scarcely imagined by Christians who remained in England, Ireland, France or Scotland. This multicultural environment would only increase in its diversity as Canada became the home of peoples and faiths from other parts of Europe and other continents of the globe. Finally, Canadians would become increasingly aware that they were often caught between the competing claims of the "auld countries" and those of the republican colossus to the south. Thus, it comes as no surprise that, in his explorations of Church-State relations in the pre-Confederation era, John Moir would become attracted to more fundamental questions of Canadian Christian identity. Would churches merely replicate the Erastian vision of the old world or perhaps adopt the Enlightenment principle of the "separation of Church and State" as outlined in the American Constitution? Would religion be a badge of loyalty or disloyalty in British North America? Would Catholics be tolerated in the realm of a Protestant king or queen? Would the voluntary principle prevail, making all religions equal, with special privileges extended to none? Could one embrace a vision of "His Dominion" regardless of one's denominational affiliation? How was religion formative in the making of the Dominion of Canada?

Such questions, born of his early work, have been evident over and over again in later essays and monographs. Two of John's most influential essays, "The Canadianization of the Protestant Churches" (*Canadian Historical Association, Historical Papers*, 1966) and "The Problem of a Double Minority: Some Reflections on the Development of the English-speaking Catholic Church in Canada in the Nineteenth Century" (*Histoire sociale-Social History*, 1971) delve into the difficulties faced by Protestants and by English-speaking Catholics as they come to terms with the evolution of Canadian society from colonial status to emerging nation. Upper Canadian Protestants emerged from the pre-Confederation period with greater autonomy from Europe, a more "indigenized" clergy, and a stronger adherence to the voluntary principle, all of which led to a greater sense of the "Canadianness" of their denominations. Similarly, Anglo-Celtic Catholics came to regard themselves as a linguistic minority in their own Church and a religious minority within Canada itself. They proceeded to carve out a unique Canadian identity which in some ways complements but does not conform to the expectations of either of the dominant majorities they face.

Much of John Moir's work would revisit questions of identity and national vision, perhaps reflecting his own times in the 1950s, 60s and 70s, when our collective preoccupation with "Canada's identity" was rivalled only by a certain obsessiveness about "the Constitution." In many of his essays, Moir reminded us that there was a time when most Canadians were "religious" and that their belief systems and church polity had a significant influence on how they saw that country as it was, and how they might envision it to be:

Religion has played a central role in shaping the Canadian character and making the Canadian experience. In obvious, but also in subtle, almost indefinable ways, the influence of the Christian church has made Canadians into religiously motivated individuals. The Judeo-Christian tradition is so deeply infused into the fabric of Canadian life that even modern secularists have unconsciously accepted its values and its forms of expression. Religion has been such a vital life force in creating present-day Canada that no apologies are needed for our attempts to examine and explain its influences on ourselves. [5]

A sense of this religious influence on Canadian identity could be evident in interdenominational associations like the Laymen's Missionary Movement,[6] in the religious press,[7] or simply within the changing perspectives of individual Canadian Christian churches.

Consequently, the second great stream of John Moir's scholarship—the evolution of the Christian denomination— is very much related to issues of identity and national vision. Of particular note has been his ongoing research and writing of the history of the Presbyterian Church in Canada. His great work in this regard, *Enduring Witness: A History of the Presbyterian Church in Canada* (1974), was described by its author as an effort to "illuminate in some measure the particular contribution of Presbyterianism to our national growth." One reviewer was less modest, describing this book as "based on thorough research" and "concise, thoughtful and balanced." Goldwyn French added: "All those who share an interest in the role of religion in the shaping of Canadian society and culture are in his [Moir's] debt for this skilful study of one major element in our Christian tradition."[8] With *Enduring Witness* as his diving board John continued research and teaching the history of Canadian Presbyterianism resulting in the publication of several biographies of noted Canadian Presbyterians,[9] contributions to the *Dictionary of Canadian Biography*, the edition of several essays by his late colleague and fellow Presbyterian historian, the Reverend Allan Farris,[10] and John's on-going participation in the Canadian Society for Presbyterian History. Most recently, his *Selected Correspondence of the Glasgow Colonial Society, 1825-1840* (Champlain Society, 1994) wedded his interest in Presbyterian mission with the editing of primary documents, a task that John has undertaken many times in order to encourage further research in religious history. After his official retirement from the University of Toronto, John continued to teach the history of Canadian Presbyterianism at Knox College. In sum, a researcher would be hard pressed to endeavour research in the history of Canadian Presbyterians without reference to John Moir's monumental work. Although John had begun his life as a member of the United Church, and had studied

Methodism with Donald Creighton, at that time a fellow member of the United Church, John's passionate curiosity for the other major denominational stream that entered Church Union, Canadian Presbyterianism, is explained, in part, by his wife Jacqueline who recounts that the Moir family embraced Presbyterianism in 1972, because they felt more at home "in their form of service."[11]

While his reputation as Canada's premier scholar of Canadian Presbyterianism has been well earned, John's scholarly endeavours have by no means been exclusive to Scottish Calvinism. John's work has had remarkable ecumenical breadth, something evidenced early in his career, when he selected a minor doctoral field in the philosophy of Thomas Aquinas—the most revered of Roman Catholic thinkers. True to this curiosity about all Christians and their relations with one another, John's articles and books have covered issues and episodes in the history of Canada's Methodists, Presbyterians, Anglicans, Baptists, Huguenots, Evangelical Christians, and Roman Catholics. In the process, he has uncovered frameworks for understanding the relations between denominations and the political and social reference points that historically have inflamed sectarian passions or have provided workable compromises. He has examined interfaith relations through the interpretation of marriage laws, editorials in the secular and religious press, and the public debates over sectarian education. Once again, within the context of individual denominations and their relations to one another, John has discovered elements reminiscent of his original work on church and state: how churches grapple with their identity in relation to the nation and within a pluralistic social and religious context. Moreover, he has introduced useful categories to discuss sectarian relations—confrontation, toleration, parallelism, and reconciliation.[12] He himself has rejected the confrontation school as having created "a historicized mythology of conflict," although he has not embraced a completely irenic view of denominational relations, suggesting perhaps contemporary reconciliation may well be the result of religious indifferentism in a secular society wherein religion has become increasingly privatized. In what his late colleague and friend Pierre Savard described as his "Moiresque" style, John issued challenges to scholars to delve deeply into the sources and question the popular stereotypes of Protestant-Catholic relations. As John often put it himself, "I sent up another balloon to see what might happen."

Some of these denominations have recognized his talents more formally. In 1975, John received a Doctor of Divinity degree from Presbyterian College in Montreal in recognition for his groundbreaking *Enduring Witness*. In 1991, the Archdiocese of Toronto honoured John with one of its few Sesquicentennial Jubilee Medals for his edition of *Church and Society: Documents on the Religious and Social History of the Roman Catholic Archdiocese of Toronto from the Archives of the Archdiocese* (1991). The Jubilee Medal was presented to John by Archbishop (now Cardinal) Aloysius Ambrozic, who has maintained a warm correspondence with John ever since. That same year, 1991, John Moir was awarded the George Edward Clerk Medal from the Canadian Catholic Historical Association in recognition of his outstanding contribution to Canadian religious historical scholarship. Such recognition from Christian adherents of both Knox and Rome are a fitting tribute to a scholar whose curiosity, energy, and perspicacity have never been marked by sectarian narrowness nor denominational exclusivity.

"Teaching" has often been underestimated in its value to the scholarly pursuit of history. Nevertheless, most good professors will acknowledge the close relationship between one's endeavours in the classroom and one's labours in the archives. His graduate students may recall that, as he began his senior seminar, "Canadian Religious Traditions," John would preface all remarks with "I wonder what John Moir will learn this year." His enthusiasm for the materials and for the questions posed in the seminar was obvious, if not infectious. The papers written within the context of his graduate courses were often "new studies" in the field of religious history and, subsequently, many of these were published. John had the quality to pull questions out of students where one thought few existed and he was as excited about them as was the student. Perhaps this enthusiasm also derived from the fact that John remained a student at heart; during his years teaching at the University of Toronto he often took courses to upgrade his knowledge in certain areas—especially Calvinism,

Biblical Studies, and Patristics. In his classes, students were always exposed to the "wonder" of historical "discovery."

In conjunction with his vocation as teacher, John Moir took an active interest in publishing materials that could be used within the classroom or could help students to use and interpret primary documents. The volume you are holding in your hands is a perfect example of Moir's teaching ability. Although his dozens of scholarly articles, monographs, and chapters established his scholarly reputation, other works and speeches made his name recognized in post-secondary institutions, undergraduate tutorials, and to the non-academic community at large. He served as author or co-author of three general texts on Canadian history, produced several useful collections of primary documents relating to Church history, and most notably co-edited a popular undergraduate reader, *Changing Perspectives in Canadian History.* [13] This innovative volume confronted students with questions and debates in Canadian history, exposing them to various points of view as expressed in both primary documents and more contemporary historical interpretations of the events in question. John and co-editors Kenneth MacKirdy and Yves Zoltvany regarded *Changing Perspectives* as "an experiment" since the "problems approach to Canadian history had not been attempted before."[14] Four years after its first printing, a revised edition of *Changing Perspectives* appeared. Concisely written, with updated bibliographies and carefully edited primary documents with introductory commentary, this slender volume stimulated hours of discussion and debate on the salient issues and questions of Canadian history. Endeavours such as these allowed John to create his own tools for more effective teaching.

John's road to the classroom, however, was not particularly easy. When he graduated from the University of Toronto in 1954 there were few academic jobs to be had. As was the case with many young academics of his day (and ours), history-related employment was "where you found it." The winding road from job to job was made much more tolerable by the companionship of Jacqueline Heyland, to whom John was married in 1952. Together they witnessed John's brief pilgrimage through the Archives of Ontario, Ontario Hydro, and Queen's University Library. In 1956, John joined the faculty at fledgling Carleton

University in Ottawa, where he remained until 1965. John was lured away from the nation's capital by an offer from historian J. Maurice Careless to become a faculty member at the University of Toronto's new campus in Scarborough. The Moirs left Ottawa, purchased a house in Markham, Ontario, and John spent the rest of his full-time teaching career at Scarborough College. Before his retirement in 1989, however, John had expanded his teaching to include cross-appointments to the School of Graduate Studies at the University of Toronto, the Department of History at U of T's St. George Campus, the Ontario Institute for Studies in Education, and the Toronto School of Theology. He also became a sessional lecturer at Knox College. All of this teaching activity was kept in balance by his "other" life, which included Jacqueline, eight children (Christine, Sheila, Allison, Ian, Gillian, David, Andrew and Michael), and a menagerie of animals, not the least of which were stray canines who happened to show up at the Markham abode, were offered Scottish hospitality, and then never left.

John's "other children" have been his graduate students —some twenty of whom he supervised or co-supervised to the completion of their studies. Many of these can relate to John's concern for "the whole student," as he supervised the actual research and writing of theses, but also took an active interest in the student as a person. This author can remember many times when the revising and editing of a thesis chapter was also an excuse to bring spouse and children to Markham for a social or a supper. John had the insight to know that graduate study was only one dimension of a person's multi-faceted life, within which one had to establish some semblance of balance and sanity. In this respect, John and Jacqueline were co-supervisors. Nor was such hospitality and concern extended exclusively to "his students"; there were many others who, though not directly "supervised" by John, bore the imprint of his classes and his concern for their projects. Little known is the fact that many professors sit on dissertation committees as second and third readers. These labours are rarely accounted for in one's curriculum vitae or in the Dean's office. Many owe a debt to John for his vital, yet uncredited labours. There are several such students, some who followed programs in other universities with more detached supervisors. These other students have acknowledged

John as having given them confidence and support when they most needed it. John, like the grandfather who inspired him, has been "the teacher" to many.

His active participation in many scholarly societies has also given him a presence among his peers. He served as President of both the Ontario Historical Society and the Canadian Association for Scottish Studies and was a founding member and President of the Canadian Society for Presbyterian History and similarly of the Canadian Society of Church History. In conjunction with many of these associations, John has spent numerous hours volunteering as archivist, editor, and consultant to scholarly journals, church societies, and special projects, including serving as an editor of commemorative anthologies for his friend and colleague John Webster Grant and his supervisor Donald Creighton.[15] In 1989, John Moir retired from teaching, although, as he admitted shortly thereafter, he was as busy as ever researching, writing and participating in at least half a dozen scholarly associations.

Certainly the release from administration and teaching gave him a greater opportunity to spend time with a family that was ever expanding. To the ranks of eight children were added eight grandchildren. Family members were spread out across the continent—Ontario, Nova Scotia, Florida, and the Northwest Territories. John and Jacqueline have been frequent travellers across the continent and abroad, a penchant for tourism likely having originated from sabbatical leaves in England (1958-9) and France (1971-2). Nevertheless, the research and writing has continued. Retirement to Port Dover, Ontario, has given John new interest in the local religious history of southwestern Ontario and several local congregations have had the benefit of tightly written and interesting histories.[16] Currently, with Paul Laverdure's help, John and Jacqueline have been translating the works of Father Emile Petitot, OMI, the multi-talented, yet controversial, Roman Catholic missionary in Canada's northwest.

This volume, *Christianity in Canada*, is but a taste of the questions posed in the scholarly work of John Moir. Several of the essays are well known and oft-cited. Others have never appeared in printed form, because they were originally conceived and delivered as talks or public lectures. The collection and this appreciation have been gathered and edited by Dr. Paul Laverdure, one of John's former students. These essays only encompass a portion of John Moir's work, but they offer an important portal into the themes and issues that permeate all of his scholarly pursuits. As John might modestly say, these are "the balloons" for others to target and deflate; not surprisingly, many of these balloons are still afloat, having weathered much scrutiny. Many of us owe John a great debt, not only for the balloons, but for teaching us how to launch our own balloons.

Mark G. McGowan

Christianity and Culture Programme
St. Michael's University in the University of Toronto

I

Religious Determinants in Canadian History

This paper, delivered at the University of Lethbridge in 1980, was an attempt to give an overview of religious forces operating in Canadian history.

I see five religious determinants in Canadian history, and they are so interwoven and interrelated that their categorization and division is artificial and unsatisfactory for an historian's holistic approach. Nevertheless, in an attempt at simplification, I would list those five determinants as centrality, mission, indigenization, churchliness and activism. In each of these categories one can find to a greater or lesser degree an opposite tendency—secularism, parochialism, catholicity, sectarianism and withdrawal—and each of these will also be mentioned here. In my opinion, however, the determinants have been more important in forming a Canadian religious tradition or ethos than their opposites.

My first contention therefore is that religion has played a central role in the development of Canada, that religion has acted as a social cement when and where secular, political or economic forces and institutions have failed or been lacking in the total process of nation-building. At least until a generation ago it was confidently assumed by most Canadians that Canada was a Christian country, and that this was God's providential intention. Thus the Canadian churches viewed themselves as the conscience of the state—politicians were expected to judge all matters by Judeo-Christian values and Canadians of all walks of life were expected to witness to their belief by regular church attendance and by practice of the Golden Rule. The facts of Canadian life in any given period may seem to belie the concept of a Christian nation, and it is best to ask for a detailed explanation of what brand of Christianity God had chosen for Canada. Nevertheless the indisputable fact remains, even if Canada was a less than perfect example of a Christian nation, Canadians believed it was Christian, and belief can count for more than fact.

As yet no scholar has explored the religious dimension of our faith that we are a chosen people. Perhaps this is because our covenanted condition is so obvious that comment seems superfluous. A leading Canadian Protestant churchman once wrote, "In the beginning God created Canada," and a Canadian victory over a Russian hockey team was hailed as proof that God is a Canadian. My point is that although Canadians are not and seldom have been marked by outstanding religiosity in the practising sense, nevertheless we are prone to frame and express our stated ideals, of political leadership or national destiny for instance, in terms that reflect the central role of religion in the making of Canada.

As for the practical centrality which I mentioned earlier that the churches have promoted, I have at times suggested, not wholly tongue in cheek, that membership in a Canadian denomination can be a kind of surrogate nationalism. An Albertan arriving in Toronto may understandably feel that he or she is *in partibus infidelium* (among the infidels), but one can always find (even in Toronto) kindred religious souls, fellow denominationalists whose fellowship will suggest that there is in Canada a unifying force not of this world that binds Canadians together.

My second determinant, the mission impulse, is as old as Canada itself, and is both cause and effect of centrality. A religious motivation—to convert the native Canadians—vied with French interests in exploration and profit from the moment Jacques Cartier planted a cross on Canadian soil in 1535. Furs and missions together built New France—it was no accident that one third of all Frenchmen in the country were employed in the Jesuit mission to the Huron tribes in 1634. The failure of the early French missions nonetheless provided the European colonists with hospitals and schools as the sense of mission was redirected to build a new and purified French society in France's New World—Bishop Laval hoped to keep New France as a mission forever. That combination of a sense of identity, racial or national, with a belief in a providential destiny for French Canadians, was reactivated by Louis Riel when he sought to establish a new papacy and state in western Canada.

Mission was a determinant in the lives of Loyalists too, although in the negative sense of a counter-revolutionary destiny to preserve in North America the superior institutions of the British way of life in the face of disloyal but successful republicans. That high sense of calling found its positive form again after Confederation when unified, affluent Protestant churches in Canada carried the Gospel to regions Caesar never knew—China, Japan, Formosa and India. By the turn of the century Canadian Protestant churches could count over four hundred missionary preachers, teachers, doctors, dentists, nurses, agriculturalists etc. in foreign fields. Roman Catholic Canadian missionaries are more difficult to count because they operated through international rather than national groups.

The culmination of this incredible missionary drive (which swept men, women, children of all classes into a paroxysm of fund raising, education, prayer and participation in missionary endeavours) was the Laymens' Missionary Movement, dedicated to converting Canada's allotted portion of the world's heathen (no less than forty million Chinese) within one generation. This unbridled enthusiasm drew 2,500 people from every province of the Dominion, at their own expense, to a missionary congress in Toronto in 1909. Only the destruction of European hegemony by war in 1939-45 finally curtailed traditional mission efforts in the Third World and focussed Canada's missionary impulse towards economic and social needs in underdeveloped countries.

Indigenization of religion and more obviously of religious institutions is an inevitable development wherever cultural transfer to a new environment occurs. Adaptation to new surroundings, new needs and new challenges is, in the case of religion, minimized by the maintenance of doctrine—the Nicene creed is so basic to Christianity that few have suggested replacing its theology, even if they are willing to tinker with other creedal expressions. But there is also a grey area of faith expressed as national culture where Canadianization has been both restricted and expressed. The "sacredness" of language—the apparently inseparableness of a national tongue from a nation's faith—is not new.

Today this unity is seen in certain ethnic religious organizations or denominations who reflect their own conviction of the principle expressed by the Dutch in the seventeenth century, that God can only be worshipped in Dutch. A more obvious example of religio-cultural identification in Canada was the case of that Anglican bishop in British Columbia who in the

1860s had prefabricated sheet-iron churches in the English Gothic style shipped to Vancouver Island via the Horn, to ensure the "right" surroundings for worship in the colonial church.

Indigenization, however, has affected all religious traditions in Canada and can be examined under three headings—legal, organizational and psychological. Legal indigenization has involved breaking the ties that bind internationally, becoming autonomous, out-growing a mission status, abandoning (under pressure in the case of the churches of England and Scotland) all claims to legal establishment and consequently to any social superiority that legal establishment might confer. For many denominations (since most began as missions to Canada) indigenization has often meant being forced out into the cruel cold world of self-support, a fate that seems necessarily joined to coming of age. It was the frightful spectre of having to rely on free-will offerings that drove that great Canadian John Strachan to his frantic defence of the Anglican monopoly of the Clergy Reserves, that lucrative source of clerical supplemental income.

Organizational indigenization is similarly visible to some degree in every denomination in Canada. A unique inheritance from New France is the virtually autonomous *fabrique* which manages church property in each French Canadian parish. Within the Anglican commonwealth the development of the federalistic Lambeth Conference owed much to the initiative of John Strachan who introduced diocesan synods to the Canadian church in the early 1850s as an organizational solution to previous lay non-involvement in the church's concerns. Looking beyond the institutional church one can discern indigenization in the action of the nineteenth-century Sons of Temperance who equated their own jurisdictional unit boundaries with those of parliamentary constituencies.

Perhaps more interesting than jurisdictional and structural indigenity among Canadian churches were the psychological indicators of growing Canadianization. "We are too Scotch," one Presbyterian minister complained in the 1840s. "The thistle is everywhere seen." A generation later Toronto Congregationalists pointed proudly to the fact that the trowel used to lay a church cornerstone was made in the shape of a maple leaf. But these are late evidences—as early as 1813

John Strachan had called for the ordination of Canadian men, who would understand Canada's problems, because imported British clergy showed so little interest or ability to identify with their new homeland.

Among Roman Catholics indigenization had actually started a century before Confederation. In New France the church officers, the orders of men and the more elitist nuns were French. *Canadiens* found their lowly niche in the church as parish priests or teaching nuns in the parochial schools. By removing this French upper class from the church, the British Conquest promoted the Canadianization of the Roman Catholic church by *Canadiens* and for *Canadiens*, a policy most heartily endorsed and encouraged by the British who understood the deep connections between the *Canadiens*, their culture and their land. Today the lace jabot of a Presbyterian moderator or the gaiters of an Anglican bishop seem strangely out of place in a nuclear age-Canada, even if such clothing is intended to be no more than a gentle reminder of our trans-Atlantic roots and of the principle of catholicity.

Churchliness as a characteristic of Canadian religious life is easier to say than to define. Theologically and liturgically it seems to mean avoiding either extreme emotionalism or ritualism, but falling somewhat on the conservative side of centre. Churchliness has also been evident in the quantitative way that Canadians have sought religious solidarity and unity by avoiding sectarian divisiveness, so common in the American religious experience and praised by some as the inevitable fruits of American freedom. At the 1971 census three of every four Canadians belonged to the Roman Catholic, United or Anglican churches, and one of every ten in the population belonged to the Presbyterian, Lutheran or Baptist communions—all other religious persuasions accounted for only ten per cent.

Thus, to talk of religious pluralism in Canada is misleading because over eighty-five per cent of the population belongs to just six denominations, but an additional ten per cent reported as believers covered between fifty and a hundred smaller faith groups. Social statisticians point correctly to the trend towards greater pluralism created by immigration and by the loss of adherents from so-called mainline churches in the past generation. Even assuming that this trend continues until Canada resembles the United States, at least for the present we can talk historically and more accurately of Canadian churchliness than of Canadian religious pluralism. In part this is due to our dual counter-revolutionary tradition (against both 1776 and 1789), but perhaps partly it is a reaction against the isolation imposed by a vast land on a small and scattered population. Whatever the causes, Canadians have accepted churchliness as the religious norm of Canadian life—divisiveness and sectarianism have been viewed, at least tacitly, as less than Canadian.

The equation of churchliness with loyalism (a Reformation inheritance) can be discerned in the reaction against New Light revivalism in colonial Nova Scotia and more stridently in John Strachan's denunciation of the supposed republicanism of Upper Canadian Methodists after the War of 1812-1814. Ironically, the search for religious comprehensiveness can lead through liberalism to an easy acceptance of religious pluralism, particularly as the dream of a Christian Canada faces growing secularism. Secularism, an ill-defined and perhaps indefinable word, means, according to the dictionary, concern with worldly affairs. According to the sociologists, it describes a decline of measurable religiosity; and for religious conservatives it is any alteration in the supposed religion of our grandparents. From secularism it is a surprisingly easy step, at least for the historian, to a consideration of my final determinant, social activism.

The eighth question in the Old Testament is Cain's, "Am I my brother's keeper?" To this fundamental question Canadians have from the era of discovery responded with an unequivocal "yes," although our missionary measures have not always matched our professions. For instance, Canadian protestations of caring are viewed with scepticism by third world inhabitants who have measured our foreign aid against our affluent life-style. Social activism was expressed in those umbrella-phrases, Social Gospel and Catholic Action. Under several titles it was a product of early nineteenth century evangelicalism and, equally important, the so-called theological revolution. From the emphasis on "save this individual" the focus shifted at some point around the middle of the last century to "save this individual and save this society."

That concern, which had earlier viewed social problems such as alcoholism as causes, now came to view the same problems as effects, as much as or more than causes. Why did people drink to excess? Was it simply moral weakness or could it possibly be that alcoholism was also the unpleasant and unfortunate safety-valve or escape hatch from uncontrollable social conditions? Individuals might be saved, but could they stay saved in the dark satanic mills of urbanized, industrial society? From the early temperance movement came the initiative and the organizational know-how to tackle sin on its many visible frontiers—prostitution (called the "social evil"), sexual exploitation, excessive working hours and unsafe working and living conditions, lack of sanitation, impure foods, polluted air, etc.

The Social Gospellers' concerns sound like (and not accidentally so) a catalogue of the modern environmentalists' complaints. By the time of World War I, that Armageddon of western civilization, a new imperative seemed to be developing out of the Social Gospel—save this society by legislated morality. The individual was being lost sight of; the state and society were now both the end and the means. It was ironic that what had begun as a practical here-and-now attempt to realize the Sermon on the Mount, to make His Kingdom a here-and-now affair, had become a parallel of statism— whether fascistic or communistic or merely secular. Somehow, mankind in the image of God had got shunted aside as the means became as important as the ends. The use of political power to achieve His Kingdom had been secularized to read, "the achievement of mankind's kingdom," and in reaction to this, theological conservatism and fundamentalism often swung to the other extreme of a self-centred rather than a social gospel.

Despite the apparent secularization of the Social Gospel in some quarters, I believe that the process is evolutionary, not revolutionary. The Social Gospel lives on in the very fibre of most Canadians who, if they seldom attend the formalities of organized and institutionalized religion, nevertheless are so deeply permeated by our Judeo-Christian values that they will support such movements as Amnesty International, Project North and Oxfam. I suspect, but cannot prove, that it is precisely on this issue of social activism (am I my brother's keeper?) that Canadian evangelical conservatives differ sharply from their American counterparts.

The fascinating (to an historian) topic of how and how far the precepts of the Social Gospel have influenced our relations with our neighbours in this global village begs for investigation. For instance, how did the principles of the Social Gospel inform the foreign policies of the Liberal government of Lester Pearson, that son of the Methodist parsonage and fellow-student at Victoria College in a generation imbued with Social Gospel ideals? By implication I have pointed to the corollary of the extension of the Social Gospel —from home mission to foreign mission and then to ecumenism, and thus that particular Canadian religious determinant leads full circle to Canada's missionary origins.

My theme is simple, that no one can fully understand Canadians and Canada's history if they do not include, examine and take account of the role of religion in our past and present. Religion has been a major factor (certainly not the only factor but undeniably a major one) in Canadian history. It deserves attention, perhaps equal attention, with such other factors as economics, politics and the arts. All are interrelated, despite the present tendency to stress particular aspects of our history in isolation—urban history, labour history, women's history, etc.—to the detriment and even the exclusion of other facets of history. It is devoutly to be hoped that history will soon return to the condition of holism where everything is grist to the historian's mill and all aspects of our history receive due attention.

II

The Search For A Christian Canada

The following text is a slightly truncated version of three presentations given as the Birks Lectures at McGill University in 1991 and published the following year in Volume 20 of Arc, the journal of McGill's Faculty of Religious Studies.

I

By the time Columbus sighted the New World in 1492, Europe was ripe to explode in a way impossible five hundred years earlier when Vikings reached the American hemisphere. New political and economic structures, religious ferment, "modern" science and printing made the sixteenth century one of the most dynamic periods in world history. Columbus's discovery brought wealth to western Europe, and from this wealth flowed greater power to the new, centralized and bureaucratic governments of Spain, Portugal, France and England. Motives for promoting exploration and exploitation of the new world soon became complex, but the primary reason for seeking the fabled Orient had been to replace the profitable caravan routes lost by the Turkish conquest of the Byzantine Empire in 1453. Besides wealth, European explorations also brought a comfortable conviction of cultural superiority while the Christian churches were confronted with the missionary challenge of other religious systems.

As discovery developed into settlement, it became the practice of all the European colonizing nations to reproduce in the New World a mirror image of the mother-nation. A galaxy of "New" creations appeared, such as New England, New Scotland, New France, New Netherlands, New Sweden —evidence of a nostalgic desire to recreate the European mother country politically, economically, socially and religiously in this different environment. Whatever the material incentives of their Most Christian Majesties, Ferdinand and Isabella, for supporting Columbus's first westward venture, religion had played a major role, thanks to the influence and conviction of Spain's minister of finance, Gabriel Sanchez. Sanchez actually specified that the undertaking was for the

9

salvation of the souls of many lost nations, and after the "great Discovery" of 1492, credited by Columbus to "the holy Christian faith," priests were present in all of Columbus's expeditions.

When it became clear that Columbus had not reached the "lost souls" of Asia but had, in his words, found a "new land," then difficult theological considerations followed. Who or what were these inhabitants of this unknown world? Where did they fit in the simple and rigid schema of the Biblical creation story taught by the church for more than a millennium? Were these tribes lost from history and were they subject to original sin or were they created before Adam—pre-Adamites? Were they even humans, like Europeans, or products of some separate and unrevealed creation? Whether pre- or post-Adamite, however, they were clearly in need of the gospel and of salvation. In 1537 Pope Paul III ended much of the theological discussion by announcing that "the Indians are truly men" who wanted to be Christianized. Therefore the Macedonian cry, "Come over and help us," imposed an obligation on Christians to evangelize the New World as part of the process of Europeanizing it.

It would be too much to expect that in the 1500s, when nationalism and the Reformation were sweeping Europe, the exploring and colonizing nations would do anything else but recreate in the New World whatever form of Christianity their nation-state followed. Europe's wars of religion are proof of deep religious conviction—a Saint Bartholomew's Day massacre and its Protestant counterparts were not the product of religious indifference. Thus, for three centuries the pattern of religious development in the North American territories of the European nations evolved from the moment of Columbus' great discovery. For both the European settlers and their native neighbours that meant the religion of the colonizing nation, whether Roman Catholic or some nationalized form such as the Church of England.

Canadian history is no exception to these European developments, attitudes and policies. A French *mission civilisatrice* to Canada's natives began tentatively in the 1540s. Francis I had first sent Jacques Cartier to find "great quantities of gold and other riches," but the missionary motive was clearly stated at Cartier's third voyage in 1541. The king noted then that Cartier had already brought Indians to France, "to instruct them in the love and fear of God, his holy faith and Christian doctrine," before sending them back as missionaries to their own people. Now, however, the creation of a French colony was being planned, "so that we may better fulfil our intention and to do actions agreeable to God" in a typical merging of national and divine designs.

Permanent French settlement was delayed, however, until the beginning of the 1600s. With France and its monarchy weakened by a half-century of domestic religious warfare, the new missionary initiative, first in Acadia and later at Quebec, seems to have come largely from Samuel Champlain. His "great project"—to make New France European—aimed to convert the natives to Christianity and French culture. For this purpose he brought Récollet friars in 1613, and two decades later the larger and more famous Jesuit mission to the Huron Indians began. Eventually, however, the church's methods were criticized even by contemporaries for reducing the mysteries of the Christian faith to agreeable proportions and for using questionable tactics and tricks that might damage or even destroy the goal of creating Christians.

Religious facilities for the few French settlers in Canada were only incidental to the missionary programme. Even at Quebec City the institutional structures of the church were directed primarily at the native peoples, not the French. When Montreal was founded in May of 1642, the motive was again missionary, inspired by the Jesuits' letters home, the *Relations*. For the small and beleaguered French colony on the St. Lawrence, its physical salvation was Louis XIV's decision in 1663 to make it a province of France as suggested by Quebec's missionary bishop, Laval. Thereafter, colonization officially replaced the missionary motive, although the first step in this direction had been taken more than three decades earlier at the siege of the Huguenot stronghold of La Rochelle in 1627. There Louis XIII had signed a charter for the Company of One Hundred Associates, creating a new and exclusively Catholic trading consortium and ordering that "none but French Catholics" live in the settlement.

This emigration policy embodied the Reformation principle that, for political stability, the religion of a nation must be the religion of its ruler, and in the last four decades of the

1600s this policy bore full fruit when extensive emigration created social, religious and linguistic cohesion in the colony. As New France grew demographically and economically, the dream of christianizing the native people took second place to maintaining a Christian society among the settlers themselves. Louis XIV underlined the shift by declaring that his interest in France's North American territories was "the re-establishment of commerce." As for the church in New France, its attention turned increasingly to a displaced European society that seemed to ape the worst aspects of European life. The church promoted moral rigorism in its quest for a Christian New France and tried to use the power of the state to enforce church decrees.

Instead of a theocracy, however, increased royal attention to New France introduced Gallicanism—the political claim of near autonomy for the church in France—to justify interference with the church. The king's officers in the colony searched nunneries for contraband furs and parish priests were required to be unpaid civil servants of the central government. As surely as Henry VIII was a self-made pope-king, Louis XIV exercised control over the Catholic church in his realms. The degree to which New France became a Christian society may be contested, but whatever was achieved probably owed more to the efforts of French- Canadian society and the parish clergy drawn from that society rather than to France, since the episcopal seat at Quebec was empty for about a third of the century before the British Conquest.

II

The Conquest opened a new and more complex phase in the christianizing of Canada. Britain's new subjects—francophone and Roman Catholic—became part of an anglophone and legally Protestant empire. The Acadians had been deported for strategic reasons, but with the French threat to the English colonies now removed, the proposed solution to the Canadian question was assimilation to the conquering culture. Religion, not language, was the stumbling block in making the *Canadiens* British. The military administrator of the conquered colony reported that, because French Canadians were tenacious of their religion, the best way to make them loyal Britishers was to guarantee their freedom of religion.

The 1763 peace treaty promised that freedom "as far as the laws of Great Britain permit," but those laws denied political rights to Catholics. Later, Governor Carleton estimated the disfranchised "new subjects" at more than ninety-five percent of Quebec's population, and in 1767 he assured the British government that *Canadiens* would people the country forever, "barring a catastrophe shocking to think of."

Meanwhile, a plan to Anglicanize the new subjects by providing French-speaking Protestant clergy was begun in the belief that religious conversion would ensure political allegiance and religious uniformity, perhaps under a new slogan, "none but francophone Protestants." This scheme was negated by an equally official policy to maintain and Canadianize the Roman Catholic Church, also in the interests of political stability. Because a new Roman Catholic bishop was appointed with British connivance, that church survived institutionally. The imported French Protestant clergy were ignored by francophones for religious reasons and by anglophones for linguistic reasons.

Presumably the catastrophe that Carleton had feared in 1767 was an American revolution. In 1774, on the eve of that Revolution, the Quebec Act gave the Catholic church in Quebec legal recognition along with Anglicanism, the religion of the monarch and supposedly of his subjects. The Act's purpose was to keep Quebec British by keeping it French and Roman Catholic, but it became one of the four Intolerable Acts condemned by the American Declaration of Independence and denounced by the Continental Congress for establishing in Canada "a religion that has deluged England in blood, and dispersed bigotry, persecution, murder and rebellion through every part of the world." Nevertheless, thanks to the Quebec Act the colony now had two established churches, and later two bishops of Quebec—one Anglican and the other Roman Catholic.

The American Revolution reshaped the North American colonies both religiously and demographically, and its most immediate impact was the arrival of the Loyalists. As long as French Canadians were a majority, they felt secure in their religious rights, but the Loyalists changed the religious complexion of Canada. The presence of so many anglophones justified dividing the province of Quebec into predominantly francophone and Roman Catholic Lower Canada, and into Upper Canada: anglophone and Protestant, or at least non-Catholic, but with the Church of England legally established. Although double "establishment" irritated the Church of England, it did reflect political realities. The Roman Catholic Church had supported Britain in the Revolution, and for his loyalty during the War of 1812-14 its Bishop, Plessis, received a government salary and a promise that royal supremacy would not be imposed on his church. Thus, after legal recognition, the Roman Catholic Church regained an independence lost in 1663, while the Church of England was still treated as a branch of government.

In Upper Canada the Church of England by its own estimate could claim only twenty percent of the population, and by unfriendly estimate just two percent, yet it monopolized the income of the Clergy Reserves—almost two and a half million acres of the richest lands in North America set aside for the Protestant Clergy when Upper Canada was created. Church establishment and religious pluralism already co-existed in the Maritime colonies, but without the temptation of such loaves and fishes as the Reserves. Was it realistic to expect that a pluralistic Upper Canada would become Anglican, or that Lower Canada could reconcile two rival establishments? Such questions remained irrelevant to an imperial government already convinced that a major cause of the American revolution was the absence of church establishment.

Upper Canada's difficulties with church establishment began indirectly in December 1813, when the Americans burned Niagara-on-the-Lake. After the war the Presbyterians of the town rebuilt their church, a Canadian architectural gem, but faced with this heavy expense they petitioned the crown to provide a salary for their minister from the income of the Clergy Reserves. When the government took no action, leading Canadian Presbyterians pointed out the political advantages of co-establishing the national Church of Scotland in the colonies to ensure loyalty. They claimed their case was also patriotic because other denominations were Americans who "disseminate political disaffection." The Anglican Clergy Reserves Corporation responded that "Protestant clergy" meant Church of England—if "Protestant clergy" included others, where would such an interpretation end?

In retrospect, state support for religion seemed warranted when the poverty of the early pioneers made outside support at the least desirable if not necessary. Clerical salaries were low, never certain to be paid in full, and the custom of partial payment in kind left some ministers saddled with quantities of inferior and unmarketable produce. The objections to the Church of England's privileged position regarding the Clergy Reserves, marriage laws and education, political appointments, and the selection of military and legislative chaplains came from rivals for such preferred treatment, but more importantly from voluntarists eager to abolish, not share, an establishment which was unbiblical, political, and injurious to other denominations. When John Strachan, Anglican archdeacon and educator of a generation of conservative leaders of the colony, defended establishment in a famous sermon and in letters to the British government, voluntarism became a political issue in the colony.

Strachan equated religious dissent with disloyalty, which provoked an effective defence of non-established patriotism from the young Methodist Egerton Ryerson on behalf of all voluntarists, including Baptists and low church Anglicans. An unrepentant Strachan insisted that a state without an establishment was a contradiction. This Strachan-Ryerson exchange opened a decade-long battle over the proper form for a Christian Upper Canada as opposing political factions joined the fray. On one side was the conservative and establishment-minded "Family Compact"; on the other were voluntarists ranging from the moderate Anglican Robert Baldwin to the unbalanced William Lyon Mackenzie.

Strachan continued to assure the British government that there were only two kinds of Upper Canadians—Anglicans, and those who wished they were Anglican and who would become Anglican if given the opportunity. That opportunity would come when the mother country provided adequate economic support for clergy of the established church and, by thus ensuring loyalty, would end the threat of republicanism and irreligion. This assessment of the religious situation in Upper Canada was wrong because Strachan assumed that all Anglicans supported the establishment principle, and that non-Anglicans could not be happy outside his Church. Even if his dream of an established colonial church had ever become a reality, religious uniformity was unlikely to follow in pluralistic Upper Canada. In the early 1830s Lieutenant-Governor Colborne noted that something in the North American air made establishment an alien idea, but in 1836 he aided the establishment cause by endowing forty-four Anglican rectories with 400 acres each from the Clergy Reserves.

The voluntarist reaction to this development was immediate and loud—the rectories were illegal and provocative. Strachan, however, persuaded the imperial government to save the rectories because they were part of a long-standing policy for church establishment. After the Rebellions of 1837, less than two years later, Lord Durham reported that in Upper Canada the Reserves and rectories had been contributing causes of the unrest. The next governor, Lord Sydenham, was directed to settle the Reserves issue locally, but when his efforts failed, the imperial parliament enacted his proposal. A compromise was struck between the establishment principle and denominationalism—current income from the Reserves would be shared by those larger churches already receiving government aid and any future additional funds would be divided among the smaller denominations. Thus, the Church of England was joined at the Protestant Clergy Reserves banquet by the Church of Scotland, Roman Catholics, Methodists, and potentially by all non-voluntarist religious bodies.

III

Multiple establishment was supposed to create a nominally Christian colony by including the major denominations and hence a majority of the population. British North Americans had, however, been politicized by the controversies of the 1820s and 1830s, and by the 1850s many were ready to use the state to create their version of the righteous nation. One radical reformer wanted to tax church property—"Why shouldn't God pay taxes? Everyone else does!" Another view of Christian nationhood came in 1844 in a short-lived law of the United Canadas that disenfranchised all clergy. Then suddenly the Reserves' policy of share and conquer collapsed in 1848 when the new Lafontaine-Baldwin Reform government announced that extra loaves and fishes were now available on demand for the smaller churches who would thus join the colony's hydra-headed religious establishment. Immediately, voluntarists repeated their decades-old demand that the Reserves' income be used for education.

This renewed mêlée over the Reserves was only one of the issues unsettling the Canadas in the late 1840s and early 1850s. Responsible government, the University Question, seigneurial tenure, rapid technological change, government corruption, the collapse of the Reform party, the rise of radical fringe groups, and several religious controversies linking language and religion combined to make the 1850s one of the most chaotic decades in Canadian history. Among these disputes the campaign to end the Clergy Reserves was bitter and noisy, and involved the first use of a public opinion poll in Canada. Finally, a bill to secularize the Reserves was introduced by John A. Macdonald's Conservative government in 1854, the same year that seigneurial tenure was abolished and Canada got an elected senate. The Act states its intention to "remove all semblance of connexion between Church and State," the only such reference in Canadian law.

The establishment version of a Christian nation seemed to die with the Clergy Reserves, but so too did the voluntarist ideal of the separation of church and state. The four "established" churches received cash settlements for their vested interests in the Reserves, money that the churches of England and Scotland promptly turned into perpetual funds. To this day the Anglican Church of Canada in Ontario still has an income from the defunct Clergy Reserves, but the Presbyterians lost theirs in bad investments. Thus, voluntarism's victory was incomplete, even more so when that second vestige of establishment, the rectories, was perpetuated in 1856. When the validity of the rectories was tested in the courts (using public funds), British jurists declared that, even if the Rectories were "objectionable on grounds of public policy, and offensive to the feelings of a portion of the people," their patents were legally sound. To this day Ontario possesses endowed Anglican rectories, a reminder of that abortive plan for a church establishment.

Despite pre-Confederation preoccupations with issues of church and state, a Christian Canada in the broader sense was not forgotten. Pioneer life was characterized by excessive drinking, gambling, swearing and violence, but into the harsh, lonely and irreligious pioneer existence Christianity came as a civilizing influence. The first denomination to appear in the field probably attracted and retained many for whom denominationalism had become meaningless. All the churches preached a shotgun attack against such time-wasting (and hence ungodly) leisure activities as dancing, card playing, the theatre, reading novels, or ice skating.

If Canadian churches have a chequered record of religious intolerance, at the very least they can claim an enviable tradition of denominational co-operation and concern for social problems. Stemming from the spirituality of the nineteenth-century Evangelical Revival and from colonial conditions, two religious and social concerns, cutting across denominational lines, emerged before Confederation. The first was the temperance issue, the second sabbatarianism, or keeping the Sabbath holy as required by the Fourth Commandment. Grain was grown in vast quantities, but when distilled it became a smaller and more profitable product, which made liquor a major economic consideration. At 25 cents a gallon, and fifty per cent stronger than the modern product, whisky was the major cause of wide-spread alcoholism. In some families whisky was given to all members every morning to prevent colds. At residential schools boys drank "small beer" (recently rediscovered and renamed "lite").

Christian clergymen generally believed in moderate drinking but alcoholism became so common, even among men of the cloth, that importing the temperance movement from Europe and the United States was a natural response. By the 1830s temperance societies appeared in every colony, a coincidence in time that proves the seriousness of the problem. Because alcoholism leads to abuses of persons and property, first temperance and, later, teetotalism became a persistent theme in the search for a Christian Canada, and when anti-alcohol education seemed fruitless, the campaign demanded state-enforced prohibition. Legal prohibition was proposed in the Maritimes before the 1830s, and in Upper Canada by 1840, where temperance was also recommended as a test for church membership. Some denominations did not believe that sobriety could be legislated, but all agreed that governments should fire intemperate civil servants. As late as Confederation, however, colonial society was not ready to legislate a sober Christian Canada into existence.

If temperance was the particular enthusiasm of the Methodists, Baptists and evangelical Anglicans, the Presbyterian passion for keeping the Lord's Day holy earned from Roman Catholics the nickname "the Covenanters' hobby." The sabbatarian crusade to achieve a Canadian Sabbath by forcing the closing of post offices and canals on Sunday by law began in the 1840s. In 1853 over seventeen thousand persons in Upper Canada, but only three thousand in Lower Canada, petitioned parliament for a Lord's Day law. One Toronto newspaper objected that a law against Sunday labour would contravene the separation of church and state, but almost every year for a decade George Brown introduced unsuccessful private bills to compel Sabbath observance. Canadians apparently still did not feel that a Canadian Christian Sunday was so threatened by commercialism as to justify government intervention.

IV

By the era of Confederation the search for a Christian Canada was moving away from the issue of establishment towards a popular consensus about what constituted a righteous nation. This new vision was interdenominational and assumed that Canadians shared a common Christianity because, with the church-state issue buried, a sort of omnibus Protestantism emerged. This transdenominational consensus on such topics as evangelism, temperance, sabbatarianism and political responsibility combined with a sense of dedication and activism flowing from the Evangelical Revival, pointing to a new, enthusiastic, aggressive and co-operative search for a Christian Canada. The beliefs that the Christian church is the conscience of the state and that the state's power can and should be used to create a Christian Canada, underlay two parallel movements, the Social Gospel and Catholic Action.

Temperance and sabbatarianism were only two thin edges of a wedge of traditional Christian social concern rekindled in Canada as elsewhere during the mid-Victorian years when the church again found its prophetic voice. The Evangelical Revival began this new search for a Christian Canada by stressing personal conversion, with proof of conversion measured in purity and piety of life. Next, a theological revolution gradually and subtly shifted emphasis from redemption to incarnation. Attention was redirected from the individual to the group. To save the individual, society must also be saved, so the goal of this world became the Jesus-like life in terms of moral and physical living standards, or the quality of life.

Now, the reconciliation of God and Humanity seemed to come more through the Incarnate Word than through Christ the Redeeming Lamb—Jesus became a more human, dedicated, sociable, even clubbable activist. Where societal concerns were involved, the range of social and moral problems expanded infinitely. To deal with an alcoholic was to deal with one person—to deal with alcoholism was to face a galaxy of interrelated social issues in an urbanizing and industrializing community. In Canada, however, the long post-Confederation recession delayed public response to urbanization and industrialization until the 1890s.

In the generation after Confederation the main Protestant development was the unification in 1875 of the Presbyterian and in 1884 of the Methodist churches that together claimed a third of the nation's population. By then the emergence of an economic middle class was spreading a veneer of culture over Canada. For the churches this brought new buildings of classic design and dimensions to replace older and plainer meeting places. Educated clergy ousted those who were merely inspired. Robed choirs now sang at the congregations rather than with them. Auxiliary organizations enlisted women, youth, and children in physical and social as well as spiritual development and home and foreign mission enterprises.

By the end of the century large-scale industry was drawing youth from the security of country life to the temptations of the city. The church was already there, preserving Christian Canada by easing this cultural transition for immigrants from the farms, and from overseas. The vast numbers of New Canadians arriving in eastern cities and in the West posed a second challenge to a Christian Canada. At the great 1909 Protestant Mission Congress in Toronto, Charles W. Gordon (of Ralph Connor literary fame) declared that non-anglophone newcomers must be Canadianized through evangelization. The Congress's slogan, "Evangelize the world in this generation," also assigned Canada, the lynch-pin of God's Anglo-Saxondom, forty million Chinese to convert.

Whether the nation's mission was abroad or at home, whether to old Canadians or new, the response of the Christian churches to the challenges of immigration and industrialization was "practical Christianity," the application of Social Gospel principles. The Social Gospel movement was not an organization but a collective answer to the worst results of urbanization and industrialization. It was also an umbrella-term for special interest groups with social concerns. Yet the Social Gospel philosophy was never codified, and only popularized after it was a generation old. The degree of involvement in the Social Gospel by each Protestant church seems directly proportional to the Evangelical Revival's influence on that denomination. Methodists took an ideological approach to the Social Gospel, Presbyterians and Baptists were more pragmatic, and the Church of England adopted an essentially conservative strategy.

What the Social Gospel was for Protestants, Catholic Action was for the Church of Rome, whose involvement in social action has a long tradition in Canada. Both English and French churches have shared that tradition, but the latter has been less willing to co-operate with non-Catholics. The crusades of the Social Gospel and Catholic Action reflected contemporary problems—intemperance, Sabbath desecration, unsafe working conditions, child labour, long working hours, abuse of women and children, poor housing, impure food and water, crowded and polluted cities, moral impurity in politics and sex, and the ghettoization of New Canadians in a Christian Canada. Leadership came willingly from the clergy, but more importantly from well-to-do Christian Canadians with time, money and organizational experience. As leaders diversified their Social Gospel interests, networking became an operational norm even in family and social life.

The Social Gospel's influence on Canadian life changed the tone and objectives of the nation irrevocably. In retrospect the Social Gospel was more preservative than revolutionary as it aimed to save the existing Christian Canada from the anti-religious and anti-Christian forces loosed against society by the industrial revolution. Thanks to the war-time demand that grain be consumed exclusively as food, the manufacture of alcohol was banned in 1918. Without a patriotic and militant war effort, however, even this short-lived legislation might never have become law. The story of legislated

Sabbath observance in Canada shows how effective organization by the Lord's Day Alliance won the Lord's Day Act of 1906, but that Act, too, was an incomplete victory. The Alliance had depended on the help of organized labour, which was more interested in a day of rest than in enforcement of the Fourth Commandment.

The Lord's Day Act itself gave industry profitable loopholes, and a concerned Alliance warned that if reverence for the Sabbath were lost not only a Christian Canada but civilization itself might disappear. During the inter-war years the Alliance successfully prosecuted small shop owners, the Hart House String Quartet, ice cream vendors and movie house operators—with wealthy corporations it was less fortunate. The sabbatarian cause was further weakened by disorganization and distractions during both World Wars, by the divisions of Protestantism, and by the leakage of denominational support into newer crusades. Church union cost the Alliance more church backing, as did generational leadership changes, and by the end of the 1940s the future of Canada's Christian Sunday was in doubt. Increasingly sabbatarianism was challenged by commercialism and a pluralism of non-Christian religions until by the 1960s Sunday was definitely a holiday, and only partly a holy day, even for most Christians.

V

In the crucible of World War I Canada had become a nation and so, in the opinion of many Protestants, it needed a national church. A union of the Methodists, Presbyterians and Congregationalists, planned for almost two decades, would help to win the world for Christ and create a collective conscience for the Canadian nation-state. A big, unified church could save Anglo-Saxon and Protestant values and institutionalize the dream of a Christian Canada. Church union would be both the natural and the national answer to change; it would be the Social Gospel at collective prayer. Ironically, the union of 1925 was also a return to the establishment principle—one nation, one church—that denominationalism had defeated almost a century earlier.

In part, church union had been a response to earlier clashes between Protestantism and Roman Catholicism. Religious violence had ended but, in the late 1880s, papal involvement in dividing the Jesuits' Estates funds allowed Protestants to protest "foreign" interference in Canadian affairs and challenge Catholics' loyalty to Canada. Militant Protestants organized the "equal rights" movement but failed to make their point with Canadian politicians or the Canadian public. The issue of Roman Catholicism's role in Canadian life arose again when the papal decree *Ne Temere*, issued in 1906 to prevent clandestine marriages, was used in civil courts to annul some mixed marriages. Although Roman canon law is part of Quebec's Civil Code, Protestants insisted that the law of Canada must have precedence over denominationalism.

Despite these religious confrontations, a common language proved to be a greater reconciler of competing visions of a Christian Canada than a shared denominationalism. As English-speaking Catholics and Protestants moved closer together, relations between English and French Catholics became more strained. The Abbé Lionel Groulx offered francophones a divinely destined, Roman Catholic Quebec in place of a Christian Canada. It would be a French-Canadian homeland shaped by faith and heritage. Preaching a sacralized French-Canadian nationalism, he became godfather to *Action Française* and Quebec sovereignty, yet this very dream of a regional and cultural Christian society was desacralized in the Quiet Revolution.

Was there ever a Christian Canada, or was it an impossible dream? What had begun as a mission to Canada became a mission in Canada, and then a mission of Canada. Today the values of Canada's Judeo-Christian heritage still inform the nation, and politicians employ such Social Gospel phrases as "the just society." At home and abroad Social Gospel and Catholic Action ideals are proclaimed and practised by numerous Canadian organizations. Individually Canadians retain their passionate thirst for justice as the highest Christian virtue. They voice their concern for the welfare of others and their disapproval of discrimination against those less well-off.

At the very least, Canada remains numerically Christian, since nine out of every ten citizens claim adherence to one of the six largest denominations. As recently as 1981, when the proposed new constitution omitted all references to the

Creator, thousands of letters protested this oversight and the preamble of the bill was rewritten to acknowledge "the supremacy of God." Admittedly, only one Canadian in four attends a church with anything approaching regularity, but the Christian churches report a more intense spiritual life. Religious pluralism, first seen as a threat to Anglo-Saxon values, now seems to offer a further bulwark against secularism. The search for a Christian Canada has taken some unexpected turns in the twentieth century, but after four hundred years this legacy cannot be denied as one of the most formative influences in modern Canadian society.

III

The Sectarian Tradition in Canada

About 1960 the "Faith and Order" section of the World Council of Churches produced a volume on The Christian Tradition *which did not include Canada. Over lunch in Montreal, when the Canadian societies for church history, theology and biblical studies were meeting together at McGill University, a plan for such a volume was mapped out and chapters assigned to historians of various major denominations. The denominational focus of the proposed volume was in keeping with popular religious opinion of the day, although we were unaware of the revolution in inter-church relations about to be unleashed by the Second Vatican Council.*

John Moir was asked to write a short chapter on all of the other religious groups, and was assigned the title "The Sectarian Tradition," a title suggested by Ernst Troeltsch's sociological work, recently re-translated into English and introduced by Richard Niehbuhr.

The result of this decision to produce a collection of papers on Canadian denominational traditions was The Churches and the Canadian Experience, *edited by John Webster Grant and published by Ryerson Press with money from several denominations and interested groups. While the sociological term "sectarian'" has fallen out of favour (or has never been in favour) with historians of "smaller" denominations, Moir's discussion of Canada's "other" denominations and their role in Canadian politics remains illuminating.*

In Canada sects have been exclusively of Protestant origin, although sectarianism is not a distinctively Protestant or even Christian phenomenon. Every religious movement, as soon as it begins to adapt or accommodate to its terrestrial environment, tends to produce its own sectarian echo. The aim of the sect is to restore the original purity of the true faith by returning to the source of the movement, ignoring and rejecting all that has happened in the meantime, namely the accumulation of tradition.

But if tradition is the memory and conscience of the church, does a sectarian tradition also exist in Canada? Is

there a distinguishable Canadian tradition? Any answers to
these questions cannot hope to receive complete acceptance,
if for no other reason than that even scholars do not agree as
to what constitutes a sect.

From the point of view of the sects, and of the law, sects
do not exist. However small or large, however inconsequen-
tial or important, however pagan or Christian, all religious
groupings seem to be incorporated as churches. Nevertheless,
the sect can be differentiated from both the church and the
cult by several criteria.[1]

A "sect" can be defined as a body of persons agreeing
upon religious doctrines usually different from those of an
established or orthodox church from which they have separated and usually having distinctive common worship. But the
inclusion of the qualifier "usually" limits the utility of this definition and the reference to doctrinal differences opens vast
areas for discussion. A second definition, "a nonconformist
or other church as described by opponents," begs the question of the relation of sect to church, but does point up the
common pejorative use of the word. Another definition, "a
religious denomination," is too generalized to be useful, but
the description, "a party or faction in a religious body," does
provide a base for this inquiry since it preserves the sense of
the Latin root secta—a faction or following, with connotations of separation, distinction and protest. The common definition of "church" as "an organized Christian society at any
time" would cover the sect too, but it reminds us that we are
concerned only with Christian sects and justifies the exclusion
of several groups that pass for sects in common parlance.

"Sect," then, involves division, protest and separation,
and popularly implies smallness of numbers. The North American sect is fundamentalist, evangelistic, Bible-centred and
traditionally anti-traditionalist in its emphasis. It stresses the
necessity for conversion as a condition of membership, a fact
which leads Richard Niebuhr to say that the true sect exists
for only one generation.[2] The sect is totalitarian in its demand
for strict behavioural conformity and, like the totalitarian
state, is aggressively militant in its symbolism and defensive in
its outlook. It requires total obedience and loyalty, opposing
membership in other organizations as contaminating. The sect
stresses proselytization, particularly through overseas mission,
and it affords a larger role to women in its democratic,

congregationally autonomous organization. It combats worldliness in all its aspect—dress, amusements and possessions—reminding its members of the imminent needle's eye.

The sect is anti-clerical, anti-intellectual as shown by its reliance on a God-ordained ministry, anti-scientific especially in its response to the theory of evolution, and anti-state in its disregard for national boundaries and, at times, for national laws. To these factors the sociologist adds more general characteristics. The sect is "the church of the disinherited," of the economically inferior and socially uprooted. Hence, the sectarian will be found most frequently in the lower class, less often in the middle class. Movement from the former socioeconomic group to the other should normally be accompanied by transfer from sect to church in the case of the individual or mutation of sect into church if the bulk of the sect membership is involved in a change of status. Today, however, "disinheritance" is frequently social rather than economic. The sect member driving a Cadillac or power-boat reflects the disparity between Canadian class structure and income level.

Obviously, the sum of these characteristics will rarely if ever be found in one sect. Nevertheless, the sect is clearly distinguishable from the church. The church is bureaucratic in organization, either individually or corporately hierarchically structured, accommodated to society, latitudinarian in ideology—it accepts different ethical standards for different social classes—and more or less traditionalist by comparison with the sect. But between the abstracted church and the idealized sect lies a spectrum of churchy sects and sectarian churches. Sects become respectable by accommodation as expensive buildings and more worldly behaviour reflect the economic success of members. In many churches evidence of sectarian influence can be discovered, whether inherited from previous sect status or acquired by adaptation to local conditions.

On the North American continent, which early provided a refuge for European sects, sectarianism has found particularly fertile soil for its ideals and techniques. Historically, the sects have been numerous on this continent, although their individual membership has encompassed only a very small proportion of the total population. Despite a paucity of members, the sects have frequently exerted a disproportionately large influence on social and political developments.

E.T. Clark[3] has grouped American sects into seven categories which deserve attention as they apply to Canadian sectarianism. The "pessimistic" sects include the Millerites and their successors, the Seventh-Day Adventists and the Jehovah's Witnesses, though the last-named can be ignored on the grounds that it has departed from Christian doctrine. The next group, "perfectionist" sects, historically includes the Methodists and their ideological offspring such as the Holiness Movement and the Church of the Nazarene. Of the hundred or so sects in the United States, about one-half grew out of Methodism. By the mid-nineteenth century the Wesleyan Methodist churches in North America—to distinguish them from the small sects—had progressed from sect to church, a process which Wesley himself had foreseen when he wrote, "The Methodists in every place grow diligent and frugal; consequently, they increase in goods."[4] The next category comprises the "legalistic" sects who claim to be sole heirs to the true and early church. By such practices as foot-washing and plain dress, they stress the primitiveness of their Christianity. The sects noted as legalistic—for example the Reformed Episcopal and Primitive Baptist—have had no significant place in Canadian church history. Similarly, "charismatic" sects as the Church of God and the "holy rollers" who stress tongues and prophecy have made no noticeable contribution to any sectarian tradition in this country if for no other reason than that "perfectionist" sects have accepted such phenomena as part of their own sectarian tradition.

"Communistic" sects such as Hutterites and Doukhobors have an important place in our collective national religious life, more so than in the melting pot of the United States. Here is the ultimate in the rejection of accommodation, and the same form of withdrawal can be seen in early Mennonite and Lutheran communities in eastern Canada. Perhaps a clue lies in the broader field of cultural rather than religious separation. Canadian communistic groups are invariably of non-English, non-French extraction, and language preservation is a large part of their motivation. If such groups are sects, the language barrier has prevented them from contributing to any general Canadian sectarian tradition, but they may be treated more conveniently as a separate church tradition outside the scope of this study.

Finally, two sect-types that can be dismissed as being either non-Christian or non-sect are the scientific, hedonistic "egocentric" groups such as the Christian Science Church or "The Great I Am," which are best defined as cults, and the "esoteric" groups such as the Baha'is and the Rosicrucians, which are not even Christian.

In the two centuries since the bulk of present-day Canada came under British sovereignty, at least three distinct periods of sectarian activity can be distinguished. The first period is in the Great Awakening of the Newlight movement. The second is in the Great Revival in Upper Canada. The last period begins contemporaneously—and not coincidentally—with Confederation, with the church unions, with intensive industrialization and urbanization in central Canada, and with the opening of the West. In each of these periods, sectarianism was a reaction or protest against different things: in the first period against the political involvement of the New England establishment, in the second against the privileges of the Anglican establishment in Upper Canada, and in the third against the latitudinarianism, social respectability and service-club "togetherness" of the modern conventionalized churches.

Canada is the product of two counter-revolutions. The Counter-Reformation stamped New France with that religious zeal and piety which gives French Canada its distinctive character to this day. British reaction to the American Revolution ensured that the Second Empire in North America would differ markedly from the American republic to the south. These counter-revolutionary traditions have worked against the growth of sectarianism in Canada—the French tradition by its exclusivism and ultramontanism, the British by its equation of religious dissent with republicanism and treason. Thanks to the Counter-Reformation, the province of Quebec neither produced nor shared to any great extent in any sectarian tradition until after the Second Vatican Council period.

Nova Scotia had been British for almost half a century before a change in imperial policy introduced the elements in which the Newlight movement was to grow. The so-called "Charter of Nova Scotia," issued in 1759 to encourage settlement, attracted enough immigrants from New England to make the colony a projection in time and space of New England. The promise of religious freedom for Protestant dissenters was not the least of the attractions. New England

Puritanism had but recently lost the sectarian characteristic of accepting members by conversion only, a characteristic which had produced in those colonies an oligarchic theocracy with little room for dissenters. This immigration to Nova Scotia was ended after a decade by the opening of the Ohio Valley with all the opportunity and freedom from institutional limitations that accompany a new frontier.

In New England, Puritanism was rapidly accommodating itself to a society of the remaining "half-saved" when the Great Awakening reached Nova Scotia in 1775. This date in itself might suggest some connection with the political events of the Revolution. All the evidence is to the contrary, however, for the Great Awakening which had begun with Whitefield in the colonies to the south swept into Nova Scotia apparently in total disregard of political considerations. Indeed, the Great Awakening in Nova Scotia seemed to profit by the Revolution, for it fed on Nova Scotian Congregationalism sympathetic to rebellion.

The Newlight movement offered the neutral Yankees of Nova Scotia a religious solution to their political neutrality. Henry Alline had found his own escape from chill Calvinism in personal conversion in 1775. His charismatic qualities and the sectarian nature of the Newlight provided a catalyst for elements of religious dissatisfaction already present in the colony. As a sectarian movement the Newlight cut across established denominational lines; its divisive effects were soon condemned by Anglicans, Presbyterians, Methodists and even some Congregationalists. Here was the first Canadian encounter between British ecclesiasticism and the inherent sectarianism of the New World with its frontier conditions. Loyalists arriving in Nova Scotia brought with them or soon absorbed the Newlight, which in turn they spread as they opened new frontiers of settlement in the colony. Despite Alline's death in 1784 the Newlight movement continued to spread in Nova Scotia—to the distress of the Anglican Bishop Inglis, who in 1799 was complaining about these "enthusiasts." But this first great North American sectarian movement had run its course in Nova Scotia by 1810. Its close alliance with Baptists, stemming from their common Calvinism, ended in the absorption of the Newlight into the Baptist churches, a victory for ecclesiasticism in spite of the inherent sectarian tendencies of the Baptists. But the element of

Calvinism in the Newlight movement was unusual if not unique, and certainly was a distinctive ingredient of Canadian sectarianism.

Whereas the Newlight movement had succeeded in Nova Scotia because it was accepted as politically neutral (which Congregationalism was not), the Great Revival in Upper Canada was from the outset identified rightly or wrongly with the American Revolution. Perhaps it was the reassuring British presence and influence in the person of military forces and government functionaries that made Bishop Inglis somewhat less critical of the Newlight movement than were his colleagues in the Canadas of its counterpart there. After the dimming of the Newlight, the people of Nova Scotia, sects included, tended to look eastward for inspiration, to receive a distinctly European outlook which thereafter put a quietus on sectarian agitation by accommodating sectarianism to Erastian tradition (that is to say, the state being supreme in church matters). In Upper Canada, however, official criticism of sectarians began when it might have been least expected.

Methodist influences in the colony had been from the outset of American origin. Though early and spontaneous Methodist class meetings had been organized among the Loyalists, the sect owed its organization in Upper Canada to Nathan Bangs and other American Methodists of the Genesee Conference. Imperial authorities had professed to find a causal relation between sectarianism and revolution in the Thirteen Colonies, and to ensure the loyalty of the truncated Second Empire in North America, gave the Church of England a preferred position if not a full establishment. Imperial policy was intended to establish in North America, albeit belatedly, the European principle of *cuius regio, eius religio* (the religion of the ruler is the religion of the realm), which had been transplanted so successfully a century before in New France. In the two Canadas, British policy included the reservation of one-seventh of the surveyed land for the profit of the "Protestant" clergy. It therefore seems strange that there had been no official objection to American Methodist infiltration during the War of 1812 or immediately afterwards when legislative action severely restricted the legal position of American citizens in the province. Anti-American pressure was, however, felt strongly within the Canadian Methodist body; it led to the move in 1824 by the Canadians for com-

plete separation from the Genesee Conference, a move completed in 1828 by the establishment of an autonomous
Canadian Methodist organization. But no open attack on sectarianism was made until 1826 when Archdeacon Strachan's
memorial sermon for the late Bishop Mountain was published.

Two explanations may be offered for this sudden official
interest in sectarian growth. In the first place, the hegemony
of the Church of England had already been challenged by the
Church of Scotland's claim to co-establishment in the Empire
and a share of the Clergy Reserves. This was a direct threat to
the Anglican monopoly, but it did not involve sectarianism.
The second explanation may lie in the vast numerical increase
of Methodism. Its use of itinerant preachers and revivalistic
camp meetings was rapidly winning a frontier population
from the sedentary churches by default. In Prince Edward
County, for instance, its organizational advantages enabled it
to take over the highly decentralized and incohesive Quaker
groups. It has been estimated that in the mid-1820s perhaps
more than half of the colony's population was attached to the
Methodists. Thus it may have been simply the challenge of
numbers from the sects that prompted Strachan's outburst.
No such problem faced his bishop in Lower Canada.

The publication of Strachan's charges—that the Methodist preachers were uneducated, unsettled, politically minded, American (hence anti-monarchical), and hostile to "the
parent Church"—provoked a reply from the young Egerton
Ryerson defending some of the main sectarian characteristics.[5] In summary, he claimed that the Methodist preachers
are God-inspired men preaching the gospel without government subsidies and education is acquired in other ways and
other places than in colleges. Seven-eighths of the Methodist
preachers are British born, and of the rest all but two are naturalized citizens. They are serving God, not Mammon—it is
Strachan who is politically minded! Ironically, while Strachan fulminated, his Bishop recognized that this opposition
was not directed against Anglicanism but against the church-
state relationship which gave the Church of England "the
character of an establishment."[6]

The argument was destined to assume a political tone
that would mark out the boundary of sectarian tradition for
coming generations. Strachan had said that a Christian nation
without an establishment is a contradiction, and around the

issue of establishment versus voluntarism the basic Canadian sectarian tradition grew up. On the one side were the churches, particularly the Anglican, equating religious protest with political disloyalty in the best Royalist and Tory tradition. Opposed were the dissenters upholding what had become a New World tradition in itself, the separation of church and state. The fact that separation was embodied in the First Amendment to the Constitution of the United States was, understandably, not cited by sectarians already smarting from the accusation of republicanism! But in any case, the accusation was largely groundless, as the sectarians had proven in the American Revolution and in 1812, and were to prove again in 1837. The six Ryerson brothers, five of whom were Methodist teachers, could claim the title of United Empire Loyalist (U.E.L.) as Strachan could not. Upper Canadian sectarians of the colonial period were in the awkward position of holding two contrary traditions—those of the British and loyalist counter-revolution and the North American voluntarist revolution. The established, co-established and semi-established churches of England, Scotland and Rome were virtually unencumbered by North American influences.

During the next quarter-century the churches held firmly to vestigial remains of establishment, but one by one their rights (or were they privileges?)—the monopoly on marriages and church burials, direct political representation in the legislative councils, control of the educational system, and enjoyment of the Clergy Reserves and Rectory lands—were swept into the limbo of undenominational nationalization or, equally obnoxious, shared with the sectarians. As late as 1841 membership in the Legislative Council of Canada was divided equally between the three churches, but three years later the Methodists could boast that the appointment of Ryerson as Superintendent of Education gave them their first public office. Strachan might charge that to infringe the Anglican university endowment monopoly was to equate Christian truth with sectarian error,[7] but the forces of sectarianism seemed irresistible. New strength to the sectarian cause came with the Disruption of the Kirk. Now, remarked one anti-clerical Presbyterian, the followers of Knox would have a choice of religion other than St. Giles or Canterbury.[8]

But the growth of sectarianism in the province—the appearance of the voluntarist Free Church, the Methodist New

Connexion, and other groups—was in fact transforming the Wesleyan Methodists into a church. The old Methodists were accommodating themselves to the new order of possession as their church acquired physical structures and their members' wealth. The torch of voluntarism passed to the other sectarian groups when their Methodist college took government money and when the Methodist Church shared in the spoils of the Clergy Reserves. The turning point for sect and church was reached soon after mid-century. Officially no establishment remained and the Canadian sectarian tradition had lost its *raison d'être*.

For the Churches of England and Scotland the loss of status was a blessing in disguise. True, they would continue to preserve their trans-Atlantic orientation, though in an ever-diminishing degree, but the way was now open to the forces of indigenization. The Church of England in Canada soon received self-government and set a pattern for church organization in the rest of the Empire. The Church of Scotland soon acquired its first native-born minister. The only aspect of sectarianism in Canada that was distinctively Canadian seemed to pass into the realm of tradition. But tradition is a persistent thing. The rectories still exist in law and fact. The Church of England stands first on the ladder of precedence, with the Church of Rome on the next rung and occupying its peculiar position in the province of Quebec. United Church buildings are still referred to by some as "meeting houses," and conservatives have discovered a close relationship between the United Church and the political left. On the occasion of royal visits the suggestion is heard that the religiously divisible Crown should patronize the almost-national church!

In the generation between the secularization of the Clergy Reserves and the Methodist and Presbyterian unions, British North America achieved political unity, and Darwin produced a crisis in the course of the scientific revolution. The arrival of the railways and telegraphs, the founding of industrial enterprises, the growth of metropolitan centres— all these and other forces changed the very fabric of Canadian society. Within religious organizations the centralizing tendencies were obvious and reflected the disappearance of the frontier that had bred sectarianism. But the move from sect to church was not to go unchallenged. A new phase of sectarianism, the modern phase in Canada's history, began in reaction to those very changes in religious, social and economic organization. As was the case in the Great Awakening which brought Newlightism to Nova Scotia, the modern period of sectarianism in Canada is North American, rather than Canadian, in origin. Such sectarian movements as have begun in Canada in the last century parallel similar movements in the United States. They must be considered as similar reactions to similar conditions, and they have been deeply influenced by and closely connected to their American counterparts. The sole exceptions to this North Americanism are the Salvation Army, which reached Canada from Britain eighty years ago, and the Plymouth Brethren, a "come-out" sect of the Church of Ireland which arrived a few years earlier.

Like the Great Awakening, the Holiness Movement which appeared in the United States in the 1850s was at first interdenominational and professed no desire to establish yet another sect. Two generations earlier, certain "Scotch Baptists" in British North America had started a similar movement towards apostolic Christianity and Christian unity which ended in the separate existence of the Disciples of Christ. Now, the expulsion of the "holy" nucleus from the Methodist Episcopalians for criticizing the "easy, indulgent, accommodating, mammonized" church[9] created the seemingly inevitable sectarian structure—a new "church." It was no accident that the Free Methodists should arrive in Canada in 1876, just two years after the major Canadian Methodist churches had merged in an organic union. In their move to regain initial principles, to restore the sectarian tradition of "old-time religion" with its non-material symbols, the Free Methodists drew their support from the "more disinherited" of the rural poor. For this economic group, the unskilled or semi-skilled, there was even a special beatitude—"Blessed are the horny hands of toil." At the same time and for the same reasons the Mennonites were split by the sectarian force that created the United Missionary Church.

But one more factor must be credited with creating the sectarian revival—the new frontier in the West. Here the religious conditions of the East a half century earlier were recreated, and the modern phase of sectarianism in Canada remains to this day more obviously and intimately connected with the agrarian West than with the settled and industrialized East. Thus at the end of the First World War over 100 sects were noted

in the Canadian West.[10] Of 480 Pentecostal Assembly congregations, 415 are west of the Niagara Peninsula. Similarly,
the Christian and Missionary Alliance and the Church of the
Nazarene draw their greatest strength in Canada from the
western provinces.

Two aspects of sectarianism in the Prairies deserve special attention, for they support the contention that sects
attract the disinherited and that they are international rather
than territorial. In the first place, the sects have had great success among foreign-born people—more than ten percent of
all the Pentecostal Assemblies in Canada are non-English-
speaking. Secondly, all of the sects operating in the Prairies
have close connections with the neighbouring states to the
south and several have their headquarters in the American
Mid-West.

It is noteworthy that the Holiness Movement made no
impression on the Maritime Provinces, where no significant
sectarianism or sectarian tradition has appeared since the
death of Alline's influence. But the Holiness Movement did
lead to a belated sectarian development in Ontario about the
turn of the century. The expulsion of the charismatic R.C.
Horner from the Methodist Church because of his highly
emotional evangelical campaigns resulted in 1895 in the
establishment of the "Wesleyan Connection." This movement
reversed the usual historical process by expanding into the
Eastern United States. Internal sectarianism within the Wesleyan Connection in turn produced in 1969 the Standard
Church, a body whose influence is largely confined to Ontario.
The only other sectarian bodies that have failed to gain a
foothold on the Canadian Prairies are the "legalistic" Reformed Episcopal Church, which has only six congregations
in the whole country, and the Calvinistic, millenarian, sub-
sected Plymouth Brethren whose 6,500 adherents are concentrated predominantly in Ontario and British Columbia.

Paradoxically, the Prairies, which have been the hotbed
of this modern phase of sectarianism, also provided the impe-
tus for the church union of 1925. In Alberta, the Great
Depression and to some extent church union intensified sectarian activity. At the same time the Depression produced the
Social Credit Party. This has led Canadian scholars to suggest
that the sects of Alberta are the Social Credit Party at a
prayer meeting. If there was any truth in this proposition a

generation ago, it seems untenable today when eighty-five percent of the province's population belongs to seven denominations that cannot conceivably be called sects, and when thirty-five percent of the population are city-dwellers. Nevertheless the Social Credit Party drew heavily on the sects for party leadership material and on sectarian attitudes within the larger churches for political support on the hustings. If the Prairie sects, so weak in numbers, have not produced a new type of theocracy in Alberta, at least they have developed forms of inter-sectarian co-operation in the exchange of preachers, combined promotion of evangelical rallies, and joint support for the Youth for Christ Movement and similar organizations. The strength of Social Credit in Alberta and British Columbia is to be found not solely in the sects but in sectarian attitudes shared by members of the larger churches. The appeal of Social Credit (and of later political organizations, such as the Reform and the Canadian Alliance parties) is reminiscent of the religion-based political conservatism of early Victorian Canadian Methodism, when support for Christian measures and Christian men, in that order, was advocated to replace partisan politics. Revivalistic spirit and techniques had a prominent place in Social Credit gatherings, but a less blatant non-denominational Christian religiosity is readily discernible in Canadian politics generally.

Is there a sectarian tradition in Canada? The answer must be in the affirmative, but with the qualification that in its broadest aspects the tradition is more properly described as North American. It is the tradition of the sect on the frontier—perfectionist and, excepting the strong Calvinistic overtones of Alline's Newlightism, drawing most of its ideology and practices from the Methodist heritage. "Legalistic" sects have had little appeal to Canadians, probably because such sects are more traditional than emotional. "Pessimistic" sects have not held any early gains made, for hope deferred maketh the adventist sick. "Charismatic" sects have tended to be absorbed into "perfectionist" sects, because charisma is but one proof of holiness. Since the "communistic" sects in Canada—if they are sects—have not communicated any tradition, there remains only one vital North American sectarian tradition in Canada—the tradition of the "perfectionist" sects, drawn either from the Arminianism of the Methodists or the Calvinism of the Baptists. But the sects in Canada have

never been so numerous or the membership so large as in the
United States. The sectarian tradition in Canada repeats the
old dictum about "Canada, the double negative"—not
American, not British, but a peculiar amalgam of both. North
American sectarianism and British ecclesiasticism have been
mutually circumscribed within Canada.

Is there also a sectarian tradition that is peculiarly Canadian? Here the answer is undoubtedly affirmative. What
H.H. Walsh described as the projection of the church-sect
controversy into the form of the church-state controversy is
peculiarly Canadian.[11] This sectarian tradition could not exist
in the United States, and in England it had died with the
Puritan Commonwealth. Anti-establishmentarianism seems
to be the only sectarian tradition which has a national foundation in this country. Canada, to paraphrase one Canadian
sociologist, has preserved churchism to preserve itself.[12]
Whenever military, economic, political or cultural absorption
by the United States threatened as in 1776, 1812, 1837, 1911
or even 1957, Canada has turned to its counter-revolutionary
tradition for inspiration. And ecclesiasticism is a traditional
part of that tradition. The sect serves the function of providing a counter-weight to the over-centralizing tendencies of
ecclesiasticism. In Canada this function has been moulded
into a Canadian sectarian tradition of religious egalitarianism
in a semi-Erastian state.

IV

The Canadianization of the Protestant Churches

This paper was presented at the annual meeting of the Canadian Historical Association at Sherbrooke in 1966 and was published in the Association's volume of papers for that year.

Applying the term "Canadianization" to the development of the Christian churches in this country before Confederation is begging the question whether any demonstrable Canadianism existed in that period. Still, one can admit that nationalism did not exist in the Province of Canada before 1867 without thereby denying that some sense of Canadian identity was assuming nascent form at least from the War of 1812 onwards. The political results of that War suggest one possible interpretation of the Canadianization of the Protestant churches, namely the reconciliation of divided loyalties in the politico-religious sphere. Another interpretation may be that Canadianization in the religious sphere reflects a stage in the growth from sect to church, a form of ecclesiastical anti-colonialism.[1] While this latter interpretation can be applied to denominations that began in undeniably sectarian form in Canada, it is impossible to discuss the colonial position of the British national churches in these terms.

Perhaps the process of Canadianization in the Protestant churches can be formulated in this way: the churches of England and Scotland, as institutional projections of the established churches in Britain, were slow to accept Canadianization because their mission status involved such strong physical, financial and ideological dependence on the mother churches that the umbilical cord seemed almost to be made of iron. In contrast religious bodies without such dependence could indigenize rapidly provided they rejected the sectarian view that national boundaries are immaterial to His Kingdom. The Protestant sect that could think Canadian had more freedom of structure and spirit to Canadianize than the established church-missions that were historically tied too closely to Old World nationalism for the good of their overseas development.

The process of Canadianizing the Protestant churches in Canada—effectively in Upper Canada—has three major aspects. The first is the training and employment of a native clergy—a Canadian-born or at least Canadian-resident clergy—that would understand Canadian problems and Canadian ways better than British-trained missionaries. The second aspect is the legalization of church bodies to organize church courts and hold property—the creation of jurisdiction. This involved the structuring of churches to meet specific Canadian conditions. The third major aspect can be defined as psychological Canadianism—the acquisition and manifestation of attitudes reflecting identification with the land and people of Canada and with the Canadian outlook—in a word the growth of a Canadian sentiment or identity in the life of the churches. This was marked within the churches by certain liturgical changes and increased lay participation in church government, and in the secular realm by an overt interest in the aspirations of the nation. The three interconnected aspects do not appear at the same time or in the same order within the various churches. As legally established churches in Britain, the churches of England and Scotland had legal status in Canada before dissenting bodies, and partly as a result of this preferred position, partly because of their mission connection with the mother churches, they were late in achieving Canadian identity.

The types of ecclesiastical polity had an important bearing on the rate of indigenization. Frontier conditions left many persons and families denominationally uncommitted for years. They would probably respond to the ministrations of any denomination that could reach them physically. Congregationally organized churches would seem to have a greater flexibility for adaptation to local conditions than presbyterial—or episcopal—structured churches. In the Canadas, however, the two main congregationally structured groups, the Baptists and the Congregationalists, both failed before 1867 to become significant forces for similar reasons. Jealously guarded congregational autonomy impaired any mission outreach on a significant scale. The lack of any effective organization above the individual congregation localized the influence of the Baptist and Congregational fellowships. Frontier conditions, in fact, demanded centralized control and flexibility. Not the congregational but the episcopal system—either individual or corporate episcopacy—

best filled the needs of church organization to reach the uncommitted pioneer. But establishmentarianism and too rigid adherence to the European parish system blighted the policy-making powers of progressive bishops and presbyteries. Thus it fell to the Methodists to achieve the most successful combination of centralized control and local flexibility through their Conference and circuit rider system, and through their lack of establishment status.

The spirit of political loyalism resulting from the War of 1812 forced Canadian Methodism to end its tutelage under the American Methodist Church. In Lower Canada Methodism came under direct control of the English Conference in 1820; this mission connection, providing preachers and funds, prevented any development of Canadianism. A handful of Methodists in an overwhelmingly Roman Catholic population found survival possible only through dependence on a mother church. Essentially, this was the condition of all Protestant churches in Lower Canada. In Upper Canada, political loyalism was an even stronger force in cutting the American tie, but the absence of any predominant denomination comparable to the Roman Catholic Church in Lower Canada made independence a practicable alternative to connection with the English Methodist Conference.

The movement of the Upper Canadian Methodists for autonomy was begun in 1824 and completed in 1828. The Upper Canadian census of 1825 showed a total population of 158,000 and, allowing conservatively a four to one ration of adherents to full members, the Methodist total would be almost 34,000, or more than one in five of the population. Just three years later when independence was achieved, that total had increased by 10,000, and the number of preachers had risen from thirty-three to forty-six. Obviously, Methodism was reaching and winning the settlers. At exactly the same time, John Strachan's strictures, expressed in his famous sermon on Bishop Mountain's death and in his Ecclesiastical Chart of 1827, forced Methodism to clarify its Canadianism.

Strachan had attacked "the uneducated itinerant preachers" who were "almost universally Americans." The devastating reply of the young Egerton Ryerson showed that all but eight of the Methodist preachers were British-born and educated, and six of those eight were naturalized citizens.[2] The real issue, however, was church establishment—Strachan's demand for more effective government support of the Church of England—and here Methodism took the lead in promoting voluntarism or complete separation of church and state as a Canadian ideal. Strachan's statements had opened the Clergy Reserves controversy that was to bedevil Canadian religious and political life for the next thirty years. They also led to the establishment in 1829 of the *Christian Guardian*, the official voice of Methodism and the most influential newspaper in the province until George Brown's *Globe*. In succeeding years, the *Christian Guardian* and the Methodist Conference spoke for most dissenters when they denounced church establishment as un-Canadian.

Strachan's embroilment in the Clergy Reserves controversy and his related claim that loyalty was a peculiarly Anglican attribute have, unfortunately, veiled his own forceful Canadianism. As early as 1815 he had attempted to train a native ministry which he saw as essential to Anglican success in Canada.[3] The charter of King's College he obtained in 1827 was remarkably liberal for its day and would have been even more liberal if Strachan had had his way. The fact that the charter imposed no religious tests on students was his tacit admission of the religious pluralism already existing in Upper Canada. Even in the structure of the church, Strachan was already advocating a synodical form of government with lay representation as better adapted to the Church's Canadian needs.[4]

The militant voluntarism of the Methodists became quiescent in the early 1830s after the government-encouraged incursion of the English Conference into Upper Canada led the Canadians to accept union with that body. This sharply curtailed their autonomy and freedom of action. Despite the promise of the 1833 Articles of Union to "preserve inviolate the rights and privileges" of the Canadian Methodists, the English Conference henceforth appointed the President of the Canadian Conference, controlled all Canadian missions, and enforced English standards for ordination—this last a downgrading of the laity since it ended ordination of local preachers. The final article was the English Conference's version of the Colonial Laws Validity Act.[5] The conservative influence of the English preachers, more Wesleyan than Methodist in their deference towards the established church, was further enhanced in 1834 by a unanimous Conference resolution to exclude discussion of political questions from the *Christian Guardian*.[6] The union of 1833, though short lived, was a victory for ecclesiastical imperialism and a defeat for the Canadian experience. The Canadianism of the Methodists thereafter was more evident in the continuing Methodist Episcopal Church that had chosen separation in preference to union.

Coincident with union, the supposed coalition of voluntarists and radical reformers in Upper Canada was terminated by Egerton Ryerson's denunciation in October 1833 of William Mackenzie's ungodly associate, Joseph Hume. Mackenzie had mistakenly assumed that the Methodists were political reformers—he was equally mistaken after 1833 in believing that they had all "gone over to the enemy."[7] The aims of the Canadian Methodists were simply religious equality and political independence. The violent reaction of their English Conference brethren to the Rebellion of 1837 revealed the deep differences in outlook of the two groups. The English Conference dissolved the union in 1840 because the majority of Canadian Wesleyan Methodists would not abandon voluntarism.[8] In the end Governor General Lord Sydenham's magic wand achieved what the English Conference could not. By offering a modicum of state support through the Clergy Reserves Act of 1840, Sydenham and his "high priest,"[9] Egerton Ryerson, effectively stopped the mouth if it did not destroy the voluntarism of the Canadian Wesleyan Methodists. When the English and Canadian conferences were reunited in 1847 on virtually the same terms as 1833, it was on the clear understanding of "no politics" in the *Guardian* or Conference. So, in the final phase of the Clergy Reserves controversy that was about to begin, the voice of Canadianism in the Methodist Conference was muted.

Beginning in 1834 the reform movement in Upper Canada became secularized and when the cause of voluntarism was next taken up at the end of the forties, the torch had passed to the Free Church and its two journalistic lay spokesmen, Peter and George Brown. The hope of creating a single comprehensive Canadian Presbyterian organization was explicit in the formation of the Presbytery of the Canadas in 1818 by sixteen ministers from four different churches and three national backgrounds,[10] but these hopes had been destroyed by the divisive missionary work of the Church of Scotland's

Glasgow Colonial Society in the 1820s and by the resultant 1831 creation of the Synod of the Presbyterian Church of Canada in connection with the Church of Scotland. The Church of Scotland in Canada soon challenged the Anglican monopoly of the Clergy Reserves on the basis of its claim to co-establishment in the Empire, a claim that was, of course, a rejection of voluntarism.

The retributive disruption of the Canadian Church of Scotland Synod in 1844 was unrelated to Canadian conditions—the authority of the Scottish church courts did not extend beyond the quay of Greenock.[11] Against the divisive activities of the Free Church agents in Canada, they protested in a similar vein: "Placed as we are in a position entirely different from that of the Church of Scotland—exempted from all the grievances, either real or imaginary, which gave rise to the disruption there; and possessing a full, free and unquestioned right of jurisdiction."[12] Nevertheless Disruption shattered the Kirk in Canada with important results for the Canadianization of Presbyterianism.

In the first place, the Canadian Free Church immediately drew away about a quarter of the clergy of the old synod and thereafter increased its strength by leaps and bounds. The Church of Scotland needed a generation to regain its pre-disruption numbers. In a handful of years the laity of the Free Church, spurred on by its journalistic voices, the *Banner* and the *Globe* of the Browns, assumed the leadership of the voluntarists in Canada even though the Free Church in Scotland still favoured the establishment principle. Equally important in the Canadianizing of Presbyterianism, the Free Church seminary, Knox College, opened in 1844 with thirteen students—by its sixth session, 1849-50, it contained fifty-six students and eleven graduates had already been licensed to preach.[13] Thus the stage was set for the final all-out drive against the Clergy Reserves with the Free Church donning the mantle laid down by the Methodists over a decade earlier.

Several other developments in the 1840s were also hastening the process of Canadianization within the Protestant churches. Tractarianism, though only mildly promoted among Canadian Anglicans, divided that Church sharply into low and high church parties that generally reflected differences in national origins—the low church element predominating among Irish settlers in western Upper Canada, the same region that had gone most solidly Free Church.[14] Tractarianism presented the Anglican Church in Canada for the first time with an issue involving loyalty to the parent church and to establishmentarianism. The conversion of leading English Tractarians to Roman Catholicism prevented any open disruption within the Anglican Church while strengthening the self-confidence of the low church party. Ironically, the anti-Erastianism of the Tractarians looked very much like the practical voluntarism of the Canadian low church party.

While Tractarianism was shaking the Church of England (or the United Churches of England and Ireland as the low churchmen insisted on calling it), its Roman trend challenged all Reformed churches to closer co-operation for mutual self-defence. With the rise of the "Papal Aggression" controversy (caused by the establishment of Roman Catholic dioceses in England) in the early 1850s, co-operation began to assume the proportions of an urgent necessity. The Protestant reaction to Papal Aggression, already foreshadowed by the reaction to Tractarianism, resulted in a sort of Protestant ecumenism in Canada, in which Anglicans, Presbyterians, Methodists, Baptists and Congregationalists drew together to prosecute social reforms dear to Protestant hearts, such as temperance, sabbatarianism, and Sunday school movements. Only the continuing presence of the Clergy Reserves seemed to stand in the way of a Protestant rapprochement leading to eventual church union on the basis of a commonly shared Canadianism.

The great crisis of Canadianization, especially for the semi-established churches, arrived with the Great Ministry of Baldwin and Lafontaine. For the Anglican Church, the implications of the new order were made evident in the nationalistic legislative programme of the Reform government. King's College, popular symbol of supposed Anglican privilege in education, fell before the forces of secularization despite Strachan's protest against such "opposition to Religious truth" and "striking enmity" to the Church of England. Baldwin's "impious" University Bill was but the religious twin of the Rebellion Losses Act passed two weeks earlier. Worse was to follow—by the summer of 1850, the left-wing reformers of Upper Canada, having tasted clerical blood at King's College, were in full cry for an end to the Clergy Reserves. The forces of the voluntarists were now united in the newly-formed interdenominational Anti-Clergy Reserves Association.[15]

There is no need to retrace the chequered path to secularization of the Reserves. What is of more immediate interest is the remarkable reaction by the Church of England in the direction of Canadianization when faced with the possible loss of this last vestige of establishment.

In April 1850 John Strachan went to England in search of funds for Trinity College. There is no evidence that he discussed the Clergy Reserves question there but it would be surprising if he had not. His actions on his return to Canada suggest that he had discussed it with church authorities at home and discovered little willingness on their part to defend the Anglican share of the Reserves. As early as 1832 Strachan had proposed a diocesan synod as the best means to "obtain that influence on public opinion, or with the Government, or with the Bishop himself,—that we ought to possess, till we have frequent Convocations, composed of the Clergy and members from their several congregations. To such assemblies the Episcopal Church in the United States owes almost everything."[16]

In May 1851, Strachan initiated the first step in such a plan by inviting lay representation to his visitation. Strachan's biographer connects this move directly to the renewed agitation against the Clergy Reserves. The assembled clergy and laity of Toronto diocese passed resolutions protesting the threatened secularization and recommending legal creation of a diocesan synod.[17] Five months later, five of the seven British North American bishops met privately in Quebec to formulate a detailed plan for such synods and for an ecclesiastical province to govern the church in Canada.[18] This was but the fulfilment of the petition of Strachan and his ad hoc synod to the Archbishop of Canterbury: "The time has arrived when we must look to our local resources for the maintenance of the Clergy and the extension of the Church."[19]

Before legal stature was obtained for synods, the Clergy Reserves passed into history. The Church in Canada had not really expected the imperial House of Commons to save the Reserves, but it did place "the fullest reliance" in the House of Lords.[20] Yet even the peers proved to have feet of clay. "What could we expect," lamented Strachan, "when nine Bishops out of nineteen voted for the total confiscation of the Church Property in Canada."[21] By separating church and state, the Canadian Clergy Reserves Act of 1854 imposed voluntarism on all denominations. Equally as important as the final settlement of that long-festering sore were the resultant advances towards Canadianization made by the Protestant churches. The impact can be seen first as affecting the churches collectively. The major obstacle to Protestant co-operation was now gone and expressions of approval for intra-denominational and even for interdenominational unions began to be heard. No doubt the destruction of the Clergy Reserves road block also consolidated the latent anti-Romanism so recently awakened by the "papal aggression" controversy.

For the Protestant churches, the remaining decade before Confederation marked a continuation and intensification of the Canadianizing process begun years before. But this intensification was also the result of developments other than the ending of the Reserves. Of the mass of interwoven revolutionary changes that began about 1850, probably the most pervasive, if subtle, were the revolutions in communications and transportation. The same telegraph that provided rapid news services for the new daily papers increased the Canadian churches' awareness of things Canadian and global. The same railway that carried goods and people rapidly from one part of Canada to another increased by an equal degree the mobility of the clergy. The age of iron and steam would later present the churches with complex challenges in an urbanized and industrialized society but its first impact on the Protestant churches was to heighten their search for identity with the new and more secular Canada, and to create internal pressures in favour of laicization, decentralization and democratization.

Since the shadow of church establishment ended with the Reserves just as these physical and psychological revolutions were occurring, it is not surprising that the Churches of England and Scotland were the most obviously affected by the change of intellectual climate. Their church-state connection and mission status had been a form of ecclesiastical mercantilism. Their preferred position in the colony had depended on an imperial concept of the church and, as long as benefits—financial and other—flowed from that connection, their loyalty to the mother churches and the Empire for which they stood was entirely understandable. But just as the adoption of free trade and responsible government had caused the violent reaction of those Montreal Tories who burned the Parliament buildings and promoted annexation to the United States in

1849, the indifference of the established mother churches to the plight of their Canadian offspring led to measures of Canadianization in the Churches of England and Scotland.

Since the reduction of the imperial parliamentary grant to the Society for the Propagation of the Gospel (SPG) in the 1830s, Canadian Anglican leaders had clung the more desperately to the Clergy Reserves. At the same time they had tried to enlist the laity in more extensive voluntary giving through the organization of diocesan societies that included laymen. Addressing the Archdeaconry of York in 1852, A.N. Bethune had emphasized this obligation to self-help in conjunction with a government "provision for the maintenance of religion which shall be beyond . . . the capriciousness and risk of the voluntary system."[22] Anglicans generally failed to respond to such appeals and church finances continued to pose a problem. By contrast, the Church of England was embarrassed by a surplus of clergy and had to turn away applicants from outside Canada.

One purpose of diocesan synods was to take over financial aspects of administration, including supervision of the commuted Clergy Reserves Fund. Strachan had called his episcopal visitation of 1853 a synod even though legislation for Anglican self-government was not obtained until 1857. The Toronto Synod of 1856 foreshadowed the new order with a canon for the election of bishops by clergy and laity. The unseemly races for the mitres of Huron and Ontario, however, caused Whitaker, the high church provost of Trinity College, to advocate synod delegation of its electoral power to the authorities of the Church in England. Strachan's Canadianism showed in his reply that Whitaker's proposal "ignores the claims of the whole Canadian Clergy and neutralizes the very powers of self-government which the Church in the colonies has been so anxious to possess."[23]

In 1860 the Church in Canada achieved autonomy and territorial integration a full seven years before Confederation with the appointment of a metropolitan and the erection of a provincial synod. Preaching before the Toronto synod in 1865, H.C. Cooper emphasized the peacefulness of this evolution to church self-government, achieved "without any rupture, or even weakening, of those ties of loyalty and affection" that bind Anglicans to the mother church and to the Crown. Royal supremacy remained unimpaired by accepting the principle of a religiously divisible Crown. The fact that the Church in Canada was both "self-acting and self-reliant" exemplified the spirit of the commonwealth, namely self-government without separation. Within the Anglican communion the problem of divided loyalties had been solved by the same methods and on the same principles that achieved self-government for Canada. Finally, as Cooper noted, voluntarism had left the Church unrepresented in the provincial legislature and therefore the presence of the laity in synods was a necessity for the Canadianized Church.[24]

The last legal tie between Canadian Anglicanism and the mother church—the royal recognition of bishops—was destroyed, not by Canadian anti-colonials or secularists, but by the 1864 decision of the Judicial Committee of the Privy Council in the case involving Bishop Colenso of Natal. The validity of royal patents for colonial bishops was now denied. The granting of responsible government, it was held, ended royal authority over the colonial Church.[25] After the initial period of confusion caused by the Colenso case, the Canadian Church reacted to its new separated status at its third triennial provincial synod with a unanimous resolution requesting the Archbishop of Canterbury to form a General council of the Anglican communion.[26] This proposal was not accepted by the Archbishop but the action of the Canadian synod did lead directly to the calling of the less formal first Lambeth Conference.

The results of nationalizing the Clergy Reserves were not as painful for the Church of Scotland as for the Church of England. The reversion to the Church of Scotland of Reserve stipends previously paid to ministers who joined the Free Church at Disruption had increased the per capita share of the Church of Scotland. Since the Church of Scotland did not grow at anything like the rate of the Free Church or even the Church of England, the loss of the Reserves in 1854 did not have the same quantitative impact on that Church as on its sister establishment, but it did free the Kirk from the main obstacle to Canadianization. A correspondent to *The Presbyterian* struck the note of Canadianism for the Kirk. "Let us as British North Americans feel that this is our country, that our interests are here, that its institutions are our institutions. Let us have a British North American Presbyterian Church, that will extend from Newfoundland to Vancouver's Island: and only one Presbyterian Church."[27]

William Proudfoot, Secessionist church missionary, had spoken for all Canadian Presbyterians when he wrote in favour of a native ministry. "We are too Scotch—our habits, our brogue, our mode of sermonizing are all too Scotch. The thistle is everywhere seen . . . our mission is a foreign affair. And so it will be until we employ the country born, divest it of its Scotch character, and make it Canadian."[28] Similarly, the Free Church magazine, the *Canadian Presbyter*, favoured Canadianization. Canadian Presbyterianism should not "follow in a slavish spirit the forms and customs of older churches." Like their immigrant members, the colonial churches must learn new lessons.[29] Months later the same editor, complaining of lack of support for Knox College, remarked, "We are in fact a Missionary Church." "It is obvious that we Presbyterians in Canada have to make progress at least in one direction, and that is the direction of Union."[30]

Union talks between the Free Church and the smaller United Presbyterian Church synod had in fact begun coincidentally with Disruption. Noting that the six Presbyterian bodies in British North America together had 300 ordained clergy, the Free Church magazine called for an end to racial, national and sectional prejudices. "Our Church must open her doors and bid all Canadians enter."[31] For a new, comprehensive Canadian Presbyterian communion, the editor proposed the title, "The United Church of Canada."[32] Union of the Free Church and United Presbyterian as the Canada Presbyterian Church was consummated in 1861, on the neutral ground of the Montreal Wesleyan Methodist Church.

The new Presbyterian body had nearly two hundred thousand members. The Synod of the Church of Scotland with only 108,000 was increasingly unable to finance church extension and meet the demand for ministers.[33] In 1865 the average weekly contribution of members was less than one cent. Since eleven of one hundred and sixty-six congregations gave almost half of the total collection, the remainder were putting one half cent per head on the collection plate.[34] "We need not try to hide the truth, ours is a Voluntary Church," noted a Report on the state of the Kirk.[35] Despite the establishment of Queen's College in 1841 to train Canadians for the ministry, of one hundred and twenty-five ministers and licentiates active in Canada in 1867 only twenty-two were Canadian-born. In a quarter century, Queen's had granted only fifteen degrees in Theology[36]

The revival of the Clergy Reserves Question in the early 1850s reawakened briefly the old tensions within the Wesleyan Methodist Church. The Conference of 1851 reacted to popular pressure with resolutions condemning the Reserves as "wholly at variance with the sentiments and feelings of the Canadian people, and most unjust to the Wesleyan and several other religious denominations."[37] But the Conference would not join in the public agitation of what was now considered to be a purely political question, and the *Christian Guardian* was at some pains to disclaim any rift between the laity and Conference over the Clergy Reserves Question.[38] Thereafter the *Guardian* remained editorially silent to the chagrin of all voluntarists. An attempt by John Ryerson to force the Conference of 1854 to support secularization was defeated by the conservative forces.[39] That same Conference, however, assumed responsibility from the English Conference for the work in Lower Canada and for the western (Hudson Bay and Rocky Mountain) missions, evidence that Canadian Methodists were awakening to Canada's manifest destiny in the west.[40]

One year later the Wesleyan Conference gave laymen an equal voice with clergy in the management of church funds[41]—certainly a small measure of democratization in the church but as far as the Wesleyan Methodists were prepared to go in the period before Confederation. Active Canadianism had passed from the Wesleyans to the smaller Methodist Episcopal and New Connexion churches, just as the Church of Scotland had lost its initiative in Canadianization to the Free Church.

The Baptists comprising in 1861 less than five per cent of the population and the Congregationalists comprising less than one per cent expressed their Canadianism mainly in opposition to the Clergy Reserves and separate schools. Congregational home missions had been placed under Canadian control in 1853 but two-thirds of the churches still depended on outside help.[42] The announcement that in 1861 the Colonial Missionary Society would reduce its support of Canadian missions elicited bitter comments about desertion by the mother country. Congregationalism faced the financially bleak future with the same despair that the Church of England had greeted the decline of SPG support decades earlier, yet the columns of the *Canadian Independent* reflected no sentiment of Canadianism. Perhaps the silver trowel shaped like a maple leaf used to lay the cornerstone of a Toronto Congregational Church in 1863 indicated some covert psychological Canadianization, but the financial crisis of the missions suggested that Congregationalism was not yet physically ready for Canadianization.

At Confederation, the smallest Protestant churches—Lutheran, Mennonite, Tunker and others—together held at most five per cent of the Upper Canadian population. Being ethnic churches, their Canadianization has been more difficult because of Old World national and language traditions that were deemed essential to their existence. The story of their accommodation to the Canadian environment belongs to the post-Confederation era.

Reviewing the incomplete Canadianization of the Protestant churches before Confederation, it is obvious that the Clergy Reserves acted as a catalyst in the process. For the churches of England and Scotland the loss of the Reserves had imposed the unavoidable necessity of self-reliance. For the voluntarist churches the Reserves had symbolized an old world conception of church-state relations for which, they sincerely believed, there was no room in Canada. For them Canadianization—psychological and legal—was a reaction against evidences of an establishmentarianism that claimed a monopoly of loyalty and true Christianity. For the supposedly established churches of England and Scotland, the existence of the Reserves was a block to Canadianization. For the voluntarist churches, nationalization of the Reserves inaugurated a second phase of Canadianization that was less obvious if no less real than its earlier expression. Within a generation after Confederation, all Canadian Presbyterians were joined in one nation-wide church and the Methodist bodies had been similarly united. Principal Grant of Queen's prophesied a future union of all Christians of this country in a single national church.[43]

A second factor was undoubtedly the achievement of responsible government. If a double political loyalty to colony and mother country was possible, why could there not be self-government for colonial churches? This realization, added to the apparent indifference of the parent church of England towards its colonial branch, proved decisive in Canadianizing the Anglican Church.

The contribution of the "Papal Aggression" issue to the Canadianization of the Protestant churches is more difficult to assess. Canadian echoes of the Papal Aggression controversy were more usually expressed in political rather than religious terms, as being connected with separate schools, representation by population or "rep by pop," and sectional deadlock, the inability of the Canadas to work together.[44] Religious reactions to the controversy were expressed simply within the framework of traditional Protestant-Roman Catholic antagonism. Polarization between Canadianism and ultramontanism had only just begun to appear in 1867. Before Confederation, only the Free Church had felt any compulsive duty to make the French better Canadians by making them Protestants. Only after the Protestant churches had themselves achieved a measurable degree of Canadianization did they see ultramontanism as a supra-national and un-Canadian loyalty. Undoubtedly the most potent force in their own Canadianization before 1867 was the spirit and practice of voluntarism. It required political Confederation to create the geographical setting and breadth of vision that enabled the Protestant churches to make the first step towards church union by forming ecclesiastical organizations that were denominationally unified and nation-wide in jurisdiction.

V

American Influences on
Canadian Protestant Churches
before Confederation

This paper was presented to a meeting of the American Society of Church History in Toronto in 1966 and was published in Church History *the following year.*

American influences on Canadian Protestant Churches before Confederation do not present any simple historical pattern. As any student of Canadian history would expect, the responses of the Canadian Protestant denominations vary widely, not only from one denomination to another but from one region to another. Indeed, regionalism seems to be the most important factor in determining the degree of American influences, both positive and negative, on Canadian Protestantism. Canadian historians have examined or at least noted separate aspects of American influences, particularly in a denominational context, but no one has apparently attempted a survey approach to the wide range of such influences—wide both geographically and topically.

It has been customarily and confidently assumed by Canadian historians writing general accounts of the interplay of Canadian-American relations that the dominant motif in the religious sphere as in the secular is or ought to be anti-Americanism. Close scrutiny of American religious influences during roughly a century preceding Confederation suggests that anti-Americanism is a minor and in some areas insignificant factor in the development of Canadian Protestantism. Admittedly, it is difficult to disentangle anti-Americanism from the attack on and defence of the incomplete and eventually futile efforts to create an Anglican establishment in the British North American colonies. In other words, Anglican opposition to the demand of Protestant dissenters for religious equality seems to have been credited by historians to anti-American sentiments because the religious equality sought in British North America was parallel to and, hence, supposedly inspired by the United States' acceptance of the principle of the separation of church and state. This is not to deny that expressions of anti-Americanism can be found in the writings and speeches of the defenders of establishmentarianism, but such expressions seem to be secondary to their main theme of defending state-churchism—after-thoughts offered as additional but not basic arguments for maintaining legal distinctions between conformity and dissent. More importantly, in several aspects of religious development American influences were not challenged but were accepted even by the Church of England and, taking a regional perspective of the whole question, anti-Americanism seems to have been virtually non-existent as a factor in Protestant history in the Maritime colonies.

Up to the American Revolution the old province of Nova Scotia had all the appearance of being a demographic and hence religious frontier of New England. Congregationalism had been introduced by the New England settlers who constituted the bulk of the population. At least seventeen ministers had come either with, or at the invitation of, Congregationalists. By contrast, the Church of England, established as the state religion in 1758, had only three missionaries of the Society for the Propagation of the Gospel, including one serving the "foreign Protestants" of Lunenburg. Presbyterianism had come from Ulster, mostly by way of New Hampshire thanks to the colonizing efforts of Colonel Alexander McNutt around 1760.[1] Eight days after landing at Truro these Ulstermen organized a congregation and began a church building. Their appeal in 1763 for a minister was answered by the Presbytery of New Brunswick, New Jersey, which sent James Lyon in 1764.

Before Lyon arrived, however, a separate appeal had been sent to the Associate Synod of the Secession Church in Scotland which sent out Samuel Kinlock as a missionary. Three years later Kinlock was replaced by two men who remained in Nova Scotia. A fourth missionary, James Murdoch of the Ulster General Associate (Anti-Burgher) Secession Church, arrived in 1766 but eschewed any future connection with either Burgher or Anti-Burgher presbyteries in Nova Scotia. The important point here is the predominant connection of Nova Scotian Presbyterianism with Britain. When James Lyon returned to the United States at the outbreak of the Revolution, the single tie with American Presbyterianism was broken. Henceforth Presbyterianism in

Nova Scotia looked exclusively to Britain and no American influences can be discerned.

For Congregationalism in Nova Scotia the breaking point of American ties was both painful and destructive. The fifteen congregations organized before the Revolution were apparently served exclusively by New England ministers. One of these joined with three Presbyterians to perform the first Protestant ordination in 1770, an ordination whose irregularity simply reflects the Congregational custom of establishing "gathered" churches through the initiative of local groups who drew up their own covenants based on New England models.[2] The inherent separatism of Congregationalist organization and the general poverty of the settlers had already seriously weakened Congregationalism in Nova Scotia before it collapsed under the double blows of the Revolution and the Newlightism of Henry Alline.

When the challenge of loyalty came in 1775 pro-American sympathies were displayed in rural areas where Congregationalism was the dominant denomination. Upon the outbreak of hostilities a number of leading Congregational laymen returned to New England. The abortive revolt at Maugerville on the Saint John River was led by the Congregational deacons and by the minister who later escaped to the United States.[3] All but two or perhaps three of the Congregational ministers left the province at the earliest opportunity, one exception being William Seccombe who was ordered to desist from preaching and to post a £500 bond.[4] Despite Seccombe's known sympathies for the Revolution he remained in Nova Scotia and died there in 1792.

The political liability of Congregationalism in Nova Scotia was only one factor in its virtual disappearance during the Revolution. The *coup de grâce* came from Henry Alline's divisive preaching of Newlightism, beginning contemporaneously with but unrelated to the Revolution.[5] Newlightism split virtually every congregation in the colony, just as it had in the other seaboard colonies when it spread northward during the preceding generation. Only four congregational churches in Nova Scotia survived the onslaught of Newlightism and they can barely claim a continuous existence[6]—churches that accepted the New Light became Baptist congregations or, in a few cases, Presbyterian churches. As a religious force Congregationalism disappeared from Nova Scotia for generations; yet the question remains: would the outcome of the impact of Newlightism have been any different had the Revolution not occurred?

In any case the Congregational polity at least made the change easier because the concept of the "gathered church" was also basic to Baptist ecclesiology. Not the organization but the theology of Congregationalism had changed as Calvinism, antipaedobaptism (the doctrine opposed to infant baptism) and closed communion became dominant.[7] With the exception of the loyalty issue the problems of the pre-Revolutionary Congregationalists were also those of the post-Revolutionary Baptist fellowship in Nova Scotia. This exception is evident in the Baptist ministry in Nova Scotia—not one of the Baptist "fathers" was an American national though several had come to Nova Scotia in the pre-Revolutionary migration.

Perhaps the fact that the Baptist fellowship in the Maritime colonies as a post-Revolutionary growth, uncontaminated and hence untrammelled by the loyalty issue, accounts for the extensive evidence of American influence in its growth. "Messengers" were regularly exchanged with the Massachusetts Association and undoubtedly such fraternal visits introduced American religious ideas. Maritime Baptists profited from American experience in organizing associations or inter-church co-operative undertakings. The model of the Nova Scotia Association was avowedly the Danbury Association in New England. Baptist statements of faith were frequently verbatim copies of American covenants. Like the Maritime Baptists, the Baptists of Massachusetts were struggling for separation of church and state. Further American influences on Maritime Baptists can be seen in their mutual interests in developing educational facilities and later in pioneering co-education. A final influence can be seen in the temperance movement that developed in the late 1820s. After 1800 the attention of Maritime Baptists was absorbed by their own denominational developmental problems, yet one of their historians is able to state categorically that, "The course of Baptist history in the Maritime Provinces during the early nineteenth century continued to be greatly influenced by the relations maintained with the Baptists of New England."[8]

After its tenuous beginnings in Nova Scotia the Church of England grew rapidly thanks to the American Revolution. How many Loyalists were Anglican cannot be established, but with the great migration of 1783 came thirty-one Anglican clergymen, although only ten remained in the province.[9] The opinion of Thomas Carleton, brother of Sir Guy and first governor of the new province of New Brunswick, that the lack of a proper Anglican establishment had been a factor contributing to the revolution and therefore a condition not to be repeated in the remaining colonies, was an opinion shared by many, including William Knox, under-secretary for the Colonies, and by Carleton's secretary, Jonathan Odell, Loyalist and former SPG missionary.[10] While Carleton hopefully laid out Anglican parishes in the colony and his first legislature reenacted the Nova Scotia statute establishing the Church of England, Knox was prepared to tolerate Roman Catholicism if it would provide an additional bulwark against republicanism.

The same anti-American sentiments might reasonably be expected to appear in the shrunken province of Nova Scotia, particularly after Charles Inglis' appointment as Bishop. Instead, Governor Parr boasted of his policy of "unlimited toleration"[11] and the Loyalist bishop maintained close and friendly relations with leaders of the Protestant Episcopal Church in the United States. As probable author of that petition from eighteen Anglican clergymen to Sir Guy Carleton, composed at New York in 1783,[12] asking him to support the establishment of a bishop of Nova Scotia, Inglis continued to view the clergy of the Protestant Episcopal Church, his former associates, as slightly and accidentally separated brethren.[13] Samuel Seabury, Loyalist, became the first bishop of the Protestant Episcopal Church and T.B. Chandler, who refused the see of Nova Scotia, returned to the United States in 1785.[14] Charles Inglis and later his son, Bishop John, maintained a steady correspondence with Bishop J.H. Hobart of New York, son-in-law of Chandler, and John was a guest and travelling companion of the Hobart household. Other Anglican leaders in British North America shared these fraternal feelings. Charles Stewart preached his first sermon after his consecration as bishop of Quebec in Inglis' old church, Trinity, where Hobart now had his throne and, in 1828, even extended a preaching engagement at Buffalo in order to meet the Hobarts and Inglis who were visiting the Falls together.[15] Similarly, John Stuart, Loyalist "father of Anglicanism in Upper Canada," carried on an intimate correspondence with Bishop White of Philadelphia.

The surprisingly restrained anti-Americanism in the Church of England remained even after the emergence of Methodism in the Maritimes. Methodists, like the Baptists, could date their beginnings in Nova Scotia from the time of the Revolution but, unlike the Baptists, the Methodists came into existence as an organized body in North America as a result of the Revolution. The necessity of providing continuity for Methodism in the revolted colonies finally forced John Wesley into making the long avoided and unwanted break with the Church of England by sending Coke to consecrate Asbury as the bishop of the Methodist Episcopal Church in the United States. Where the Church of England was hampered by the imperial statute that denied American-ordained clergy the right to officiate on British soil,[16] Wesley had no reluctance in leaving Nova Scotia as a mission of the American Conference or in directing William Black, founder of Methodism in the Maritime colonies, to obtain preachers from that conference.[17]

Freeborn Garretson, first American volunteer for Nova Scotia, arrived in Halifax in 1785 to a warm welcome from Governor Parr and from John Breynton, the Anglican rector. Travelling through the colony, Garretson encountered no anti-Americanism—Anglican, Presbyterian and Congregational pulpits alike were opened to him—but he did discover that "a number of people would prefer an Englishman to an American," while others took offence at the mere suggestion of an English connection.[18] James Wray, the first English missionary, came in 1787 and was soon complaining that the Methodist Discipline was not being fully observed because of American influence. Wesley seemed to agree with Wray's estimate of American influence when he wrote, "O American gratitude! Lord, I appeal to thee."[19] The same complaints regarding non-observance of the Discipline were still being voiced in 1817.[20]

American Methodist missionaries—as many as six in one year—arrived in the Maritimes without any charges of creeping republicanism being voiced. Bishop Inglis' later confused equation of the New Lights and Methodists as "fanatics" and "enthusiasts" stemmed from the hardening of denominational lines around the turn of the century.[21] There was never an overt suggestion of disloyalty imputed to the Americans among the Methodist preachers, but increased opposition to

Methodism and other forms of dissent may have influenced Black's decision in 1799 to seek missionaries exclusively from the British Conference. The deferential attitude that Black, like Wesley and Coke, showed towards the national church became a characteristic of Maritime Methodism. This, combined with the small numbers of Methodists, who never exceeded ten per cent of the population in those colonies, is a partial explanation for the belated, non-political and restrained antagonism to Methodism on the part of the established church. Other factors that counteracted any potential anti-Americanism were, no doubt, the year-round communications with Britain that kept Maritime eyes turned eastward rather than southward, and the lack of any post-Loyalist American immigration. In the Maritime colonies the Loyalist fact was so deeply and dominantly fixed in the social fabric that American influences could be received and absorbed by the Protestant churches without fear of political repercussions.

If the American Revolution contributed in these several positive ways to the religious development of the Maritime colonies, its importance to the evolution of Protestantism in the Canadas was even more marked and decisive. It is a commonplace of Canadian history to say that without the Revolution there would have been no Upper Canada—the axiom deserves to be repeated occasionally as a reminder of its basic and formative importance to the Canadian experience. Loyalists who stayed in what was to become Lower Canada generally fitted into a pre-established religious pattern. Presbyterianism and Anglicanism were already functioning in the Province before the Revolution but this did not preclude the appearance of American influences among the Protestant denominations in the post-Revolutionary period. St. Gabriel's Street Presbyterian congregation, organized in 1786 by the Loyalist chaplain John Bethune, received as its second minister John Young, licensed in Scotland but ordained by the presbytery of New York. From 1791 to 1793 Young and his congregation belonged to the American Presbyterian Church. The calling of the Scot James Somerville to St. Gabriel's Street, Montreal, in 1802 split the congregation along national lines of Scottish fur traders versus former Americans. In forming a separate congregation the latter group obtained aid from American Presbyterians and also a Scottish minister, Robert Easton, who came via New York where two fellow missionaries of the Scottish Associate Synod had settled.[22] The same national tensions continued inside the new congregation until a further splintering of the American Presbyterian group created the nucleus of the present-day Erskine and American United Church. By 1817 the four Presbyterian ministers in Lower Canada and the nine in Upper Canada together represented five different Presbyterian bodies, three from Britain and two from the United States.

The Baptist communion began in the Eastern Townships in 1793 when two missionaries from Vermont organized a church and ordained a Loyalist as preacher. This early contact with the United States stemmed from American initiative and was not repeated until 1806 when the Massachusetts Baptist Missionary Society began to send preachers on annual visits to the Townships.[23] This practice ended in 1811, not apparently because of any anti-American feeling. Since the missionaries ordained local men whenever churches were organized, Baptist congregational polity precluded any possibility of charges of American domination. The small number of Baptists in Lower Canada made the communion's development dependent on outside sources and at the same time this retarded growth saved them from the kind of jealousy created by the burgeoning influence of Methodism in Upper Canada.

In the upper province no less than nine missionaries of six different American Baptist associations or missionary societies began work during the first score of years in the nineteenth century. The majority of pastors seems to have been post-Loyalist settlers—only two of eighteen served in imperial or provincial regiments during the Revolution.[24] The settlement of the Ottawa Valley after the Napoleonic wars introduced a group of Baptists who were almost exclusively Scottish. Whereas the Baptist church established under American influence along the Ontario strand were solidly of the "closed communion" school, the Ottawa Valley Baptists held to open communion. Yet it was the closed or strict communion custom that had won general acceptance among Canadian Baptists before Confederation. That more evidences of American influence are not found among Baptists in the Canadas must be attributed to divisive forces, both human and natural, that frustrated their educational and missionary efforts during the period.[25]

American Presbyterianism entered Upper Canada soon after the creation of the province when Jabez Collver of New

Jersey, a minister of the "Cambridge Presbyterian Order," settled in Norfolk County at Governor Simcoe's invitation.[26] Collver's congregation, though Presbyterian in name, was still independent of any higher court when Collver died in 1818. More important than this isolated case were the contacts established with the Dutch Reformed Church and the Associate Reformed Church of the United States. The latter body sent several missionaries into the province but formed no churches. The Niagara region, scene of a later incursion of American Presbyterianism, received Daniel W. Eastman from the American Associate Presbyterian Church in 1801. Eastman, whose Canadian ministry lasted sixty-four years, did not join the indigenous Presbytery of the Canadas when it was formed in 1818, but this presbytery did absorb Robert McDowall, survivor of the two ministers from the Dutch Reformed Classis of Albany who had served several congregations between Glengarry and York counties over a number of years.[27]

The Presbytery of the Canadas had barely been formed from these disparate elements when missionaries of the Glasgow Colonial Society of the Church of Scotland reached Canada and drastically altered the development of Canadian Presbyterianism. Appealing successfully to the bonds of tradition and old-world nationalism, these missionaries won a majority of the Presbyterians for the Kirk and imprinted on Canadian Presbyterianism a conservatism that it never lost. The significance of this Britishness and conservatism becomes apparent upon examination of the rise and fall of the independent Niagara Presbytery that was formed in 1833 with substantial support from the American Home Missionary Society of New York City.

A.K. Buell, one of the earliest of seven or eight American Presbyterian missionaries who formed the Niagara Presbytery, noted in 1831 the presence of an anti-American heritage of the War of 1812. "We must be British or the cry is raised against us."[28] The religious enthusiasm of American Presbyterianism found a strong echo in the Niagara region at first but soon caused friction when it encountered the conservatism of British-oriented Presbyterianism. The Niagara Presbytery, which, unlike the Kirk, accepted voluntarism and used Isaac Watt's psalms and hymns, barely survived the anti-American reaction to the Rebellion of 1837.[29] Enthusiasm, voluntarism and liturgical liberalism went down to defeat in 1838 when most of the ministers of the presbytery deserted its twenty-five congregations to return to the United States because of "suspicion of disaffection to the Government."[30] The later voluntarism of the Free Church in Canada owed nothing directly to American influences, for the Free Church in Canada was as much a product of Britain as was the establishmentarian Church of Scotland. American influences had been purged from Canadian Presbyterianism a long generation before Confederation, thanks to a combination of religious and political conservatism.

The long church-state controversy, in itself an aspect of church-sect relations in Upper Canada, has long attracted the attention of historians, so that the existence of the issue and of the part played by the Methodists in the campaign for religious equality is well known. The isolated activity of such Methodists as the Hecks and Emburys constitutes only a prelude to the story of Canadian Methodism. Of greater significance was the entry of American Methodists into Upper Canada at the invitation of certain Canadian settlers because the preacher William Losee had visited his Loyalist relatives in 1790. The circuit that Losee formed the following year became an integral part of the New York Conference of the Methodist Episcopal Church. The rapid growth of Methodism that followed was made possible primarily by the failure of the British-based churches to provide for the spiritual needs of the settlers. Most Upper Canadians were religiously uncommitted; John Langhorn, Anglican missionary at Bath, reported he had only eleven communicants in a settlement of fifteen hundred souls.[31] Into this institutional vacuum American Methodism carried its dynamic message and its highly mobile organization. Its success was also due no doubt in part to the post-Loyalist migration from the United States which swamped the Loyalists numerically in the space of a generation.

Between 1790 and 1812 the Methodist Episcopal Church sent at least seventy-six missionaries into the Canadas—not more than seven of them were Canadian-born.[32] The bulk of their labours were concentrated in Upper Canada—only in 1806 did they mount a concerted drive in Lower Canada by organizing a three-circuit district. By 1811 these Lower Canadian circuits had increased to five but reported only 242 members.[33] Upper Canada had 2,800 members on seven circuits.[34] Given the Loyalist tradition of anti-Americanism, the lack of any strong reaction against this incursion of the Methodist

Episcopal Church may seem surprising. The explanation, I suggest, is that the Loyalist tradition is a half-truth. The anti-
Americanism credited to the Loyalists was largely a creation of
the post-1812 War period. Lieutenant-Governor Simcoe,
whose British enthusiasms are indisputable, was anxious to
have a fully established church in Upper Canada "to loosen the
weight of democratic influences" and preserve "the Connection between Great Britain and her Colonies" in the face of the
anticipated American demographic expansion,[35] yet he never
suggested that Methodism's American connections constituted
a loyalty risk. The anti-Americanism later directed against
American influences on Canadian Methodism can be
explained only as a product of the War of 1812.

In 1812 the Lower Canadian Methodist district joined
the Upper Canadian district as part of the Genesee Conference, which met on the American side of the Niagara River
one month after war was declared. The bishop proceeded to
make circuit appointments to the Canadas, but American
preachers had already been ordered out of the upper province and no Canadian-born preachers attended that Conference. The bishop's circuit plan existed on paper only, for
no Methodist preacher remained in Lower Canada and eight
of the thirteen still in the upper province located, that is,
ceased to itinerate, before the end of the War.[36] Thus the work
of the American Methodists virtually disappeared during the
war and there is no indication that the preachers who remained
in Upper Canada were under suspicion for their previous
American connection.

When peace returned the Methodist Episcopal Church
began rebuilding its Canadian work. Three Upper Canadian
preachers who had not located were again on circuit and of
the twelve preachers appointed to Upper Canada by the
Genesee Conference in 1815 all but two or three were of
British birth. The rest were Americans "of moderate politics
and prudent in conduct."[37] Methodism in Canada had thus
been largely purged of American preachers. The war had
removed them on account of their citizenship, not because of
any political activity, for the Methodist Episcopal Church had
eschewed politics in Canada even more carefully than it had
in the United States.

The war diverted Upper Canadian Methodism into new
channels and laid the groundwork for the creation in 1828 of

Canada's first indigenous church. But the war also created
the climate for the politico-religious conflict that raged in the
province during the next two decades. The loyalty issue arose
first in Lower Canada where three missionaries of the English Conference had arrived in 1815 in response to an invitation from some Montreal Methodists. Bishop Asbury's
protest against this intrusion was answered by the London
Missionary Committee with a reference to the Lower Canadians' preference for English preachers, "not to mention
their political relation to this country."[38] Probably the deaths
of the diplomatic Coke and Asbury prolonged the settling of
this confrontation between English and American influences.
Before the concordat was reached in 1819 giving Lower
Canada and Kingston to the English Conference, six English
missionaries had split several Methodist congregations as far
west as Niagara and had drawn off about ten per cent of the
membership on those circuits by their appeal to British loyalty.[39] English missionaries in the field considered the Missionary Committee's decision to leave Upper Canada to the
Americans as an ill-timed and unnecessary retreat, and they
continued to complain of it for a decade.[40]

Freed of the English challenge, the Upper Canadian
Methodists began to Canadianize rapidly. The Genesee Conference, meeting at Niagara, Upper Canada, in 1820, advised
the bishops to establish an annual Canadian Conference if
expedient, and resolved that its preachers in the British province should "behave themselves as peaceable and orderly
subjects."[41] The bishops postponed the formation of such a
Conference, but when the General Conference of 1824 was
informed by petitions that its eastern Canadian circuits were
"all in a blaze for separation,"[42] separation was granted. The
Canadian Conference immediately memorialized the American conferences for full independence on the grounds of geo-
graphic necessity, of political prejudice in Canada against
American influences, of jealousies awakened by the provincial government as a result of the recent English Conference
activities, of the possibility of a future Anglo-American war,
and of the desirability to obtain legal status and religious
equality in Canada.[43] The desired independence was obtained
in 1828, and, interestingly, the new Canadian Wesleyan
Methodist Church abandoned the American title of "bishop"
for the more republican-sounding office of "president of

Conference." The Canadians would have liked the famous American Nathan Bangs as first president, but he was an alien and "too democratical."[44]

The effects of this two-stage achievement of independence were soon apparent. From thirty-three preachers and 6,150 members in 1824 the Church grew to sixty-five preachers and 15,000 members in 1832.[45] Soon after this growth began, and largely, I suggest, in response to it, Archdeacon John Strachan inaugurated the era of religious conflict in the province with the publication in 1826 of his sermon on the death of Bishop Mountain and his open letter and Ecclesiastical Chart to the Colonial Secretary in the next year, both intended primarily to elicit more financial aid from the imperial government. Criticism of the Chart by dissenters concentrated on its faulty denominational statistics, but what really fired the heather was Strachan's characterization in his sermon of dissenting preachers as "almost universally from the Republican States of America," from whose "hostility to our Parent Church" their hearers would soon "imbibe opinions anything but favourable to the political Institutions of England."[46] The reaction of indignant Methodism was the occasion for Egerton Ryerson's debut in the stormy politics of Upper Canada.

Despite Ryerson's refutation of Strachan's charges and despite the adverse report on Strachan's Chart by a select committee of the Assembly, persons close to the government were instrumental in having the Methodist English Conference break the concordat of 1819 by sending missionaries once more into Upper Canada. The promise of £900 from the Casual and Territorial Revenues was an added incentive for this step.[47] To forestall a repetition of the divisions of 1817 the Canadians proposed and in 1833 completed a union with the English Conference. By this step the Canadian body came under English control and their influential journal, the *Christian Guardian*, was effectively gagged. The secretary of the English Conference's Missionary Committee boasted to the Colonial Secretary that, thanks to the union, "the influence of the United States will therefore be utterly shut out."[48] Whether real or imaginary, American influences on Canadian Methodism were indeed suppressed until the English Conference dissolved the union in 1840 because of alleged Canadian hostility to the Anglican establishment. By that date it was obvious that

Canadian Methodists were motivated solely by Canadianism, and in attacking their voluntarism Methodist opponents were confusing a North American religious outlook with supposed American influence.

After the Rebellion of 1837, charges of republicanism simply could not be made to stick to the dissenters who had incontrovertibly proven their loyalty during that crisis. In the next decade defenders of the Clergy Reserves might accuse voluntarists of behaving like Americans regarding church establishment but not even John Strachan suggested that they were under any direct American influence. Instead, during the quarter century between the Union of the Canadas and Confederation, religious controversy in the province centred on two entirely local issues, education and the Clergy Reserves, and on the "papal aggression" controversy. In these three issues both evidence of and charges of American influence were virtually nonexistent. John Strachan defended Anglican control of King's College and the Anglican share of the Clergy Reserves by claiming the religious decline in the United States resulted from the separation of church and state and the consequent failure of government to endow the churches.[49] With equal justice he could and did point to the same alarming tendencies in Britain, epitomized in that creation of secularism, London University, and in the progress of Erastianism which the Oxford Movement was opposing.[50] Genuine anti-Americanism appeared only in the political sphere as responses to the Annexation Manifesto and Fenianism. Canadian Protestantism had reached a degree of maturity where American influences could be received and absorbed without the old loyalty cry being raised.

Such influences are to be found in the area of socio-religious thought rather than in church organization, although the Anglican adoption of synodical episcopacy with lay representation is a notable exception to this generalization. As early as 1832 Strachan had proposed the creation of an Anglican convocation in the colonies but his fellow clergy remained resolutely opposed to lay participation in church government until the re-opening of the Clergy Reserves question in 1849 seemed to bring a change of heart.[51] Now Strachan hoped that involvement of the laity in Church government might save the Anglican interest in the Reserves, and the inclusion of laymen in his unofficial "synod" of 1853 was certainly inspired at least in form by the practice of the American Protestant Episcopal Church.[52]

In the broader sphere of public morality American influences on Protestantism in both Canada and the Maritime provinces during that quarter-century are numerous and clearly distinguishable. The Maine Law became the ideal of the widespread Canadian temperance movement and the model for several abortive attempts at parallel legislation in the provincial parliament.[53] American efforts to stop "Sabbath profanation" were equally inspiring to British Americans, who, after 1840, faced the same problems regarding Sunday mercantile operations in connection with railways, canals, post offices and markets.[54] Along with the Protestant churches of the United States and Britain, Canadian churches shared the enthusiasm for foreign missions that arose in this period. Alexander Duff, apostle of missionary enterprises, toured Canada in the course of his visit to North America, and colonial Christians for the first time began to look beyond their own local scene to the conversion of Africa and Asia.[55] Economically unable in most cases to support independent missionary efforts, the Protestant churches in British North America usually associated themselves with missions established by their American counterparts, and in contributing funds and personnel to joint enterprises they established a pattern of co-operation that has continued to this day in many mission fields.

In two American religious conflicts—the Protestant Crusade and the antislavery movement—the Canadian churches were not directly involved, although they were far from neutral observers. Throughout the 1830s and '40s Canada was untouched by the nativism that disgraced the United States. When Canadians took note of such American community projects as burning nunneries, it was to raise hands of praise for their own exceptional virtue.[56] Virulent nativism did not beset Canada until the end of the nineteenth century and even in the midst of the papal aggression controversy Canadian Protestants did not refer to Maria Monk. Although occasional references were made to Protestant-Roman Catholic controversies in the United States, more attention was given to European religious events and especially to current operations of the Inquisition in Italy.[57] Canadians did not identify with the Protestant Crusade of American nativism because the religious aspect of nativism was not differentiated from its secular or political aspects. Mob rule and the violence that characterized American life (in the opinion of Canadians) were abhorred in all their forms, even in their anti-Catholicism, as being un-British. No avowedly anti-Catholic papers were published in Canada, and when anti-Catholic feeling did appear in the 1850s it was inextricably intertwined with the sectional difficulties inherent in the political Union. Perhaps in the fifties anti-popery did replace anti-Americanism as one focus of Canadian Protestant interest.

Canadians viewed American slavery and nativism with the same pious horror, and even before the Fugitive Slave Law their efforts to aid escaping slaves had been organized largely on denominational lines. The appearance of *Uncle Tom's Cabin* led to the formation of the Anti-Slavery Society of Canada at Toronto in 1851, although the book was not published in Canada until a full year later.[58] The slavery issue proved to be a very disruptive factor in Canadian-American church relations, although it never divided Canadian churches internally. In 1845 the newly organized Free Kirk in Canada admonished the American Old School Presbyterian Church about its "sinful apathy" regarding slavery. Resolutions in the same synod in 1851, 1853 and 1857 condemned slavery while disclaiming "any design of officious intermeddling." In 1856 the Synod further resolved to examine its candidates for the ministry on their attitude towards the peculiar institution. A delegate from the New School Presbyterian Church at the Synod in 1859 was questioned minutely on the slavery stand of his own church with the result that the Canadian Synod found the American body wanting and so no return delegate was appointed.[59] An additional reason for this decision was the discovery that the New School Presbyterian Church was doctrinally unsound, in other words theologically liberal. Here is another area where American influences are noticeably absent, for most Canadian Protestant churches remained theologically conservative throughout the nineteenth century.

Canadian Baptists had expressed condemnations of slavery as early as 1838 and Congregationalists and Anglicans shared their sentiments.[60] Alone among Canadian Protestant bodies the Wesleyan Methodists refused to pronounce decidedly on slavery, solely because of their close and sympathetic ties with the American Methodist Episcopal Church. In general Canadian Protestant churches reflected the stand on the slavery question taken by their American counterparts. All Canadian churches disapproved of slavery; most were zealous in promoting such anti-slavery activities as assisting in the settlement of escaped slaves;[61] a few denominations even went so far as to reject fellowship with pro-slavery American churches.[62] Thus, in varying degrees, American slavery proved to be a disruptive factor in limiting other influences on Canadian Protestantism, but not a disruptive factor within the Canadian churches themselves because of their unanimity on that burning issue.

From this brief review of American influences on Canadian Protestantism before Confederation it is obvious that there were marked differences in the reaction of particular denominations to such influences, and differences in the degree to which those influences affected the Protestant churches in the various provinces. The "moderation and harmony" that historians have noted in the political development of the Maritimes was largely repeated in the religious attitudes of the churches in those colonies. By contrast, Upper Canada, where politics always assumed a more violent form, was the only area where American religious influences produced anti-Americanism. Despite and because of the limited establishment of the Church of England in British North America, Protestantism never became territorialized in Canada—the denominations persisted in viewing themselves as part of the church universal to which political boundaries are inconveniences. For religious ideas even more than for political ideas this world constitutes a single parish. Canadian churches, including the Church of England, manifested their eclecticism in accepting or rejecting external influences on intrinsic merit rather than country of origin.

VI
Loyalism and the Canadian Churches

This address was given to the Ontario Mennonite Historical Association meeting at Conrad Grebel College, University of Waterloo, on 25 November 1976.

To venture to give a paper on the Canadian churches and loyalism is to risk double jeopardy. In the first place, to the best of my knowledge, no one has ever set out deliberately to show the relationship between religion and loyalism in Canadian history, although many scholars have touched on the theme in connection with wider considerations of the tradition of loyalism. Next, and more awesome, is the horrendous truth that no one seems able to provide a generally acceptable definition of loyalism. In fact, the persons least capable of defining loyalism seem to be the historical experts writing about loyalism. It should follow logically, then, that the average non-expert person-on-the-street is more likely to reach an agreed and satisfactory definition of that elusive term.

One Canadian historian defined loyalism as "a fervent and sometimes highly emotional faith in the superiority of things British, particularly monarchy, the English constitution and British justice." It is fair enough for me to take issue with that definition today, since I am the historian who wrote it! And my comments thereon are twofold: first there is no direct reference to the role of religion as an ingredient of loyalism, and second, I have not, at least in the passage just quoted, distinguished between Loyalism and loyalism.

Let me answer my second self-criticism first, since my comment regarding religion and loyalism is the subject of this paper. Loyal, with a capital "L," means anything connected with the United Empire Loyalists directly, be it their motives for migration, their actual trek to Canada, their experiences as settlers, or even their own traditions as kept alive by the U.E.L. Association and by passages in history textbooks. By loyalism with a small "l," I wish to be understood as referring to a larger bundle of ideas, drawn in part as general deductions from the experiences of the U.E.L.s, but transmitted and transmuted into a philosophy, or a view of life which emphasizes things Canadian within a British context. This loyalism views society in eighteenth-century terms as an organic unity, an integration of society itself, civil and religious, according to an orderly scheme which, it is believed, should produce a more stable, more law-abiding, happier and more God-fearing people than any non-British way of life can ever do.

If this sounds racist, it sounds so because it is, because it is based on a confidently assumed superiority of British institutions and an unquestioning belief in the God-given mission—or responsibility—of the British people to share those blessings of the Almighty with, as Kipling called all other peoples, "lesser breeds without the law." Ideologically, the mantle of the Old Covenant was seen to have fallen, willy-nilly, on British shoulders. The basis of this view of nineteenth-century loyalism lies in the writings of Blackstone, Burke and Warburton. To those authors, church, state, and government were interrelated and interdependent through a natural system of checks and balances whose purpose was to produce social stability, harmony and happiness. Such a system had the divine approbation of Heaven as proven by its monarchical form and hierarchical structure. Thus, John Beverley Robinson of Upper Canada could write that the ends of this system were "integrity and independence in public servants, . . . peace and contentment in society, . . . security for property, confidence in the Laws, and attachment to British Institutions."

Unfortunately, a frontier society composed of a handful of settlers in a vast land lacked two features of this idealized social system. It lacked established institutions—"everything was to be made" as John Strachan said—and it lacked social classes, an aristocracy imbued with a belief in noblesse oblige. Time would remedy the first lack, if only the proper framework were established, and in place of an aristocracy, the colony could and did get a meritocracy of ability and character, remembered familiarly as the "family compact." Leadership, said Robinson, must come from those who are worthy, loyal, intelligent, morally upright, devout, wealthy, and dedicated to public service by a sense of their stewardship.

Such men, and Robinson is a preeminent example, could and did provide good government for the colony, but good government is not necessarily identical with self-government.

Such, I believe, is the philosophic basis of loyalism: an ordered society but not a closed society, and a society that prizes things British and the British connection as the best preservative for Canada. Implicit in this political structure, therefore, was a fear of the elective principle and of popular sovereignty, those two pillars flanking the doorway to that temple called American democracy. Election of all public officers assures only discontinuity, whereas the British ideal of aristocracy, the rule of the best to rule, assured the social fabric of that continuity which is the bedrock of British institutions.

After this lengthy diversion into the meaning of (small "l") loyalism, it is certainly time to turn to our basic theme of religion and loyalism. Canadian historians have developed two general arguments about the Loyalists around which a multitude of smaller issues cluster. I will mention these two arguments now, and then pass on quickly to a more historical account of small "l" loyalism. I will pass on quickly because, being a typical Canadian, I am as yet unable to make up my own mind as to which group has the better case in its particular argument.

Academics argue about whether the U.E.L.s were Tories or Whigs, or an amalgam of Tory and Whig ideals and, if an amalgam, in what proportions. Others argue over whether the Loyalists were voluntary or involuntary exiles after the Revolution. Whichever is the case, the Loyalists were losers and provided us eventually with out first counter-revolutionary tradition. At this point the story of the U.E.L.s begins to parallel that of the French Canadians for more than one reason. The French Canadians, also losers, soon had their own counter-revolutionary tradition as the French Revolution cut them off from their cultural homeland more completely than the American Revolution separated the Loyalists from their roots! Scholars have referred to Canadian history as a perpetual identity crisis. Crisis may be too strong a term, but there is a kernel of truth here, for all Canadians, and perhaps especially so for French Canadians, if we are to judge by the political developments in the Province of Quebec. The same problem has also been expressed as that of the non-nation, but either way, I suggest that loyalism has been the essential ingredient for all Canadians, anglophone and francophone, in their intermittently perpetual search for identity.

My starting point is our counter-revolutionary traditions, both of them. For French Canadians the Revolution in France completed their transformation into Britishers. The Conquest made them legally British, the execution of King Louis and Marie Antoinette made them psychologically loyal Britishers. Between 1763 and 1789 the British government deliberately fostered the Canadianization of the Roman Catholic Church in Canada so that within two generations the Church became the guardian and the promoter of a French Canadian nationalism in which religion and Britishness were inextricably intertwined. In the face of the American invasions of 1775 and 1812 and of the rebellion of 1837, the Bishop of Quebec and his clergy called on their flocks to show their loyalty to their legitimate British sovereigns on pain of excommunication should they break their oath of loyalty to God's anointed and appointed.

It was no aberration that most Quebec households, at least until a recent date, proudly displayed a portrait of Queen Victoria, who somehow ranked close to the Blessed Virgin as an example of motherhood and Christian family living. Similarly, it was no aberration but genuine loyalism which made Sir Wilfrid Laurier, Louis St. Laurent, and the late Governor General Vanier admirers of the British political way of life. On the eve of the general election of 1948, the Toronto *Star* appeared with the headline "Keep Canada British—Vote St. Laurent!!" above a picture of Mr. and Mrs. St. Laurent at mass in the basilica at Ottawa. And there was nothing incongruous therein to most Canadians.

Those two revolutions, the American and the French, changed ideologies as well as the balance of power, and while I have been suggesting that loyalism was part of the Canadian tradition of the Roman Catholic Church, I have not forgotten that the popular image of loyalism identified it especially with English-speaking Protestants in Upper Canada. We do not know the religious affiliation of the U.E.L.s. Certainly, all of the larger Protestant denominations were represented, as well as the Roman Catholic Church. But we do know two general facts about the religious composition of the Loyalist migration that are crucial to the development of a tradition of loyalism: 1. By the accounts of Anglicans themselves the Church of England could only claim less that 10% of the population. 2. A very large proportion had no denominational affiliation, or if they did, they soon lost it because the churches could not or would not, but certainly did not, reach out to them in their isolation on the frontier. Typically, a Methodist preacher exploring the Thames valley in 1808 reported meeting a family that had had no religious contact for seventeen years.

Here then was a scattered mass of unchurched people, waiting so eagerly for religious ministrations that they would respond to the first denomination which could break free of the traditional European patterns of fixed parish life and could find the means of coping with the distances and isolation of the frontier. The Methodists had that necessary technique—a neat combination of central control and flexibility in its circuit rider system which allowed them in two decades to organize from their American base and expand into Upper Canada so rapidly that they became a major denomination with 2500 members and probably 10,000 "hearers."

In these twenty years, 1791-1812, 76 Methodist missionaries had worked in Canada, and at least 69 of them were American. This presence of American representatives of an American religious body is the key to the growth of the loyalty controversy. In that confrontation the Church of England claimed, if not a monopoly of loyalty, at least a greater share actually and potentially than any other denomination. It certainly claimed far more loyalty than any religious denomination with American and republican connections should dare to claim.

Yet it is proper to point out that the clergy of the Church of England in Upper Canada maintained very close ties for many years with their opposite numbers in the break-away states. The Rev. John Stuart of Kinston, that epitome of Loyalism who had lost property and suffered two years imprisonment under suspicion of being a Loyalist, was and remained a friend and correspondent of William White, the Patriot rector of Philadelphia and later bishop of Pennsylvania in the American Episcopal Church. Religion and friendship might cross the political boundary created by the Revolution, but the presence of American influences in Upper Canada was already being protested before the War of 1812, and the Methodists had been marked out as potential traitors.

Since U.E.L. society was for many reasons not a literate society, one must search hard to find historical proof of loyalism before 1812. The most obvious source of the tradition seems to have been at Kingston, Upper Canada, where three remarkable men of different shades of loyalism created the loyalist tradition. The first man we have met in the person of John Stuart, rector of Kingston. The second was Richard Cartwright, successful merchant, leading member of Stuart's congregation, and a sensitive veteran of some of the most vicious campaigns of Loyalists and Indians against rebels during the War of Independence. Together these two men instilled their political opinions and above all their views of the United States of America, of republicanism, and of democracy in the young Scottish tutor of Cartwright's children, a man whom Stuart probably baptized and definitely started on a long career of service in the Church of England—none other than John Strachan.

Cartwright's career and his own writings as recorded by his biographer, John Strachan, show clearly the early mixture of three elements in Canadian loyalism—love of Canada, respect for Britain, and fear of the United States. Obviously, then as now, there was a potential clash of loyalties to Canada and to Britain, and for Cartwright as for other loyalists love of Canada, their new home, must always in such cases have prior claim over any wider imperial interests. Thus, Cartwright was bitterly critical of an immigration policy which granted vast tracts of land to the very rebels who had fought against the Loyalists in the recent war, and he complained too of Governor Simcoe's attempt to impose indiscriminately on Upper Canada "every existing regulation in England," regardless of the needs of the colony.

In the last analysis, however, Cartwright had joined the Loyalist cause out of "habitual reverence to the King and Parliament" and because he believed that his Upper Canada was what British support for the U.E.L.s had made it. It is this blend of Canadianism and Britishness, clearly visible in Strachan's career as well, which confuses this present generation that sees all nationalism in black-and-white, exclusivist, almost totalitarian terms. To the Canadians who lived between 1776 and 1945 there might admittedly be occasional strains between Canadian and imperial interests, but overwhelmingly they accepted with no difficulty the assumption that Canadianism and Britishness were complementary, not rival, ways of viewing life.

The same three elements of loyalism that we see in Cartwright are not clearly discernable in John Strachan until the War of 1812, when loyalism took on certain new and distinctive features. In the first place Strachan was not himself a Loyalist, and could only identify with Loyalism at second hand. But Strachan, as a result of his wartime experiences at York, became the spokesman, nay the high priest, of a loyalism that was articulated in more exclusive and anti-American terms than ever had been the case with the U.E.L.s, including John Stuart and Richard Cartwright. On that April day in 1813 when the British regulars marched out of York and left the inhabitants of this tiny town and capital of Upper Canada to the not-so-tender mercies of the American invaders, John Strachan felt the hand of destiny on his shoulder.

He was, it seemed to him, the one chosen to save Upper Canada for Britain. He was fully conscious of the position of leadership which had been thrust upon him as spokesman of the harassed citizens, and now he saw clearly how providence had picked him, because of his abiding faith in Canada and Britain and because of the influence he wielded over his former pupils, now co-leaders of Upper Canada (Robinson had become Attorney-General at the age of twenty-one!), as its divinely inspired agent to mould Upper Canada. The colony must be purged of disloyal elements by the ordeal of the war, to become a loyal, British and Anglican colony.

In the postwar years Strachan called repeatedly for more support from England for his idealized colony. He was behind the expulsion from Upper Canada of Robert Gourlay, that Quixotic gadfly who had encouraged settlers to challenge the wisdom of Strachan and his fellow-members of the Family Compact. Strachan successfully defended the *de facto* Anglican monopoly of the Clergy Reserves against the Church of Scotland's claim to a share as a co-established church. At the same time he founded King's College under Anglican control but open to all denominations. His religious loyalism was a simple proposition: that a Christian nation without an established church was a contradiction in terms.

Strachan was convinced that only an established church could inculcate loyalty to England; therefore, the Church of England should be in fact what it was on paper, namely the established church of Upper Canada. John Strachan's loyal Anglican establishment must include the vast land endowment of the Clergy Reserves, King's College, control of the elementary school system he had designed, a virtual monopoly on the performance of marriages, and influence through a near monopoly of public jobs. With all these advantages Strachan believed his church would draw to it all nonconformists, *if* only it had sufficient clergy to compete with other Protestant denominations and particularly with the ever-increasing Methodists.

In the wake of the War of 1812 the Methodists undertook to confirm their loyalty by removing all visible signs of American domination. First, they had to meet the challenge of the invasion by British Wesleyan missionaries who created deep divisions among the Canadians by their claim to superior loyalty because of their British origin. By 1820 the British Wesleyans had agreed to stay out of Upper Canada; the Canadians, under strong pressure from rank and file membership, began a campaign which, by successive legal steps between 1824 and 1828, won them complete autonomy from their American parent body. But while that Canadianizing campaign was still in progress the Methodists had to defend themselves against a charge of disloyalty levelled by the influential John Strachan.

In 1825 Strachan used his sermon on the death of Bishop Mountain as the occasion to demand more financial and ministerial support for his church. If such support was not forthcoming, he warned, the colony might fall into the hands of the Methodists who were ignorant, rabble-rousing, republican and American, or in one word, disloyal. When this sermon was published a year later the Methodists found their Joshua in the youthful preacher, Egerton Ryerson. Son of a U.E.L. soldier, Ryerson had seen his family suffer at the hands of invading Americans as their farms were burned and an older brother maimed for life by a sabre-cut in the mouth. In incisive, logical, and determined words, Ryerson refuted Strachan's allegations and struck a telling blow in the opening battle for Canadian recognition of religious equality based on the equal loyalty of all denominations.

That classic struggle of the 1820s and 1830s is an oft-told tale that need not be repeated here. It was John Strachan's misfortune to be the embodiment of a losing cause, that of a church establishment based an a presumed monopoly of loyalty. By all, except Strachan, it was already acknowledged that the time for church establishment in Upper Canada was long past, if indeed church establishment ever did have a ghost of a chance of succeeding. In 1828, a committee of the imperial House of Commons investigating the problems of the Canadas commented, "It would be unjust and impolitic to exalt the Church of England, by exclusive and peculiar right, above all others of His Majesty's subjects who are equally loyal, conscientious and deserving.... An established church cannot be necessary for the security of the Government; the loyalty of the people is deep and enthusiastic."

But time, not merely fair words, were needed to ensure acceptance of an equality of loyalism among all Canadians, regardless of their religion. The rebellions of 1837 raised again the issue of which denomination was most loyal, with interesting results for all. An attempt by British Wesleyans, now united with the Canadian Methodists, to conduct a witch-hunt for disloyalty among Methodists ended in the breaking of that union after Ryerson again successfully defended the loyalty of Canadian Methodists. Among Canadian Presbyterians, the small American-organized Niagara Presbytery was obliterated within a decade as its members reacted against American involvement in the Rebellion of 1837. And the Church of England was, in Strachan's words, "despoiled of its patrimony" when the Clergy Reserves Act of 1840 forced it to share the income of the lands with the Church of Scotland, the Methodists and the Roman Catholics, a sure sign that monopoly loyalism based on religion was near an end.

But the new, the lasting phase of loyalism was only begun by this acknowledgement that all denominations were loyal. If all shared in loyalism, to Canada and to Britain, then it followed that all denominations must share in the defence of their Christian nation against americanizing and republican tendencies. No historian has yet looked at the specific role of the churches in relation to loyalism during the annexation crisis of 1849, in the Reciprocity controversy of 1911, or in the two world wars. Nevertheless, the continuing connection of the churches to loyalism between 1840 and 1940 can be traced in general terms. Confederation, for instance, was hailed by the Methodists as a means of perpetuating our loyal connection with Britain. But loyalism, at least after Confederation, displayed a growing tendency to express itself more (but not exclusively) as Canadianism and less (but not exclusively) as Britishness. It was a subtle change in proportions, but the ideal was still expressed as loyalism.

Although Strachan's dream of a national church for Canada had come to nought, he himself was connected ironically with the emergence of a Canadian national religion even before Confederation. The secularization of King's College and of the Clergy Reserves in the 1850s not only created practical separation of church and state in Canada, these events and certain religious trends in Europe and Canada produced what can best be called an omnibus Protestantism. Most denominations, without considering any institutional union, could share in a common feeling on such social issues as temperance, sabbatarianism, slavery and evangelization. Loyalism was now taken for granted by Protestants and for Protestants. The case of the Roman Catholics was never so clear because of apparent rival loyalties that cropped up from time to time— Fenianism in the 1860s, ultramontanism in the 1870s, and Quebec's own brand of Canadianism during the conscription crises of the two world wars.

This growing community of outlook, which included loyalism, made possible the church unions of the post-Confederation period. Inspired by the dream of dominion from sea to sea, the Presbyterians in 1875 and the Methodists in 1884 created dominion-wide denominational unions with a view to growing with Canada. It was only a natural consequence that the next step should be an interdenominational union which the Church of England discussed with the Methodists and Presbyterians in 1889. Already in 1874, George M. Grant of Queen's had prophesied about a national Canadian church which would include even Roman Catholics. "Why not?" he concluded, "God can do greater things even than this. And who of us shall say, God forbid!"

The theme of loyalism may seem to be forgotten in this discussion of religion and nationalism, but I would insist that loyalism is there as an intrinsic part of nationalism. All proposals for church unions have been predicated on the assumption of God's will and a Christian nation, and of course all proposals of church union, at least until 1925, reflected not merely that community of outlook which has already been noted, but also a growing approximation to unity in organization of separate denominations. Such was the basis for the Presbyterian-Methodist-Congregational union of 1925, and the belief that spirit is more important than forms of church government has been behind each attempt to expand that union.

The fact is that Canada has always tended to churchism, and that includes bigness. We may boast of religious pluralism in Canada but the truth is that the nation's religious life has been consistently dominated by four churches—the Roman Catholic, Church of England, Presbyterian and Methodist. In 1871 Roman Catholics made up 43% of Canada's population, the other three 41%, for a total of 84%, leaving 16% for all the other religious groupings. A century later the Roman Catholics made up 46%, United and Anglicans 30%, for a total of 76%, and the Presbyterians, Lutherans and Baptists together added another 12% for a total of 88%. The remaining 12% of Canadians are divided into 30 other religious groups.

I stress this point of the "churchiness" or *ecclesiasticism* of Canadians to reinforce my closing point about loyalism and religion in this country. Because Canada is an artificial creation, because it is the second largest country in the world, and because its citizens, at least when they are not abroad, generally think of their loyalties in local or regional rather than national terms, I suggest that church membership means more to Canadians than nationality because it is easier to identify with a nation-wide church than it is to identify with a national government. This ecclesiasticism is, I believe, part of our loyalism or counter-revolutionary tradition (whether we are Catholic or Protestant, francophone or anglophone). Loyalism lives today, if not in the hearts of all Canadians at least in the hearts of many writers of "letters to the editor."

Loyalism is a sentiment, felt rather than articulated, a defensive and protective reaction that is almost second nature to a nation of "losers"—losers on the Plains of Abraham, or at Saratoga, or at the Winter Palace in St. Petersburg, or in Budapest. Loyalism has also a religious basis in the millenarian belief that after God has chastened us, His chosen people, then Canada's divine destiny will become apparent. Meanwhile, whenever we have faced the threat of military, or economic, or cultural absorption by our giant neighbour, whether in 1776, 1812, 1837, 1911 or even 1957, Canada has turned for security to its counter-revolutionary traditions in which ecclesiasticism and loyalism form such an important element.

VII

Egerton Ryerson, The Christian Guardian, and Upper Canadian Politics, 1829-1840

This paper grew out of a chapter of John Moir's Master of Arts thesis completed at the University of Toronto in 1949. In its present form it was read to a meeting of the Canadian Methodist Historical Society at Belleville in June 1984.

In March 1840, Governor General Charles Edward Poulett Thomson, soon to become Baron Sydenham, advised his friend Lord John Russell, the Colonial Secretary at Westminster, that the *Christian Guardian* was "the only decent paper in both Canadas."[1] This was high praise indeed for a weekly newspaper that had been in existence barely ten years, that was the official organ of a religious denomination, the Canadian Methodists, and that was competing with some fifty other newspapers for the patronage of readers in Upper and Lower Canada.[2] One reason for the *Guardian*'s high reputation was its comprehensive and unbiased reporting of the debates in the Upper Canadian Assembly by Samuel S. Junkin, the paper's jack-of-all-printing-trades. A second reason was its incisive editorials on current affairs during the years when Egerton Ryerson was its editor.

The year 1829 was a landmark in Canadian Methodist history because the annual Upper Canadian Conference initiated two projects that contributed conspicuously to national development. Those two projects were the founding of the *Christian Guardian*, ancestor of the *United Church Observer*, and the founding of Upper Canada Academy, forerunner of Victoria University. The twenty-six-year-old Egerton Ryerson, already a public figure thanks to his journalistic defence of the Methodists against Archdeacon John Strachan's charges of disloyalty and ignorance, was elected editor of the new connexional newspaper. In the autumn of 1829 Ryerson was sent to New York to buy the necessary press and type with $700 subscribed by his fellow itinerants.

Although the *Guardian*'s editors were elected at the Conferences held each summer or autumn, its volumes were dated from its first issue on 21 November 1829. In that first issue, Ryerson explained that he had accepted the editorship out of a sense of duty to his country and its government, and to Methodism. His policy would be to render to Caesar and God their respective interests, to publish only whatsoever things are true, honest, just and of good report. While being faithful to Methodism, the new editor also intended to "preserve and promote a spirit of unity and brotherly love among the various religious denominations of the Province . . . ." He would teach civil obedience to divincly derived authority, and at the same time he would maintain "the rights peculiar to a subject" that God guarantees.

As a public service the *Guardian* would publish local and foreign secular news, because spiritual interests are involved in politics. "But let it be recollected, that the discussion of these questions, we leave to other hands. The facts we may furnish; but for interpretation our readers must look into the resources of their own minds, or other periodicals."

Nevertheless, the first political comment by the *Guardian* came in connection with the provincial elections early in 1830. After refusing to back any candidate, the editor praised the integrity of unnamed Anglican, Presbyterian and Catholic politicians and condemned Strachan's political activities. "Our business is not with *men*, but with *things*—not with *individuals*, but *doctrines* and *practices*."[3]

Another year of silence on political issues passed by, but the *Guardian* of 12 November 1831 complained that other papers had linked its name to that of William Lyon Mackenzie. "*Not one word* has *ever* appeared in our paper in praise of Mr. Mackenzie or his measures." Within four weeks however, the famous Mackenzie libel case occurred and the *Guardian* did defend Mackenzie's actions in the name of freedom of the press.

It appears that the present measure [the expulsion of Mackenzie from the Assembly] is not taken up as principle, but as a pretext to get rid of an obnoxious individual . . . . Far be it from us to sanction the licentiousness of the press . . . but it is establishing the tyranny of party faction at the expense of the liberty of the press, public quiet and national prosperity.[4]

At the same moment the *Guardian* collided with Lieutenant-Governor Sir John Colborne. Responding to the annual
loyal address from Conference, Colborne repeated Strachan's
charges against the Methodists and denounced the *Guardian* as
a political paper backed by clergy who had neither "the experience or judgment to appreciate the value or advantage of a liberal education." Ryerson, as chairman of the Conference's
executive committee, refuted all the charges and denounced
those who had filled Colborne's ear with such "slanderous
falsehoods."[5] This failed to stop the attacks on the paper—
Allan Napier MacNab, M.P., for instance, compared the
Christian Guardian to Oliver Cromwell, "with the Bible in
one hand and the brand of sedition in the other."[6]

When reform and anti-reform meetings in the early
months of 1832 frequently ended in riots, the *Guardian* warned
against "Mobocracy"; and when Ryerson and Mackenzie were
burned together in effigy at Peterborough, the editor again
denied any connection with the radical leader, and pointed to
the public disorders as proof of the need of reform in the
administration of justice.[7] Three weeks later, on 16 May, a
Guardian editorial tried again to explain the paper's political
position.

> We have uniformly avowed our sentiments in favour
> of reform as far as it related to the enjoyment of
> equal religious and civil privileges by the several
> Christian denominations in this province . . . . On
> other points we leave every reader to judge for him-
> self, furnishing him with fair information on all ques-
> tions of importance, that he may judge of the merits
> of both sides.

This attempt to separate support for religious equality from
political reform failed, however, to convince conservative
contemporaries.

Ryerson's subsequent departure for England, where he
spent almost a year negotiating the union of the British and
Canadian conferences,[8] brought no noticeable change of editorial policy. James Richardson, the one-armed veteran of the
1814 battle of Oswego who assumed the editorship in the summer of 1832, was as liberally inclined as Ryerson. In Richardson's hands the *Guardian*'s support for the reform cause,
although expressed less forcefully than Ryerson's style, was

barely veiled. Only one incident occurred during Richardson's year in office to embroil the *Guardian* in public controversy. Another riot at Peterborough, condoned by public officials, earned Richardson's condemnation, but in succeeding months the editor almost completely ignored the political controversy about the paper's alleged disloyalty.[9] The re-election of Ryerson to the editorial chair in October 1833, when the Conference met to ratify the terms of the Union with the British Conference, coincided with a crisis in Canadian Methodism that permanently altered the newspaper and Upper Canadian politics. That crisis involved two separate and in some ways antithetical developments.

First, the Articles of Union between the British and Canadian Conferences created a conservative and anti-colonial British control over the Canadian Church. Article V empowered the British Conference to appoint one of its members as President of the Canadian Conference, and Article VII forbade the Canadian Conference to make "any rule, or introduce any regulation, which shall infringe on these Articles of Agreement between the two Conferences." Most Canadian Methodists were uneasy with this loss of autonomy, but it was the price paid to end that British poaching in the Canadian field which the colonial government had secretly encouraged to promote political loyalty. Second, Egerton Ryerson rocked the Upper Canadian political scene with a series of open letters, entitled "Impressions Made by Our Late Visit to England," that he began to publish in the *Guardian* on 30 October 1833.

The first "Impression" included an attack on Mackenzie's British friend and mentor, the radical reformer Joseph Hume, a man who espoused "Republicanism" and religious infidelity. In a "Second Edition" of his *Colonial Advocate*, printed the same day that the "Impressions" appeared, Mackenzie reacted hysterically to these damning charges. Under the headline "ANOTHER DESERTER," he announced that Ryerson, "a jesuit in the garb of a methodist preacher," had "hoisted the colours of a cruel, vindictive tory priesthood."[10] Like many Upper Canadian reformers, and Tories too, Mackenzie had presumed, incorrectly, that Ryerson was a thorough-going political reformer, but this raving response to the "Impressions" came not only from Mackenzie's customary emotional instability, but also from grief. Just four days earlier his baby son, Joseph Hume Mackenzie, had died.

Ryerson's protest of loyalty to the "perfectly mixed constitution" that Britain had achieved in the eighteenth century and to the cause of liberty fell on deaf ears in Mackenzie's case. In blind anger at what he saw as betrayal of the reform cause and a mockery of his family's loss, Mackenzie denounced Ryerson's Loyalist father as one who had "lifted his sword against the throats of his own countrymen struggling for freedom" in the Revolutionary war.[11] This riposte struck at two of Ryerson's strongest characteristics—love of family and pride in his United Empire Loyalist ancestry. After the "Impressions," no reconciliation between these two interpreters of reform was possible. In defence of his political interventions, Ryerson denied that his editorials had cost the *Christian Guardian* five hundred subscribers: "Discontinuances—16, because of our toryism," as against twenty-six new subscribers.[12]

In the next issue of the *Guardian*, on 27 November 1833, Ryerson provided a lengthy exposition of "Our Principles and Opinions." After ranging widely over colonial policies and practices, the editorial dealt specifically with three points about the Methodist church and party politics. First, Ryerson wrote, it would be "injurious to the interests of religion . . . to have our church amalgamated or identified with any political party." Next, Upper Canadian Methodists and other Christians should avoid all evidences of "a political party spirit—especially in such unsettled times as the present . . . ." In conclusion, he reiterated, "the *Christian Guardian*, as the organ of the Conference, and not the publication of an individual, ought not to discuss merely political questions, nor the merits of mere political parties . . . ." The whole document was a statement of principles derived from the Augustan constitution of eighteenth-century Britain; but, unrealistically, it ignored the undeniable fact that partisanship was integral to the politics of both the colony and the mother county.

Subsequent issues of the *Guardian* show that the recent union with the British Wesleyans was having the effect desired by its unsuspected instigators. The editor was, as he pointed out, honouring his pledge to the British Conference that all political issues, except the Clergy Reserves, would be eliminated from the *Guardian*.[13] This self-imposed editorial silence lasted for six months, until Joseph Hume's famous "baneful domination" letter appeared in Mackenzie's *Colonial Advocate*. As if Hume's "treasonable sentiments" were not enough to provoke a response from the *Guardian*, his characterization of Ryerson as a "renegade," "apostate," and "base, worthless hypocrite" ensured Ryerson's re-entry into the political arena of Upper Canada. Ryerson's response was brief. Every Christian and patriot was bound by Romans 13 to reject the treason of separation from Britain; and Ryerson noted, "In how different a sense is the term Reformer employed by the 'Mayor' (Mackenzie) and some others, now, from what it was a few years ago; and how different are the measures pursued."[14]

The 1834 annual Conference, the first involving the union arrangements, met at Kingston exactly one week after Ryerson's response to Hume and Mackenzie. The atmosphere was tense—ultra-Canadian opponents of the union had already seceded and formed a new conference, and further dissatisfaction was reflected in the loss of eleven hundred members on the circuits. Ryerson proposed that the *Guardian* be made into a "truly religious and literary Journal" by avoiding all political comments in its pages. Richardson was then elected editor, but when he refused to serve, Ryerson was re-elected to the surprise of several persons. Ryerson then reassured the Conference that the editor, not the Conference, was ultimately responsible for what appeared in the *Guardian* and announced that he would leave the editorship in one year. At the beginning of 1835, after the reformers had elected a majority to the Assembly for the first time in a provincial election, Ryerson apparently felt some statement of the *Guardian's* position was needed. Henceforth the paper's policy would be neutrality in politics, with only four exceptions to that rule—defence of the church, general education, the Clergy Reserves, and loyalty to Britain.[15]

Ryerson was as good as his word, avoiding politics in the paper and resigning as editor at the annual Conference in June 1835. His successor was Ephraim Evans, who with his brother James, more famous as a missionary and inventor of the Cree syllabic alphabet, had been trying to write novels until saved from this sinful waste of time by their conversion to Methodism.

Evans' personal political position was close to that of Ryerson, but he adhered strictly to political neutrality until the publication of the notorious Seventh Grievance Committee Report by the Reform-dominated Assembly of Upper Canada. In that massive and disorganized document, errors supposedly slandering Methodism attracted editorial attention in the *Guardian* of 27 May 1835. After this confrontation, political silence returned to the editorial page of the *Guardian* for another ten months, until the publication of Colonial Secretary Lord Glenelg's Instructions to Upper Canada's new lieutenant-governor, Sir Francis Bond Head. By releasing this hidden agenda of the Colonial Office to the reformers in both Upper and Lower Canada, Head unwittingly started the colonial political process rolling towards the rebellions of 1837.

The *Guardian*'s editor published the full text of Glenelg's despatch on 10 February 1836, introducing it as "probably the most ably written and statesman-like document which has ever crossed the Atlantic." The same editorial again denounced the Seventh Grievance Report as a misrepresentation of Upper Canadian public opinion. The editor admitted that "abuses exist, and some call loudly for redress," but he condemned those politicians, both local and imperial, who "create and foster evil surmising and jealousy in the minds of the people, and bring upon them imputations of disloyalty." At almost the same moment, Lieutenant-Governor Head added three leading moderate Reformers to his Executive Council, gaining further approval from the *Guardian*. The resignation of these new Councillors less than a month later and their replacement by conservatives who lacked the support of the Assembly majority produced the first crisis in Robert Baldwin's search for responsible government, but on all this the *Guardian* offered no substantive comment.

Instead, the editor's attention was focused on the operations of what he called the "Inquisition," an Assembly subcommittee investigating government grants to religious bodies. On 6 April 1836 Evans denounced this investigation as "one of the most determined crusades against the interests of Methodism that ever stained the records of a British Legislature since the ascendancy of Protestantism," a charge that brought the subject within one of Ryerson's four exceptions, namely, to defend the church. When Evans was interviewed by this subcommittee, the questions were not communicated in advance but had to be answered from memory by a simple "yes" or "no." With apparent justification, Evans complained about "discourteous and arbitrary treatment" at the hands of a committee who, with only one exception, supported the Seventh Grievance Committee.[16]

Mackenzie replied directly to the *Guardian*'s charges with a letter defending both the Grievance Report and the actions of the subcommittee on religious grants. This answer, said Evans, would not satisfy Methodists—Mackenzie was only trying to ingratiate himself with them. "It won't do. They know him too well, and have suffered too much from his friendship already, to place any confidence in him, or any of the party who have supported him in his unsuccessful, but not on that account less wicked, crusade" against the interest of Canadian Methodism.[17] The *Guardian*, like most Methodists and most Upper Canadians, now gave unqualified support to Lieutenant-Governor Head in his growing confrontation with the various Reform groups in the Assembly, unaware that Head was in fact manipulating public opinion by drawing the red herring of loyalty across the path of every political issue. Evans believed that his editorial policy was no more than a continuation of Ryerson's, and a letter from Ryerson, who was in England on business for the Conference, certainly confirmed Evans' belief.[18]

Re-elected editor in both 1836 and 1837, Evans continued to respect Conference's "no politics" order, although he occasionally used events in Lower Canada as a pretext for expressing opinions of a politically conservative tone. Rumours of open revolt in the lower province were reported in the *Guardian* of 15 November 1837, but were not confirmed until two weeks later. The insurrection at Toronto on 5 December, however, took the editor and Upper Canada by surprise. On 6 December, with Toronto still supposedly under seige by Mackenzie and his dwindling army of rebels, the *Guardian* issued an almost hysterical rallying cry to the loyal populace.

> *Canadians of every class! Canadian* REFOR-MERS! Are you prepared to shed the blood of your country-men? Can anything Mackenzie can offer you compensate for the guilt you must incur if you enrol under his revolutionary banner, and *deluge your fruitful fields with blood?* For God's sake pause! . . . The Royal standard of Britain yet waves triumphant, and invites the loyal and the good to unite in its defence, and still avail themselves of its PROTECTION against aggression.

Since a considerable portion of this edition was captured by the rebels, most of its news items were reprinted the following week, along with an editorial thanking providence for saving Toronto from "one of the most diabolical, and cruel plots which ever stained the page of history," namely the alleged plan of Mackenzie to burn the city, and that "at the commencement of a *Canadian winter!*"

On 20 December, when the round up of rebels was well under way, the editor expressed satisfaction at "the lenient course pursued" towards mere suspects. Obviously the rebellion had been a tragi-comic failure, but Mackenzie was now ensconced in Buffalo, receiving promises of American aid. The same *Guardian* editorial expressed shock and regret that the American press, including some religious journals, would even consider turning Canada into "a slaughter house." When Allan Napier MacNab burned the *Caroline* in American waters, an action that seemed to unleash an editorial torrent of Christian jingoism, the *Guardian* of 6 January 1838 gave its unequivocal support to this pre-emptive strike.

> That American citizens have been guilty of a gross infraction of the laws of nations, in levying forces against, and firing repeatedly upon a friendly power, must be admitted by all impartial persons. Should vigourous measures, however, be adopted by that country to prevent the recurrence of such disgraceful proceedings, it is probable that Britain, with her usual magnanimity, will ask no further satisfaction, and a national war may be averted.

Many readers took strong offence at the *Guardian*'s words, but the editor replied to their letters with self-confidence: "We are sorry for this, but really cannot help it. Our views on that point are unchanged . . . . The Americans . . . have themselves to blame for it."[19] In succeeding issues the *Guardian* continued to ring the changes on anti-American feeling. When the rebel army in exile was presented with a flag by a Rochester school where some Toronto girls were students, the editor commented on "the gross impropriety of British subjects sending their children for education to a country where hatred of British institutions is inculcated in almost every stage of their progress."[20]

As the time for the treason trials approached, the Tory press set up a cry for rebel blood, but to Evans's credit he opposed the popular demand for revenge. Answering the Tory Toronto *Patriot*'s call to execute convicted rebels and captured Americans, the *Guardian* of 21 March 1838 stated boldly, "We deny the moral right of any, especially the conductors of the press, to assume a dictatorial tone towards the courts of justice for the purpose of influencing their decisions." The trials were fully reported in the *Guardian* but without any significant editorial comment; and when, after the hanging of Lount and Matthews, a stay of execution was announced for the other criminals, the editor expressed his "cordial approval."[21]

Evan's moderation, however, fell short of liberalism. The appointment of Lord Durham as High Commissioner to investigate the recent rebellions was greeted coolly, and Durham himself was damned with faintest praise. "His politics have been considered ultra-liberal. He is, however, a nobleman possessed of a high sense of honour, and of great discernment and vigour."[22] Next, Evans printed, "with pleasure," a pastoral letter from Conference President William Harvard, calling for a purge of disloyal Wesleyan Methodists, whether guilty or merely suspect.[23] This "presidential bull," as it was dubbed, was too much for most Methodists to swallow. Ryerson promptly penned an eloquent plea for freedom of speech and opinion entitled "What is Christian Loyalty" that filled three and a half columns in the *Guardian*.

The tension between the Canadian and English elements in the Conference was further increased by Ryerson's public defence of Marshall Spring Bidwell, a victim of Head's political manipulations, a defence published under the transparent nom-de-plume of "A U.E. Loyalist." On behalf of his English Conference friends, Evans replied that Bidwell had gone to the United States of his own free will.[24] By the time that the Conference met in Kingston one week later, the storm clouds created by the uneasy union of 1833 were about to break with momentous results for the *Christian Guardian*, the Wesleyan Methodist Conference, and for Canada.

Ironically, that Conference gathered in Egerton Ryerson' church. Obviously, Evans's editorial policy of the past year and the "presidential bull" had so disgusted the great majority of Wesleyan Methodists that change was imperative. Ryerson, already secretary of Conference, was now elected

editor of the *Guardian* by a forty per cent majority over his
anonymous rival; and in the months following he made the
Guardian once more an eminently readable paper, probably as
interesting and instructive as it was ever to be. He announced
that, in civil affairs, neutrality would now be irresponsible. He
would not be neutral, "for this simple reason, I am a man, am
a British subject, am a professing Christian, and represent a
Christian community." "My decision, however, is not one of
party, but of principle." "To be explicit as well as brief, I am
opposed to the introduction of any new and untried theories of
Government."[25]

From his editorial chair Ryerson sedulously fostered
better Canadian-American relations and tried to minimize
the panic fear of further border incidents. When a second
insurrection in Lower Canada and simultaneous incursions
from the United States occurred late in 1838, the *Guardian* of
28 November expressed satisfaction with the suppression of
these dangers but warned against the vengeful attitude adopted by the Tory press: "To make the innocent responsible for
the sins of the guilty may answer the theory and interest of
political expediency, but it is . . . abhorrent to the feelings of
humanity," and to the Golden Rule.

The Habeas Corpus Act had now been suspended for
more than a year; and when examples of oppression and discrimination multiplied, the *Guardian* expanded its crusade for
justice. The rights of British citizens should not be "trampled
down and ruined in this un-British and ungenerous manner."[26]
"We suppose," the editor wrote sarcastically on 27 March 1839,
"after the French have been disfranchised, and American des-
cendants cried down, an attack will next be made upon the Irish
or Native inhabitants of the Province, by those whose loyalty is
a trade, whatever may be the land of their nativity."

In contrast to Evans' policy, Ryerson now gave unqualified support to Lord Durham and his mission. "I believe
nothing is politically impossible with the Earl of Durham in
these Provinces."[27] When Lord Durham's *Report* appeared,
the *Guardian* reprinted the volume in instalments, along with
copious notes and laudatory comments such as, "It will form
a new era in British Colonial government, and will doubtless
become a text book of colonial polity both at home and
throughout these provinces, if not in all the dependencies of
Great Britain."[28] Ryerson and the *Guardian*, however, were

soon reminded that to occupy the middle ground is to be vulnerable on both sides.

The theory of responsible government as *cabinet* government espoused by Robert Baldwin had gained in popularity since Durham's arrival and was promoted by Francis Hincks through the pages of his *Examiner*. Ryerson, however, incurred Hincks' enmity for defending the supposedly more patriotic nonpartisan coalition form of responsible government.[29] In Ryerson's defence it should be noted that many Canadian historians, as well as Governor General Thomson and Sir Wilfrid Laurier, agreed with Ryerson's interpretation of responsible government. Ryerson, like Lord John Russell, pointed to the incompatibility of colonial status with Baldwin's position, which in practice would, and did, lead to eventual independence from Britain.[30]

Since the re-election of Ryerson as editor, his political editorials and his renewed attacks on the Clergy Reserves had further widened the breach between the Canadian and British parties in the Conference. From London, the Wesleyan missionary secretaries wrote to Upper Canada's lieutenant-governor disclaiming responsibility for the *Guardian*'s policies, especially its voluntarism because the British party wanted to share in government funding of religious bodies. Ryerson only learned about this letter when it was printed in the *Patriot*. The *Guardian* of 22 May 1839 described this incident as "another illustration of the sort of confidential connexion which exists between the government house and the editor of that most vulgar and profligate journal," the *Patriot*.

The next day Conference President Joseph Stinson advised Robert Alder, official delegate from the British Conference, that he had no confidence in Ryerson's loyalty to Britain.[31] On 12 June, the same day that the Conference met in Hamilton, the *Guardian* carried a public letter from Alder and a reply from Ryerson, about recognizing the establishment of the Church of England. The battle lines were obviously drawn within the uneasy union, and the ensuing conflict in the Conference lasted a week while Alder consulted its most influential members in a vain attempt to suppress the *Guardian*. Ryerson's re-election to the editorial chair by 60 votes to 13 was a total defeat for the British party and foreshadowed the end of the union.

In the wake of that Conference, the *Guardian's* vocal support for Lord Durham's report continued unabated, but the paper did object to the proposed reunion of the two Canadas unless responsible government—Ryerson's version— was included. By December 1839, the *Guardian* had shifted its position to support for the reunion of the Canadas as the only alternative to chaos in the colonies. The deciding factors in this reversal were the personal influence of the new Governor General, C.E.P. Thomson, and Lord John Russell's famous despatch of 14 October 1839 on the tenure of public offices. This despatch was intended to allow a governor to create coalition governments, but in fact it became the tool that eventually made Baldwin's cabinet version of responsible government possible, when disciplined political parties could displace temporary alliances.

By the winter of 1840 political and economic conditions in Upper Canada had improved, thanks to Thomson's political abilities and to Russell's despatch which, according to the *Guardian* of 12 February 1840, had "purged out the old leaven of party domination." Ryerson probably penned this repetition of the classic *via media* interpretation of responsible government, yet a week later it was followed by a laudatory comment on Baldwin's character, principles and talents, and his appointment to Thomson's executive council. If Ryerson wrote both editorials, that suggests he still believed, mistakenly, that the Governor General could wean Baldwin over to the coalition version of responsible government.

Meanwhile, throughout the Conference year 1839-1840 the recriminations between the Canadian and British parties continued behind the scenes. President Stinson was convinced by the events at the last Conference that separation was inevitable. From London, Alder advised him, "If there must be violence & disunion let it come from the other side"— from those who made the Union.[32] The 1840 Conference met in Belleville between 10 and 20 June, and became a showdown struggle from the outset. Ryerson was elected secretary instead of the English party's candidate, Ephraim Evans. Next, Ryerson's editorial policies were approved in the face of an adverse resolution. Then, Ryerson relinquished the editorship as he had earlier indicated that he would.

When Ryerson had vacated the editorial chair temporarily in the autumn of 1839 to promote Methodism's centennial celebrations by touring the circuits, the religiously and ecclesiastically safe and colourless Jonathan Scott had been his chosen assistant for seven months. Scott was now elected to the editorship in 1840, and under him and his successors, the *Guardian* confined itself to "purely religious and literary subjects." Nevertheless, as the Conference minutes explained rather ingenuously, the Clergy Reserves would still be "considered a religious question as a matter of course."[33]

Late in the Conference the members, by large majorities, chose Egerton and his brother William to be their delegates to lay the Canadian case before the British Conference. Despite Alder's earlier comment about letting disunion come from the other side, the Ryersons' experience of rudeness, manipulation and hostility at the British Conference in Newcastle that August suggests that their English brethren were not averse to throwing the first stone. The unanimous vote in favour of union with the Canadians seven years earlier was now reversed by a majority of the British Conference members. Two months later, when a special Conference was held in Toronto to deal with the results of disunion, eleven preachers had already withdrawn, seven stations had been closed, and two-thirds of Toronto's Wesleyan Methodists had reportedly seceded. By the end of that Conference year, however, membership had increased by 663, a proof of survival and a harbinger of revival for Canadian Methodism.

The collapse of the Wesleyan Methodists' union, ironically coinciding with the reunion of the two Canadas, marked the end of an era for the Christian *Guardian*, "the only decent paper in both Canadas." During Ryerson's seven years as editor in three intervals, his policy demonstrated a larger measure of consistency than many historians have been willing to admit. His passionate loyalism, his idealistic admiration for the Constitution, and his genuine sense of moral obligation to declare the truth regardless of consequences have been fully appreciated by few. It has been a common historical view that Egerton Ryerson was a radical who turned Tory. This is, however, a misconception arising from the coincidence of certain aims of the Canadian Wesleyan Methodists, particularly their demand for religious equality, with the broader objectives of William Lyon Mackenzie, namely political and constitutional change for Upper Canada. Ryerson's prime interests were consistently justice and the liberal-conservatism of a previous century.

VIII

The Canadian Baptist and the Social Gospel Movement 1879-1914

This paper was presented to the International Symposium, "Baptists in Canada 1760-1980," held at Acadia University, Wolfville, Nova Scotia, in October 1979. It was published the following year, along with other papers read at that symposium, in Baptists in Canada: Search for Identity Amidst Diversity, *edited by Jarold K. Zeman. It is reprinted here by permission of Acadia University.*

Despite the acknowledgement by Canadian historians that the movement called the Social Gospel was and is one of the most important formative influences in our national development, to date only one scholarly monograph and a few articles have been devoted to its study. Furthermore, for reasons peculiar to Canadian historiography, those few articles have been usually concerned with Methodist involvement in the movement.[1] Nevertheless, it is widely suspected and now at least partially proven that reactions to the Social Gospel varied widely, not merely from denomination to denomination, but within individual denominations as well. Historians have also begun to look at the Presbyterian and Anglican responses to the Social Gospel.[2] Although several papers and Professor C.M. Johnston's recent history of McMaster University touch tangentially on the topic of Baptists and the Social Gospel,[3] as a research theme it remains virtually unexplored despite its obvious importance.

The purpose of this paper is to examine briefly the attitude of the editors of *The Canadian Baptist* towards the Social Gospel over a period of some thirty years. Clearly the constraints of time and space must reduce this to a mere overview, but perhaps even such a preliminary examination will serve to arouse interest and by suggesting certain tendencies may point the way for future research.

There was of course nothing new in the ideas of the Social Gospel—the parable of the Good Samaritan is but one of many biblical affirmative answers to Cain's eternal question, "Am I my brother's keeper?" What made the development of the Social Gospel distinctive in the late Victorian era was a change of direction from the highly individualistic evangelism that had preceded it. Basically this contrast was a shift in emphasis rather than a difference in the Gospel message or repudiation of evangelism. But the fact that the Social Gospel was enunciated in response to the problems of modern urbanization, industrialism and materialism attracted to the so-called Social Gospel so much public attention that at times it seemed that its teachings constituted some newly-revealed panacea for the ills of the world.

Historians do not agree on where and when this broad concept of religiously-motivated social improvement came into being. C.H. Hopkins, the bench-mark historian of the movement, has traced its amorphous lineage to the close of the American Civil War.[4] Certainly the writings of Walter Rauschenbusch at the turn of the century constitute not the proclamation of but the popularization of ideas already accepted by many Christian leaders in Europe and America. Thus, although *The Canadian Baptist* did not become the official organ of the convention until 1882 or, in strict legal terms, until 1887 when it was gifted by the will of William McMaster,[5] it is not surprising to find evidence of the Social Gospel ideas in its pages even while it was still a private publication.

It is vain of course to look so early for any full-blown statement of a Social Gospel philosophy. Indeed it can easily be argued that the Social Gospel never was a systematized philosophy—that at best it can be described as an umbrella concept covering a wide range of ideas and plans for social and moral improvement with which none of its advocates would be in total agreement, but from which all would draw such emphases as would suit their own purposes at any given time and under any given circumstances.

While *The Canadian Baptist* was still the property of William Muir, its editorial column frequently expressed Social Gospel ideas. On one occasion Muir called on Baptists to bear witness to "practical Christianity" in everyday life because the secular and religious worlds in fact are inseparable. On other occasions he commented on the need for purity in politics, on the church's responsibility to meet the temptations besetting youth in an urban environment, on the need for systematic care of the deserving poor, and on the urgency of combatting pornography and prostitution.[6] For Muir the simple cure for fraud, dishonesty, avarice, strikes, lockouts and even wars was to love your neighbour as yourself.[7] Such a sampling from the editorial pages of *The Canadian Baptist* does show that a tradition of social concern and activism already existed before the newspaper was acquired by William McMaster and the Standard Publishing Company in 1882, and before the Rev. E.W. Dadson was appointed editor in August of that year.

Dadson soon showed a more forceful and topical style in his editorial writings although the themes were those already bruited by Muir. Dadson continued the call for purity in politics, but he was more vocal on the subjects of prohibition and sabbatarianism, in part no doubt because each passing year made them more urgently Canadian problems. By 1884 Dadson was prepared to take a very positive position on specific social problems. Regarding poverty, he called for investigation and remedial action, and pointed to every man's right to work to avoid the humility of direct charity.[8] An annual income of only $350 constituted a bare subsistence for a worker's family, and occasional relief collections were not enough. Basic cures were needed for the economic ills of Canada. In Dadson's opinion, the law of supply and demand was "unchristian"[9]—the church must offer leadership "for the solution of all these great social problems."[10] With a modernity that would not be universally acceptable even today Dadson suggested that gambling was a disease. Similarly his steady support for prohibition— "annihilate," not "regulate" the liquor traffic—was typical of most Social Gospellers.[11]

On at least one occasion Dadson did pronounce the ultimate solution presumed by the Social Gospel—improving the social environment, he wrote, would "prevent the manufacture of criminals."[12] Nor was remedial social action to be left to private individuals. It was the politician's job to remove the "iniquitous causes" that promoted socialism.[13] Too often capitalism divorced morality from business practice—the truly Christian industrialist would ensure that each worker got "such a share in the profits as justly belonged to him."

With the outbreak of troubles in the Canadian Northwest, Dadson found yet another Christian cause to espouse, namely, native rights. Injustice had driven the Métis and Indians to rebellion,[14] and God-loving Canadians owed it to the natives to educate them so that they could share in the good life of a Europeanized, Christianized (and presumably Protestantized) Canada.[15] This theme of justice for native Canadians became a recurrent editorial topic in the columns of *The Canadian Baptist* for several years thereafter.[16]

In 1886 the growth of trade unionism also attracted Dadson's interest and sympathy. "Is it not wonderful that the toiling millions, whose lives are one long, weary struggle to keep the wolf from the door, should conclude that there is something wrong in a system which, for every one it makes rich condemns hundreds to hopeless poverty."[17] Trade unionism would redress this imbalance, Dadson believed, and he called for Christian co-operation between capital and labour.

A case in point arose almost immediately when the Toronto Street Railway Company fired all union members who had gone on strike. "There is no excuse for the Company's action in its effort to interfere with personal liberty. That was a bit of petty persecution, the intolerance of commercial bigotry."[18] The company had demanded that the workers subscribe to an "unrighteous test act," and the blame for the resulting violence lay entirely at the company's door. When the workers won their contest against the company *The Canadian Baptist* was jubilant. The combination of political democracy and trade unionism would bring future improvements in working conditions of the labouring class for whom Dadson was convinced real freedom of contract did not exist. "Justice requires that the poor man as well as the rich should have a voice in the legislation by which both alike are governed."[19] Profit-sharing was again advocated by *The Canadian Baptist* as a partial solution to industrial unrest.

Later the same year, moves to reduce working hours and to force early closing of shops were hailed by *The Canadian Baptist* as "late but sweet fruits of the goodly tree whose roots are fed and watered by the principles of the Sermon on the Mount."[20] The fact that ministers of many denominations had supported these reforms was "grand proof of the practical character of Toronto Christianity."

But Dadson used this episode as a springboard to advocate other needed social changes. The long, toiling hours of housewives deserved similar consideration, and what were Christians going to do about gambling, lotteries, professionalization of sports, child abuse, vivisection and similar debasing practices?[21] Laws restricting child labour and ensuring equal rights for working women were sadly needed in Canada.[22] Equal educational opportunities for the poor were another long-term solution to social injustice that had Dadson's blessing.[23]

By the time Dadson retired as editor of *The Canadian Baptist* in September 1889, he had unquestionably made the newspaper into an avowed vehicle for Social Gospel ideas, although his preferred description of such reformism was "practical Christianity." At the same time he had made it clear that *The Canadian Baptist* was totally the organ of the convention. No one, at least no one in the convention, disagreed with these policies—the proof lies in the appointment of Dr. J.E. Wells, an experienced lay journalist, as Dadson's successor.

It would be easy to dismiss the decade in which Wells occupied the editorial chair by saying that Wells' policies were simply a continuation of Dadson's. True, most of the same issues—prison reform, sabbatarianism, prohibition, justice to native Canadians, the need for inner city missions, purity in politics, sweat shop industries, profit sharing, protection for children, women's rights, poverty in the midst of plenty, etc. —continued to attract editorial attention, but two conjoined tendencies noted in Dadson's day became more evident under Wells. In the first place, Wells' approach to Social Gospel ideas assumed no doctrinaire position. *The Canadian Baptist* responded to specific social issues; it did not theorize about remaking society with any panacea to produce instant and total reform. The key expression, "practical Christianity," was still employed frequently. The second and related emphasis can be described as specificity. Like Dadson, Wells wrote not about abstract problems in the abstract but about specific issues as they arose, yet if anything, he was more forthright and more detailed, both in describing and denouncing social problems.

Wells' approach to the labour question shows clearly this change of degree of editorial concern. He steadily defended the right to strike and accused the churches of alienating the working class by always supporting the capitalists' cause.[24] Unions were needed to protect the white slaves in the sweat shops of the garment industry.[25] When a general strike against Carnegie Steel in the United States led to loss of life, Wells expressed sympathy for the workers and contempt for Carnegie's "considerable pretensions to philanthropy." The barons of industry were reducing the pay of "already poorly paid workmen, in order to increase their own lordly incomes."[26] The issue, said *The Canadian Baptist*, was the conflict between legal and moral rights.[27]

In 1894, when the "Industrial Army" of unemployed marched on Washington demanding work, *The Canadian Baptist* commented at length on the "cruel inequality" in the distribution of wealth. "Is there no legitimate and rightful way in which some portion of this immense national capital, itself the product of labor though now in the possession of the few, can be made available to save multitudes of laborers from destitution, by supplying them with work instead of charity?"[28]

Two months later, when violence in the Pullman strike had caused some sympathy for the workers, Wells pointed out that the power of the capitalists put the workers at the mercy of their employers. Since company unions were too weak a defence, was compulsory arbitration the answer to this "ruthless law of supply and demand?"[29] In a similar vein *The Canadian Baptist* attacked the unfair practices of Rockefeller and the Standard Oil Company. Many men had succeeded in business without resorting to "heartless" and "principleless" practices that victimize the weak in society.[30]

Wells also became increasingly vocal about the plight of the poor. He had high praise for the relief policies of the Salvation Army which provided the poor with opportunities to earn the necessities of life.[31] Baptist churches had already supported a "city missionary" to Toronto's poor and unchurched for a decade, but Wells believed the churches could and should do much more.[32] It was dishonest to say that the poor man could become rich by working hard—let churchgoers put themselves in the shoes of the poor and see how a life of poverty and oppression really felt.[33] Wells called for the creation of county houses of refuge to assist "the destitute poor, who are guilty of no crime but poverty."[34]

"The reporting of Wells," comments H.U. Trinier in his history of *The Canadian Baptist*, "was not only accurate and reliable; it was often blunt and to the point."[35] As a Christian social critic Wells had probably carried the newspaper even further in the direction of the Social Gospel than Dadson had. But Wells' sudden death in "harness" in September 1899, at the age of sixty, produced a crisis and eventually a change in the affairs of the newspaper. An editorial committee of Professor Calvin

Goodspeed, Archibald Blue and George R. Roberts was appointed. A year later the Rev. W.H. Cline replaced Roberts until Roberts was elected editor by the convention in November 1901. During those three years *The Canadian Baptist* was virtually devoid of specific social comment.

Roberts began his work in 1902 with the support of a fourteen-man editorial writing committee. Soon *The Canadian Baptist* had occasion to voice its opinion on certain social questions.[36] Two strikes, one by Toronto's street-car workers, the other by American coal miners, each drew critical comments because of the inconvenience caused to the public and because of the strikers' use of violence.[37] The main issue of the day, however, was that old war-horse, prohibition, which *The Canadian Baptist* asserted would bring an end to child abuse.[38] The provincial referendum on prohibition held in December 1903 was hailed as a mighty victory for the "drys"—in fact prohibition failed to carry by a mere 13,000 votes out of more than 300,000 cast. More significant to the historian is the fact that rural Ontarians favoured prohibition overwhelmingly, but the urban wets outnumbered the urban prohibitionists eight to seven.[39]

In April 1903 the anonymous editor was stressing the need to evangelize New Canadians to protect Canadian values, yet by the end of the year the paper was repeatedly speaking of evangelism in exclusively individualistic terms. This apparent ambivalence continued into early 1904 with a series of articles on socialism. Christian socialism was apparently acceptable because its aim was to "right the wrongs of society by the education of the working classes and by co-operative associations."[40] This was to be achieved by reforming the individual—non-Christian socialism that wanted to reform society was "largely the outcome of German rationalism."[41] In conclusion the editorial writer declared, "The price of labour, like any other commodity, is regulated by supply and demand," and unionism in attempting to alter this natural law was merely protecting incompetence.

If Roberts wrote this piece, it was virtually his last editorial word, for in May 1904 he was replaced by W.J. McKay, an acknowledged success as a scholar and pastor. In his journalistic valedictory Roberts expressed surprise at his firing and stated that his editorial aim had been "to give scant space to new theories and new theologies . . . perhaps *The Baptist* may to some have been thought to have been conservative to an extreme in this direction."[42] If the more liberally inclined members of the board of publication thought McKay would redress Roberts' conservatism, they must soon have discovered their error. McKay's editorial statements involving social questions differed very little from Roberts'. In Trinier's words, "His editorials were brief, inoffensive paragraphs."[43] In his first months McKay called for purity in politics, and at least once deplored poverty in the midst of plenty, asking Baptists to be "not too discriminating in their charity."[44] By 1905, however, a certain clarification of position can be discerned. Most striking, all references to social issues disappeared from the columns of *The Baptist*—less obvious was a conservative trend in theological statements. Evangelism was now defined simply as the conversion of the individual. Furthermore, McKay stated, "We do not believe that 'New Theology' . . . has any large or lasting place in the minds and affections of our people."[45]

Throughout the next four years McKay showed great interest in the newly-awakened missionary movements, but not until the closing weeks of 1909 did the editorial column take up again the theme of "practical Christianity." This time, the question involved home missions and, particularly, recent immigrants into urban areas such as Toronto where forty-five languages were now spoken. "These foreigners may not always be easy to reach with the Gospel, but they are our brethren, and we owe it to them . . . to make strenuous efforts to win them to Christ."[46] This was a theme to which McKay returned several times in subsequent issues, even going so far as to advocate interdenominational co-operation in inner city missions in order to cope with the New Canadian threat to the old Canadian way of life.

Early in 1910 McKay printed an editorial with the allusive title "Another Gospel?" in which he insisted that the old Gospel of personal salvation is all the world needs to hear.[47] Immediately thereafter he admitted that *The Baptist* had its critics, and named Elmore Harris as prominent among them.[48] Almost in the same breath the editor announced a forthcoming series of articles called "Some Fundamentals," and the newspaper noted the arrival in Toronto of a new pastor, T.T. Shields.[49] It is impossible to discern from the columns of *The Baptist* what were the sources of the tensions, but it must be significant that McKay's minor crisis coincided with the appearance of *The Fundamentals* and with the height of the attack by Elmore Harris on Matthews' teaching at McMaster University.[50]

During the remainder of 1910, while the Matthews case raged, and during 1911 and 1912, *The Canadian Baptist* avoided any social comment that might be interpreted as theologically liberal, but suddenly in 1913 there was a resurgence of editorial interest in the Social Gospel. Was it merely coincidence that Elmore Harris had died at the end of 1911? Under the editorial title, "Both Individual and Society," McKay commented, "We heartily agree with the conviction that the Gospel of Christ is a gospel of a saved society as well as a gospel of saved individuals."[51] The editorial continued in the same vein with a quotation from Shailer Matthews that the church must not be reduced to a social agency.

"Practical Christianity," to judge by the various projects reported in *The Baptist*, seemed suddenly to have become popular, and the trend got a further boost that year when the Rev. S. Edward Grigg was appointed convention superintendent of social service and evangelism. Grigg announced that in social service the Good Samaritan is the ideal, and he urged each congregation to form a social service committee to meet its neighbourhood needs.[52] Unfortunately, despite letters to the editor encouraging social service, mission givings did not increase and by the summer of 1914 the Home Mission Board had to borrow to pay its workers.[53] In an unprecedented fighting editorial that filled almost a page of *The Canadian Baptist* McKay asserted,

> It is the duty of the Church to preach the Gospel of love and mercy, and along with it add simultaneously the Gospel of a better day. Nay, we will go further and say that the line must not be drawn too sharply, that a full Gospel must satisfy the famine of righteousness and the hunger for the long-deferred justice of God.[54]

Two days after the publication of this Social Gospel credo Germany declared war on Russia. The international chain reaction leading to an Armageddon for western civilization had begun, and polite talk about social justice and the here-and-now Kingdom of God was drowned by the boom of guns. The story of the place of the Social Gospel in Canadian Baptist life after the First World War, during the years of the

Winnipeg strike, the "great depression" and in the two generations since the outbreak of the Second World War, are beyond the scope of this tentative and exploratory paper, but it is a subject that deserves the attention of future historians. As for the years examined here through the columns of *The Canadian Baptist*, certain general conclusions may be offered. Under the editorial guidance of Dadson, Wells and Roberts *The Baptist* displayed an awareness of and sympathy for many of the ideas propounded within the Social Gospel movement. Unlike contemporary Methodist Social Gospellers, Baptist leaders seem not to have espoused any doctrinaire approach to social and moral reform. The recurrent use of the expression "practical Christianity" suggests a greater affinity to the more pragmatic, less idealized, Social Gospel position held and expressed by Canadian Presbyterians.

The sudden removal of Roberts from the editorship and his replacement with the supposedly more conservative McKay must be viewed as another indicator of the deep-seated theological rift that was developing within the Baptist community at the turn of the century. With considerable success McKay threaded his way through some labyrinth of denominational politics, insisting that the real issue was not individual versus social salvation, but individual and social salvation as epitomized in the phrase the "full Gospel." Behind that change in editorial policy undoubtedly lies the turn-of-the-century conflict over higher criticism and modernism.

When all the data is finally assembled and analysed we will certainly know much more about the ideology of Canadian Baptists, about the ramifications of the modernist-fundamentalist confrontation and about the impact of the Social Gospel on the country's development.

IX

The Problem of a Double Minority:
Reflections on the English-speaking
Catholic Church in Canada
in the Nineteenth Century

This paper was originally prepared for the Commission on Comparative Ecclesiastical History at the XIII International Congress of Historical Sciences which met in Moscow in August of 1970. The paper was twinned in presentation with one by the late Professor Pierre Savard, University of Ottawa, who spoke on the French-speaking Roman Catholic Church in Canada within the same time-frame. This paper appeared in Histoire Sociale/Social History *the following year and is reprinted here with permission.*

Two centuries ago the population of Canada was exclusively French and Roman Catholic, except for the pagan natives and the small English settlement, less than five thousand strong, in the Atlantic seaboard colony of Nova Scotia. Today, after the large immigrations of English, German, Italian, Dutch, Russian and other non-French-speaking Europeans during the nineteenth and twentieth centuries, slightly less than one half of all Canadians are Roman Catholics, and only a third of the total are members of the French part of that church. Historiographically, the French-speaking Catholic Church in Canada has passed from an early hagiographic and chronicle stage and is now advancing rapidly into an era of "scientific" historical research which takes account of the contributions that other disciplines can make to the study of religious history. In contrast, the English Catholic Church in Canada has received considerably less attention from historians.

Some biographies of anglophone bishops have been published, most of which are now generations old; a limited number of brief parish histories have appeared; a few, very few, jubilee histories of dioceses exist, and most of those are of venerable vintage. Scholarly works on the English-speaking Catholic Church are, however, virtually non-existent. No single history has been attempted, and the main published resources consist of specialized papers printed since 1933 in the annual reports of the Canadian Catholic Historical Association.[1] If, as Professor Savard has suggested, large tracts of fallow ground exist in the historiography of Canada's French Roman Catholic Church, the challenge of the English-speaking Church resembles Canada's vast forested terrain where only a few isolated clearings have been made by the hands of pioneers. Perhaps the monumental size of the challenge has been one factor discouraging the assault of the historian on an area of Canadian development which is qualitatively if not quantitatively as important as the history of French-speaking Canada.

The nineteenth century can be conveniently defined as identical with the *Pax Britannica*, extending from the end of the Napoleonic wars, and the shorter war of 1812-14 with the United States, to the outbreak of the First World War. The first date marks almost precisely the separate organization of the English-speaking Church, the second the beginning of the period of deep social and economic changes which shaped present-day Canada in a new form. Viewed retrospectively, the nineteenth century was for the Catholic Church in Canada an age of tremendous expansion and achievement, as indeed it was for all Christian denominations in the country.

In 1814, the Catholic Church in British North America still consisted of the single diocese of Quebec, already 140 years old, containing two seminaries, some 300 priests and 450,000 members. At that date, the Church was primarily the French Canadian Church, for, although the Maritime colonies of New Brunswick, Nova Scotia, Cape Breton and Prince Edward Island contained about 435,000 Catholics of Scottish and Irish origin and the frontier colony of Upper Canada had some 15,000 Catholics recently arrived from Scotland,[2] the vast majority (over 80 per cent) of Catholics in British North America were French-speaking residents of Lower Canada who could boast of two centuries of linguistic and religious existence in the New World. One hundred years later, the "French fact" was still dominant both in the Church and the Dominion of Canada, but the Church now comprised 8 archbishoprics, 23 bishoprics, and 6 vicariates apostolic, at least 17 seminaries, some 2,500 priests, and 3 million members of whom about 40 per cent (some 20 per cent of the Canadian population) belonged to the English-speaking section of the Church.[3]

Although the Roman Catholic Church has always been the largest Christian denomination in Canada, generally twice the size of the largest Protestant Church, the fact that Canadian Catholicism has been composed of a French majority and an English minority (a minority actually comprising several distinct ethnic groups) has affected the role which the Church played in Canadian life. On occasions, language has proved itself a more potent unifying force than religion. English-speaking Catholics shared the religious aspirations of French-Canadian Catholics, but they often shared the political aspirations of English-speaking Protestants. The position of English Catholics may perhaps be described as a third solitude. They remained separated by language from their co-religionists and by religion from their co-linguists. The solitude of language was epitomized, for example, by the chasm that appeared between English and French bishops at the Eucharistic Congress of 1910 or in the controversy over Ontario's renowned Regulation XVII. The solitude of the English Catholic in relation to his Protestant neighbours was vividly expressed by G.M. Grant:

> Even in cities where there is the closest association of Protestant and Romanist in commercial, industrial and political life, the two currents of religious life flow side by side as distinct from each other as the St. Lawrence and the Ottawa after their conjunction. But the rivers do eventually blend into one. The two currents of religious life do not.

At the beginning of the nineteenth century, the position and problems of the Roman Catholic Church varied in the different colonies of British North America, but the early development of the English-speaking Church can be most easily dealt with by treating it as two separate regions—the Maritimes and the rest of Canada west of Montreal. Between these two unequal regions lies the French-speaking Church of Quebec, inhibiting by its geography the growth of a greater uniformity within the English-speaking Church as a whole, but testifying to the necessity of treating Canadian history in part as the collective experience of disparate regions.

Differences within the English-speaking Church were not, however, solely the result of geographical separation. Early settlement patterns in British North America had already, by

1814, shaped the character of the Maritime colonies. Throughout the nineteenth century, settlement also influenced the pattern of development in the western region as the Canadian frontier marched unsteadily westward from the Great Lakes across the Prairies to the Pacific Ocean. However, neither in the Maritimes nor in Upper Canada (and even later in the Church's expansion into western Canada) did Catholics from England play any distinguishable role. Thus, to speak of the English Catholic Church in Canada in the nineteenth century is to speak of national groups—Scottish, Irish, German and Eastern European—all of whom were non-English by origin but all of whom were or became English-speaking.

Recognition of post-Conquest cultural and linguistic pluralism within the Church came in 1819 with the appointment of two English-speaking suffragans to the Bishop of Quebec—Angus MacEachern for the Maritime colonies and his friend Alexander Macdonell for Upper Canada.[4] In both of these English-speaking regions the dominant national influence in the Church was, in the beginning, Scottish. As new bishoprics were successively carved out of MacEachern's original diocese, the appointment of bishops seems to have been dictated by the nationality of the majority of the Roman Catholics in those areas. Thus the diocese of New Brunswick had three Irish bishops in succession and four of the first five bishops of Halifax were also natives of Ireland, whereas Antigonish always maintained a strong Scottish influence and MacEachern's four successors in Charlottetown were natives of Prince Edward Island, but all of Scottish ancestry.[5] In both the Maritimes and Upper Canada, bishops tried to accommodate national interests of particular congregations when appointing priests. A notable exception to this practice seems to have been Toronto's Bishop de Charbonnel who was accused of banishing Irish priests from his diocese and of preferring French-born priests who flew in the face of Irish voluntarist sentiment by attempting to enforce fixed fees for admission to the mass.[6]

The distinctive development of the English-speaking Catholics in the Maritimes is more difficult to trace than in central or western Canada. A common old-world experience of landlordism and proselytizing may have been a bond between the Irish and Scots of the region, but the Gaelic language and clan traditions tended to keep the Scots separated.

There, as in Upper Canada, the Scots gloried in their loyalty to Britain; they were also notable for their piety, poverty, and clannishness. Like the Scots, the Irish preserved elements of a closed culture, but the Irish were more aggressive.[7] Lacking a frontier, the Maritimes enjoyed a more static society, and they also received a smaller proportion of immigrants than did the two colonies, Lower and Upper Canada, in the St. Lawrence Valley. Since the Maritimes did not share in the industrialism and rising standard of living enjoyed by those other colonies, it would seem that in religious development as in so many other aspects of the history of the seaboard, time appeared to pass that region by, and the Maritimes' political tradition of "moderation and harmony" had its religious counterpart in the mutual respect and generally good relations of Catholics and other Christians.

In the Canadas, the English Roman Catholic Church was the beneficiary of the peculiar freedom accorded to the Church in the old province of Quebec, whereas in the Maritimes full political rights for Roman Catholics were granted only in the mid-1820s. In Upper Canada, at least until the Irish famine migration, the Catholic population was predominantly rural and widely scattered,[8] the only block settlements being the Scots of Glengarry and the Irish in the neighbourhood of Peterborough and of the Rideau. Irish Catholics in the urban centres were well established in the middle-class professions and mercantile pursuits. Scottish Catholics held senior positions in the civil administration from the earliest period of settlement out of all proportion to their small numbers.[9] This Scottish influence in the two Canadas involved a clannishness that occasionally smacked of nepotism both in lay and Church circles, but the influence was rapidly dissipated in the 1830s and 1840s by an influx of Irish immigrants and Irish priests.[10] Unlike Macdonell and his Scots, whose ardent loyalism and respect for social aristocracy was conjoined to a form of Erastianism,[11] the Irish clergy and laity came from a background where the clan system had long since lost its effectiveness and where the historic repression of the Catholic Church had welded pastor and flock together in a distrust of the civil establishment and in a voluntarist tradition.[12] The Irish tended to reverse the priorities of Church and education held by Macdonell, viewing the Church as an extension of the school,[13] and their propensity towards independence was a major bane of Macdonell's closing years.[14] After the massive wave of refugees from the Irish potato famine arrived in the late 1840s, the various dioceses formed from Macdonell's original bishopric were predominantly Irish in personnel and attitudes.[15]

Upper Canadian Catholics enjoyed satisfactory relations with their Protestant neighbours, relations that were polite if not always cordial. The exception to this condition was the period of the "Papal Aggression" controversy. In 1841, Upper and Lower Canada were joined in a legislative union which gave equal representation to both sections despite the larger population of Lower Canada at that time. Within ten years, Upper Canada's population had surpassed that of Lower Canada, yet sectional representation allowed the Catholic Church to exert its powers through the solid bloc of French members in Parliament. Under these circumstance, religious controversies became political issues, and the "Papal Aggression" question, transported from Britain to Canada, bequeathed a legacy of suspicion and covert hostility to the next generation of Canadians, although it had no direct relevance to the constitution of the colony. The Irish immigrants could readily identify with radical Protestantism in its liberal and anti-establishment objectives, but such an alliance was strained by the separate school agitation wherein Catholic educational traditions overrode Irish Canadian nationalism. It was also strained by the contemporaneous "Papal Aggression" controversy without which the political history of Canada might have recorded the birth of a strong secular reform tradition generations before Laurier made Liberalism respectable for Canadian Catholics.[16]

Unacceptable as was the stand of the Liberal party leader, George Brown, on papal aggression and separate schools to the Church at large, Brown's reforming liberalism and his solution of "representation by population" for the sectional difficulties of the United Province attracted enough support among the laity and lower clergy to bring them into conflict with Church leaders. These leaders refused to see the political realism of Brown's proposals and condemned reformism out of hand because of its connection with the demand for an end to separate Roman Catholic schools.[17] One further Irish influence, or at least the strong suspicion of such an influence, may be detected in the disruptive but far from infrequent appearance of a penchant for semi-autonomous congregationalism at the very time when the Catholic Church was moving towards increased episcopal supervision. This independence of spirit among the Irish in Upper Canada cannot be offered as proofs of the frontier thesis, since such incidents as the William O'Grady affair in Toronto (where an Irish priest opposed his bishop's authority) invariably concerned urban congregations who challenged episcopally ordained priorities for the expenditure of limited financial resources.

From its institutional inception the English-speaking Catholic Church had the advantage of growing within an institutional and legal framework already established by and for the French-speaking Church. Undoubtedly, this fact facilitated its development, yet the difference of language from the French Catholic majority created strains. Unlike the Scots whose relations with the French were reasonably happy, the Irish Catholics seemed to harbour some kind of natural antipathy towards the French. Despite the generous reception of sick, destitute or orphaned Irish by the French, antipathy was none the less real for being subterranean.[18] At mid-century in Montreal, where Irish-French friction was endemic, the bishop prevented the creation of an Irish parish for a decade by refusing to acknowledge every request for such linguistic separation.[19]

Although language differences created strains, the English-speaking Church depended heavily on the French for the theological education of its priests. The attraction for English ordinands and their bishops of the two seminaries of Quebec and Montreal seems to have been determined largely on the basis of propinquity. Bishop Macdonell always looked to the Sulpicians of Montreal who operated that seminary for assistance, although he was often made painfully aware of the traditional, and in his day increasingly bitter, ecclesiastical rivalry of the two cities. His loyalty to the bishop of Quebec was hard-pressed not only by force of circumstances, but also by the pride of the Sulpicians who in his words tended to equate their own ambitions with the will of God.[20] The Upper Canadian connection to the Sulpician seminary grew over decades to be something more than mere tradition or convenience.[21] At the turn of the century, Archbishop O'Connor of Toronto was convinced that in the education of his clergy the Sulpicians should always have the last word.[22] Although plans for a seminary to serve all parts of the English Church in Canada had been put on foot by his predecessor, it was not until 1910 that the Archbishop opened St. Augustine's seminary in Toronto to perform the function.

While the history of the English Church west of Montreal is marked by occasional and unsought involvement in the Montreal-Quebec rivalry, there is no public evidence that the English Church in the Maritimes found itself caught in that crossfire. For the Maritimes, the Quebec seminary seemed the preferred source of theological education, to judge from incomplete statistics regarding the registration of ordinands. All students in the two seminaries learned French, but at least in Montreal the language issue of French versus English was perpetuated by the segregation of Ontario students, who for residential purposes lived on a separate floor nicknamed the "Irish corridor" and characterized by the high spirits of its inhabitants.[23] Differences between French and English were more than linguistic—a difference in life-style and affluence was noted by Archbishop Lynch who contrasted his "*Irish* habit of poor living" with the French custom of taking wine thrice daily.[24]

The Catholic Church in British North America shared with the rest of the world Church in the "great renewal" of the nineteenth century. In Upper Canada, the renewal began very modestly under Bishop Power during the 1840s. Early evidence of renewal in that decade are few, perhaps because of the relatively small and scattered Roman Catholic population and also because of the lack of any newspaper comparable to the *Mélanges Religieux* of Montreal.[25] This situation changed drastically at mid-century, coinciding closely with the arrival of the French count and bishop, de Charbonnel, and with the arrival of tens of thousands of Irish potato famine refugees. New religious communities were invited to the diocese, a host of Church-centred lay associations, both charitable and devotional, were founded, and Catholic newspapers appeared that emphasized the political liberalism and the Irishness of the English-speaking Church.[26]

The "great renewal" reached Upper Canada at the same time as the industrial revolution and its related revolutions in transportation, communications and agriculture so that the Church shared in the general up-surge of piety and of affluence. New churches were built and old ones replaced or extended; church and charitable givings increased at an unprecedented rate. In the area of the later diocese of Hamilton, only seven parishes and missions had been founded between 1820 and

1850, yet nineteen new ones were created in the 1850s alone—as many as were established there in the next half century.[27] These figures reflect the rapid economic expansion of the colony in the 1850s, despite the major depression during the later years of that decade. But they concern only one limited area and cannot reveal two basic factors in the history of Canada in the nineteenth century, namely, that the frontier continued to unfold as population moved westward and that in the second half of the century Canada was beset by recurrent and prolonged depressions which certainly slowed the growth of all Christian denominations in the Dominion.

The onset of industrialism and consequently of urbanization in Upper Canada at mid-century and the general lack of capital and skills on the part of the Irish famine immigrants combined to make their Church an urban institution to a degree unknown to the contemporary French-speaking Catholic Church in Canada. Furthermore, the fact that the English Church ministered to a large, low-income group concentrated in urban ghettos produced two further consequences. Lack of education among the bulk of the laity undoubtedly sharply curtailed the recruiting of priests from among the first and probably second generation of these immigrants. This in turn must account for the large number of clergy who, beginning about 1850, were received either directly from Ireland or from Ireland via the United States or France and who, in achieving position of eminence in the Church's administrative structure, stamped the English-speaking Church with an Irish character.

Yet the Irish influence in the Church did not so much replace as overlay older ethnic elements in the English Church. In Ontario German Catholics had settled in Waterloo County during the early decades of the century and had retained, through the medium of the Church, much of German culture[28] or, as a Protestant writer observed, "a freedom of tone" unlike the French and Irish Catholic expression.[29] At least ten separate schools in the County used German as the language of instruction. At the outbreak of the First World War, records of 213 of the 317 priests who had worked or visited in the County showed that 84 were Ontario-born, 36 were Irish, and 34 from Germany or Austria.[30] Similarly, among Highland Scottish settlers in Eastern Ontario Gaelic continued to be used in homes and in the pulpit, if not in the schools. Irish immigrants, however, seem to have spoken English only and this no doubt accelerated the process of their Canadianization. By the 1860s, Irish Catholics were among the most vocal exponents of a Canadian nationalism, thus following the example of the Irish clergy who identified easily and quickly with their new homeland.

This indigenization, when combined with political liberalism, produced at times a Canadianism that was anti-England and which dwelt on the past and present sufferings of Mother Ireland. But, unlike the Irish of Boston and New York, the Canadian Irish preserved no articulated traditions about the potato famine. It remained an episode that was neither historicized nor mythologized in Canada. One explanation of this omission may lie in the fact that their lay leaders, the few men of considerable substance, seem to have traced their emigration to a period before the Great Hunger, just as their Irish priests were a product of a later migration. Those immigrants who were immediate sufferers in the late forties, however, simply failed to preserve any strong group or individual recollection of their tragic experience.[31] Another consequence of urbanization and poverty was the remarkable response to the challenge of charity and the Church's inevitable need for funds. Poorer Church members gave generously in support of religion, and a traditional reliance on and promotion of the "widow's mite" is still in evidence. But such self-sacrifice by poor laity and devoted clergy does not sufficiently explain the impressive rise of the Church from a state of proud poverty in Macdonell's day to a condition of undeniably extensive wealth, if not opulence by the end of the century.[32] Capital expansion came from the profits of the sale of city-centre properties bequeathed to the Church in earlier years, and from large donations by the few wealthy Church members. Many bazaars and general subscription campaigns would be required to match such gifts as the half-million dollars given by one Toronto brewer to cover the cost of building and furnishing St. Augustine's seminary.[33]

The fact that at least a significant part of the Catholic Church's activities was increasingly concerned with this poorer class of city dwellers in a country steadily becoming more urbanized and more industrialized underlies the sympathetic or at least neutral attitude of the English-speaking hierarchy towards trade unionism at a time when their agriculturally-minded French-speaking brother bishops in Quebec were publicly condemning the Knights of Labor as a threat to the Catholic faith.[34] That so much of the available energy and resources of the English-speaking Church had to be channelled into essential parochial and social services before the First World War explains not only the monopoly role of the French Church in western Canadian missions, but also the belated participation of the English Church in the great nineteenth century movement of foreign missions.

Since education in Canada is constitutionally within exclusively provincial jurisdiction, the history of Catholic education must be examined within the separate context of each province. Hence, it is difficult to state simply and succinctly the nature and traditions of Catholic education in Canada, but some common elements may be identified as having a nation-wide application, at least for the English-speaking Church. One such tradition has been an emphasis on separate education of the sexes, although this is obviously in no way unique to the English Church. Another, probably of American or even Irish origin, is the stress laid on team sports and the general encouragement of participation in athletics, a tradition occasionally criticized as derogating from academic achievement.

Except for the successful demand for separate Catholic schools in Upper Canada (first voiced about 1850, and blamed by supporters of nondenominational education on the influence of Bishop de Charbonnel and his French Jesuit advisers), there seems to be no other evidence in the English Church of the ultramontanism which had been fostered in the French Canadian Church by Bishop Bourget of Montreal since the 1840s. A public letter from the Irish and liberal Archbishop Lynch of Toronto to the federal Liberal party leader, Alexander Mackenzie, in 1876 declared that, "In Ontario the priests are forbidden to turn the altar into a tribune from which to deliver political harangues or to menace electors on account of the votes they may give at political elections."[35] This pronouncement brought down on his head the ire of the extreme ultramontanes of Quebec where the "Catholic Programme" identified the interests of the Church with the Conservative party, and where sacramental terrorism was used to enforce the ultramontane will on Catholic electors. In Ontario, the same objectives of the Church were achieved by Lynch through quiet diplomacy and co-operation with Oliver Mowat, Liberal prime minister of the province from 1872 to 1896.[36]

Religious ultramontanism found a warm reception among English-speaking Catholics and especially among the Irish, but political ultramontanism of the *nationaliste* brand that distressed

the French-Canadian Church was entirely foreign to the transplanted liberal and voluntarist traditions, which thrived as well in
Canada as in Ireland.[37] The Papal Zouaves (Catholic volunteer
soldiers, many of them French Canadian, who left to fight for the
Pope in Italy) are not an organization, not even a memory, in
Canada's English-speaking Catholic Church. Irish pastors and
their flocks were at heart nineteenth-century liberals. Archbishop
Lynch was described in his own lifetime as "a devout Catholic, and a sincere advocate of Papal infallibility, he is willing to
accord . . . full liberty of conscience to those who differ from
him,"[38] a description that must have seemed self-contradictory
to some of his brother bishops in Quebec.

In western Canada, for most of the nineteenth century,
the Church must be viewed as an extension of the French-
Canadian Church. Missionary work among the native tribes
was exclusively in the hands of French Oblates, and even in the
three decades following Confederation in 1867, parish clergy
and parish life in the region mirrored familiar French-Canadian patterns. It was confidently assumed that the Canadian
West would be Catholic and French, but instead it became,
after 1867, first an extension of the English and Protestant
ethos of Ontario and then, in the last generation before the
First World War, a region of ethnic, linguistic and religious pluralism, thanks to thousands of Eastern Europeans who entered
in Canada's second Great Migration. The pattern of development in the West became predominantly English, although the
French had sowed the seeds of faith in earlier days.

As the "last, best West" grew at a phenomenal rate in the
twenty years before the First World War, the Church grew
proportionately. A federal Minister of the Interior commented
on the sudden change from "paltry sheds" to "real cathedrals,
houses, convents, schools and hospitals," which marked "the
very top of progress."[39] Local finances provided the physical
structures but the priests and institutions of the faith were
imported from the East. As the West seemed a mission monopoly of the Oblates until the coming of other missionary congregations in the late nineteenth century, so too early female
orders were offshoots of French-Canadian foundations. Tensions
between the early French and later English settlers arose when
later groups proposed to move churches closer to the transcontinental Canadian Pacific Railway (C.P.R.), a suggestion resisted
strongly by the more rural-minded French parishioners.

The decisive role of transportation routes in Church growth was again exemplified in the West by the opening of thirteen parishes in central Alberta immediately after the arrival of the C.P.R., and this pattern was repeated in the same area by the establishment of six more parishes when the Canadian Northern line was completed in 1906, and of four more when the Grand Trunk Pacific arrived soon after.[40] For both English and French-speaking Churches in the West problems were increased during the last decade before the War by the arrival of thousands of Eastern Europeans. In those ten years, seven Polish missions and two Greek Uniate Ruthenian parishes were created in the central area of Alberta alone. After sharing in the long incubation of the West, the Church had suddenly begun to flourish in the hot-house climate of the second Great Migration to Canada, but its character altered from a French to an English pattern, an English pattern that included ethnic pluralism reflecting the modern Canadian immigration experience and paralleling more closely developments in Canadian Protestant churches than in the French Catholic Church.

Through the nineteenth century, the English Catholic Church had grown in Canada and with Canada. By 1914 the Church mirrored territorially the expansion of the ambitious young Dominion. Physically, it reflected the affluence of the increasingly industrialized nation; spiritually, it shared in the "renewed" life of a militant Christendom and in the piety of the Victorian age of Western European civilization. Although dominated institutionally and perhaps psychologically by the "Irish fact," the English-speaking Church was accommodating to the ethnic and cultural pluralism of the modern period more easily than its French-Canadian counterpart. At the close of the nineteenth century, the English-Canadian Church was characterized by urbanism, "English Canadian" nationalism, and an overt loyalty to Britain shared by most Protestant Canadians. Such generalizations are admittedly of a most tentative nature. So little scholarly research on the English-speaking Catholic Church of Canada has been undertaken or published that until a new generation of historians can probe these questions through the use of basic documentation, the interpretation offered here must remain open to reservations, not only about their specific accuracy but about their validity in principle.

X
The Origin of the Separate Schools Question in Ontario

This article, published in the Canadian Journal of Theology *in 1959, grew out of John Moir's doctoral thesis,* Church and State in Canada West: Three Studies in the Relation of Denominationalism and Nationalism, 1841-1867 *(University of Toronto, 1954). In the past fifty years much rhetoric and more rivers of ink have been spent across Canada on the separate school question. Since many separate school systems elsewhere in Canada have been modelled on Ontario, this article could be renamed "The Origin of the Separate Schools Question."*

Unlike other historical problems of church-state relations in Canada, the separate school question remains to this day a very live issue. The report of the Hope Commission, an Ontario Royal Commission on education which reported in 1950, contained both an historical summary of the separate school controversy and a well-documented refutation in the form of a dissenting minority report by the Roman Catholic members of the Commission. Apparently the Canadian tradition of compromise has not been completely successful in this particular field. This paper is a brief attempt to appraise the origins of the problem in what is now the Province of Ontario.

"Protection from Insult"

The cases for separate schools in Ontario and Quebec constitute the obverse and reverse of the same coin rather than parallel situations. In Quebec the school system was religious, a heritage of New France; in Ontario common schools are nondenominational, and the existence of separate schools is an exception to the doctrine of popular sovereignty stemming from political and social conditions which arose under the Act of Union of 1841. In that year the Roman Catholic Church's control of all phases of education of its adherents in Lower Canada was complete and unquestioned. Protestant schools did exist there, but system there was none.

Traditionally, the Church of England had exercised a prevailing and, to many minds, undesirable influence over elementary education in Upper Canada, and successive attempts at legislation had failed to provide satisfactory school facilities. The most recent common school bill had been vetoed by the Legislative Council in 1836 on the ground that the province was already overburdened with taxes for paved roads, courthouses and jails.[1]

In his Speech from the Throne in 1841 to the first session of the first Parliament of the United Canadas, Governor General Lord Sydenham reminded the members that "a due provision for the Education of the People" was a prime duty of the state.[2] But realizing the potential difficulties of imposing a national system of primary education on two distinct cultures, Sydenham suggested that "steps may be taken, by which an advance to a more perfect system may be made." Before the school bill could be introduced petitions began to arrive from congregations of the Churches of England and Scotland praying that the Bible be made a prescribed textbook for all schools receiving government aid. In the Legislative Council William Morris, lay spokesperson of the Kirk, warned that if Roman Catholics found this provision objectionable, "We must part in peace, and conduct the education of the respective Bodies according to our sense of what is right."[3]

The Common School Bill of 1841 was described by Solicitor General Day when introducing it as only part of "the great general system of National Education."[4] Originally, the Bill contained no mention of separate schools of any description, thus clearly anticipating a unified national system of secular elementary education. But opposition soon made itself felt. The Roman Catholic bishops of Kingston and Quebec objected to the principles of the Bill. John Strachan, Anglican Bishop of Toronto, petitioned strongly that the education of Anglican children should be entrusted to Anglican teachers only. The result of this flood of petitions, forty-two in all, was that clauses were added to the Bill permitting any religious minority to establish dissentient schools.

Thus, while the Act ostensibly created a unitary system of elementary education for the United Provinces, it recognized the existence of Protestant dissentient schools in Lower Canada and provided equal opportunities for religious minorities in Upper Canada. The Act elicited no strong opposition but in practice it proved well-nigh impossible to administer. The attempt to obtain a uniform system in both parts of Canada was abandoned, and the principle of federation, which was growing within the Union, was also tacitly adopted for the field of elementary education. In 1843 two bills were introduced establishing a new system of elementary schools for Upper Canada alone.

The new plan provided that ten or more freeholders, Protestant or Roman Catholic, might establish a separate school only if the common school teacher belonged to the other major body of Christians. This was a radical departure from the limitless provisions of the Act of 1841. As a safeguard of consciences, however, the Bill added that no child need read any book or join in any devotional exercises objectionable to the parents. Only three of the seventy-one clauses of the Bill dealt with the religious question, but their restrictive nature marked a new and reactionary policy. The sole opposition to the Bill's passage came from Bishop Strachan who vainly requested a denominational division of all Common School funds.

The appointment of Egerton Ryerson as Superintendent of Education in 1844 was probably the most important single event in the educational history of Ontario. Ryerson intended that the educational system should be "Provincial, or National" (the terms were synonymous), and based on "the Christianity of the Bible—regardless of the peculiarities of Sects, or Parties." The principles of Christianity could be effected, he believed, without compromising the principles of any group. In his *Report of a System of Public Elementary Education* he asserted that education must be universal and practical, and therefore established on "Religion and Morality."

> By Religion and Morality I do not mean sectarianism in any form, but the general system of truth and morals taught in the Holy Scriptures. Sectarianism is not morality . . . . Such sectarian teaching may, as it has done, raise up an army of pugilists and persecutors, but it is not the way to create a community of Christians.[5]

He accepted the safeguards of the Common School Act, though convinced that mixed schools could be satisfactory to all. Clearly Ryerson conceived of separate schools as the exceptional means of protecting religious minority rights within the unitary whole of the provincial system. Judging by past events, he had no reason to think the system would develop on other lines than those he had laid out.

Ryerson drafted a remedial school bill in 1846 for his national system, without altering the existing separate school arrangements. One Anglican legislator requested for his denomination the same rights as the Roman Catholics, but otherwise the bill passed through the Provincial Parliament without any reference to the separate school question. The next step was the creation of a provincial Board of Education. Here Ryerson bowed to the advice of Anglican Premier William Henry Draper in avoiding a purely clerical Board. Strachan refused to be a member because this would only encourage opposition to the Board, but he gave his full support to the appointment of Michael Power, the Roman Catholic Bishop of Toronto, who was elected first chairman of the Board.

The lamentable death of Bishop Power from emigrant fever in October 1847 eventually proved disastrous to Ryerson's plans. All evidence attests that Power acted with other members of the Board in the friendliest and most harmonious manner. Power's successor, Armand François de Charbonnel, a French count and an ultramontanist who had seen the torch of revolution inflame Europe and who shared Pius IX's reaction against the new liberalism, was to prove himself in time a man of a different stamp to that of Power, who had shared Ryerson's view that separate schools were not an essential on principle, although circumstances in this case made them necessary. Even de Charbonnel, for more than a year after his appointment, contented himself with referring to their existence as a "protection from insult."[6]

The Common School Act of 1846 functioned reasonably well for more than two years. Bishop Strachan was, of course, still opposed on principle to mixed schools, insisting that, "he preferred *separate* Schools, *if they could get them.*"[7] But within the Church of England opposition to Strachan's plans was increasing among Low Church groups (who were largely Irish), and the outbreak of the Papal Aggression issue in 1850 accentuated this internal conflict. It is noteworthy that the aims and claims of the Anglican Bishop of Toronto were the same as those put forward by his Roman Catholic counterpart a few years later. In 1849, however, the passing of Robert

Baldwin's Municipal Corporations Act necessitated a revision of the Common Schools Act. Malcolm Cameron, radical member of the second Baldwin-Lafontaine administration, introduced the bill for what he described as "a systematic code" of Common School legislation.[8]

Cameron's bill bore directly on the religious question at two points. It excluded the clergy as visitors to the common schools, and it destroyed the separate schools simply by failing to mention them. Ryerson hastened to protest the first point; he did not protest the second. In point of fact, separate schools of all kinds—Roman Catholic, Protestant, and even a few coloured ones—were declining in number and there was every reason to expect the trend to continue. But Cameron's bill destroyed Ryerson's great plan for a provincial system of elementary education and, more important, it did away with Ryerson's position. It was well known that Cameron was but one of several enemies of Ryerson within the Reform Government, yet the results of this incident must have surprised all parties concerned.

First, despite Ryerson's protest and a government promise that the bill would be altered, it was passed as introduced. The surprised Superintendent immediately offered his resignation. At once the Government reconsidered its action. Ryerson was asked to remain at his post, Malcolm Cameron resigned from the Cabinet, and the existence of the law itself was ignored by all until another Act could be passed at the next Session as part of Ryerson's price for withdrawing his resignation.

The promised Common School Bill was introduced in 1850 by Ryerson's very co-operative acquaintance, Inspector General Francis Hincks. Forty-eight of the forty-nine clauses passed substantially without change, but on Clause Nineteen, which vested in the municipal authorities of each township the power to establish separate schools, Hincks and Ryerson were forced to accept an effective amendment. Roman Catholics were dissatisfied with this circumscription of rural separate schools, and the Vicar General at Kingston and the Administrator of the Toronto Diocese petitioned that "the Catholics of Canada West (may be enabled) to establish separate schools, wherever they may deem it expedient."[9]

Here was an opportunity in the eyes of High Anglicans to obtain separate Anglican schools by co-operating with the Roman Catholics. Accordingly, an agreement for joint action was reached by Assembly members of each of these churches. But the Ministry learned of the plot and turned the occasion to the best advantage by offering Roman Catholics the 1843 arrangement, a compromise that met their demands.[10] The Anglicans who had promoted the plan of united action were boasting of a majority of fourteen to twenty votes when the division was called. To their bewilderment and the amusement of the House, the Roman Catholic members voted with the Government.

Hincks admitted that he had only accepted this compromise in deference to the "strong feeling" of his colleagues,[11] and outside of Parliament there was some mild opposition to the "peculiar privileges" granted Roman Catholics at the cost of denominational equality. "The principle thus admitted," remarked George Brown's *Globe*, "strikes at the root of our whole system of national education."[12] If one denomination was entitled to such preferential treatment, then all were. This compromise, the *Globe* added prophetically, might prove to be the thin edge of the wedge. Ryerson, however, stated publicly that there was "no probability that Separate Schools will be more injurious in time to come than they have been in the past."[13] Separate school supporters still paid the local common school rates and could obtain no government aid beyond the share of the School Grant provided for the teacher's salary on the basis of the school's enrolment.

Thus, with the exception of the concession made by Hincks' Common Schools Act of 1850, the policy towards separate schools since 1841 had been increasingly restrictive and as yet the only protest of consequence had come from the Church of England. But the tide of opinion was turning as the first half of the century came to an end. Pius IX had just re-established the Roman Catholic hierarchy in Britain. He had also appointed de Charbonnel to the see of Toronto. The two incidents were pregnant with a non-celestial fire soon to fall upon Canada with unforeseen and cataclysmic results.

As the plans of the Roman Catholic Church Militant unfolded in Britain, George Brown took up the fiery cross of "Papal Aggression" on a dare, and his provocative writing soon divided the province into two hostile camps, Protestant versus Catholic. In France de Charbonnel had seen the same trends towards infidelity and indifferentism which in Italy had destroyed the early liberal proclivities of Pius IX. Yet de

Charbonnel had already laboured in Canada for several years and his elevation to the bishopric was viewed without suspicion by Canadians, so when he joined the Board of Education in Power's stead, there was no expectation that his policy would be less co-operative than that of Bishop Power. Against this background the first blow which fell for separate schools seemed at the moment relatively unimportant.

Toronto's size had been greatly expanded by recent immigration, particularly of Irish Roman Catholics, and the establishment of another separate school was requested by certain Roman Catholics.[14] The request was rejected by the Board of School Trustees as not permitted by the letter of the Act of 1850, which had been so carelessly worded as to permit the setting up of only one separate school in a town or city. The Board's decision was upheld by the Attorney General and the Queen's Bench on appeal. Nevertheless, the demand was a reasonable one. Ryerson, absent in Europe at the moment, conceded that remedial legislation must be introduced. At the same time Strachan renewed his attacks of the "intolerable degradation" of a school system which was turning Anglican children into "infidels."[15] Anglicans must have the same privileges as Roman Catholics, he insisted, and he spurred his flock to petition Parliament to this end. Roman Catholic petitions for the amendment of the nineteenth clause of the Common Schools Act were also received. The result of these actions and agitations was twofold.

George Brown, self-appointed champion of Protestant ascendancy, took up the editorial cudgel against both groups of separatists. He agreed that Anglicans should have the same rights as Roman Catholics if separate schools were to continue, but the cry of "religion in danger" was, in his opinion, just a priestly scheme to gain control of the educational system for sectarian and sacerdotal ends. Would no member of Parliament bring forward a bill to repeal the controversial Clause Nineteen and dispose of the question for all time?[16] Ironically, it was the "little Rebel," William Lyon Mackenzie, recent victor over Brown in a parliamentary by-election, who introduced such an amendment to the Government's remedial bill to eradicate those "nurseries of strife and dissension,"[17] the separate schools.

Mackenzie's amendment got only five votes; the government bill now permitting separate schools to be set up in each ward of a municipality was carried, to the avowed satisfaction of the Roman Catholic authorities. But as extremes beget extremes, so Mackenzie's abortive amendment and the *Globe's* open antagonism to separate schools aroused feelings of insecurity and uneasiness among Roman Catholics, already on the defensive because of the "Papal Aggression" controversy. No longer were separate schools a sufficient "protection from insult." A "war of total separation" had been opened between the forces of denominationalism and nationalism for control of elementary education.

The War of Total Separation

Early in 1852 several incidents occurred which brought Ryerson and de Charbonnel into open conflict. When de Charbonnel complained on behalf of the separate school at Chatham that its share of the provincial grant was too small, Ryerson defended the financial disparity by the letter of the law. Next, the bishop charged that an anti-Catholic book was used in the Chatham common school, and denounced the educational system as "a regular disguised persecution."[18] Ryerson replied that no child was forced to read any objectionable book, but de Charbonnel added the accusation that mixed schools were the "ruin of religion, and a persecution of the Church." "We must have, and we will have the full management of our Schools, as well as Protestants in Lower Canada."

To this latest demand, which set the tempo for the issue until Confederation, Ryerson retorted that it originated in the "new class of ideas and feelings" which the bishop had imported from Europe, and he contrasted it to the policy of the late Bishop Power. The existence of separate schools was in the opinion of Ryerson and the majority of the Province regrettable and inexpedient, but Ryerson denied that he had ever been unjust to Roman Catholics. When a financial problem similar to that in the Chatham case arose in Belleville, de Charbonnel threatened to use his episcopal authority to remove Roman Catholic children from mixed schools. Worsted in the argument by Ryerson's logic and superior knowledge of the facts, the bishop terminated the controversy abruptly but ominously: "I hope that by making use of all the constitutional means, in order to claim our right, I will not upset the Government of Canada nor its institutions."

Thus a corner was turned in the development of separate schools in Canada West, and the ideological bases were clearly stated. For de Charbonnel and some Roman Catholics, though not all, separate schools had become an inalienable right which must be obtained to satisfy the conscientious convictions of their religious belief. Ryerson, however, saw in the Roman Catholic demands not only a threat to his school system but to the national unity towards which it was directed. The "war of total separation," if successful, would create a nation within a nation.

In response to revived pressure put upon him under the new Hincks-Morin Reform government, Ryerson proposed in a draft of a revised bill to relieve separate school supporters of paying any common school tax and to permit them to share the provincial grant according to school attendance. But he urged that municipalities should not be forced to become tax collectors for separate schools. "The very mention of a separate column on the Tax Roll for a Separate School, excites an hostility and feeling which you can hardly imagine," he told Hincks.[19] Behind the scenes, Archbishop Turgeon of Quebec assured de Charbonnel that A.N. Morin, the leading French-Canadian member of the government, had pledged himself and his colleagues to give the Roman Catholics of Upper Canada the same advantages as the Protestants of Lower Canada enjoyed, and Attorney-General W.B. Richards also promised as much to the bishops.

In 1852 Strachan and some High Church Anglicans again petitioned Parliament against the alleged injustice and irreligion of the common schools, and that same year the Reverend Adam Townley, a convert from Methodism, abetted his bishop's efforts with a pamphlet against the school system in which he pointed to the prostitutes of Paris as living evidence of the results of secular education. Townley claimed that as the Church of England comprised one third of the population of Canada West (in fact it was only 22%), the establishment of separate Anglican schools was a "Democratic Right."[20]

In the Assembly Bishop Strachan's petition for Anglican Schools was read and ignored, while the secularizationists were petitioning for an end to Clergy Reserves, rectories and separate schools. Petitions from the Roman Catholic bishops of Kingston and London arrived praying for amendment of the Common School Act of 1850. Weeks passed and the Government showed no signs of introducing Ryerson's draft bill. At last in mid-October, Archbishop Turgeon petitioned for the same privileges for Roman Catholics in Canada West as Protestants had in Canada East. Attorney General Richards sent Ryerson a bill prepared by a French-Canadian legislator, and Ryerson hastened to Quebec to defend his system from this latest threat.

A compromise bill drafted by Ryerson was finally introduced, but too many ministerial cooks had made hash of the measure and it was returned to Ryerson for revision during the winter prorogation. Before Parliament reconvened, Richards obtained the *nihil obstat* of the Roman Catholic members and after four more months the Bill reached the Committee of the Whole. Outside Parliament, the Clear Grits and Brownite presses were loudly denouncing the bill as the destruction of the national education system. Petitions from Canada West indicated that that section of the united provinces unanimously favoured the abolition of separate schools. The only petition demanding separate Roman Catholic schools for Canada West came, significantly, from Canada East, particularly Quebec where the perambulating Parliament was currently sitting.

Despite the opposition of Brown and the Grits, the Act was passed, thanks to Lower Canadian votes. To Roman Catholics the measure gave personal pecuniary relief and sustenance for their separate schools, while leaving the conditions for establishment and division of the grant unchanged. But to "broad Protestants" like George Brown these were signs of "priestly encroachments" which threatened the very destiny of the nation.[21]

Ryerson announced publicly that the separate schools were "practically harmless" to the school system, and he still believed that experience would soon convince Roman Catholics of their disadvantages and inexpediency.[22] He could not foresee the future numerical increase of separate schools, or future Lower Canadian interference with Upper Canadian education. Many parties remained unconvinced by the Chief Superintendent's logic.

The real test of the Act's popularity, however, would be the reaction of the prime movers, the Roman Catholic hierarchy. De Charbonnel was jubilant and issued a pastoral letter commending the measure. But his tone soon changed when he discovered that Toronto Common School Trustees were hiring

Roman Catholic teachers, thus depriving his church of the legal right to maintain separate schools in that city. Hincks promised to investigate and if necessary introduce a new bill, though Ryerson was left in ignorance of this latter part of the agreement. Before the session of 1854 began, Bishop de Charbonnel issued a statement demanding equal educational rights for Upper Canadian Roman Catholics. With seven other bishops he petitioned the "aid and protection" of the Governor General "to obtain a just and equitable law in favour of Separate Schools."[23]

Before this petition reached Parliament the Hincks-Morin Government was defeated and appealed to the country in a general election. Bishop de Charbonnel wrote numerous members of Parliament requesting new separate school legislation, either in prospect or consequence of support given in their elections. Three changes were desired—exemption for Roman Catholics from paying to the separate school an amount equal to the common school rate, power to unite municipal separate school corporations into a single Board of Trustees, and direct payment of school money by the Chief Superintendent. Ryerson had no objection to the first two proposals, but he considered the third a "frivolous" attempt to place him in a vulnerable position for future agitation.[24] He went on to refute thirteen points of inequality, alleged by the Bishop, between the separate school law of the two parts of the Province. Ryerson gave Hincks a draft bill covering the desired changes at the same time advising that the policy of conciliation had now reached its limit in the eyes of Upper Canadians, for Protestants had "conscientious convictions" as strong as those of Roman Catholics.[25]

Before any action was taken the Reform regime ended and the MacNab-Morin coalition took office pledged to carry out the Hincks-Morin programme. The separate school bill was now entrusted to John A. Macdonald who promised the Roman Catholic bishops satisfaction and justice, but he put off any action until 1855. Suspicious that the delay and silence implied a scheme on the part of Ryerson and Macdonald, the Upper Canadian bishops forwarded a "protestation"(identical to de Charbonnel's statement of the previous summer) and a bill of their own.[26]

Ryerson, summoned in haste to the capital, explained that the bishops' bill was inadmissible and the protestation inaccurate. The bill would have created a special superintendent of separate schools, made the municipalities tax collectors for the separate schools, and given the separate schools an equivalent for any improvement made to a common school. Instead, Ryerson offered de Charbonnel the conditions he had outlined to Hincks, but discussion proved fruitless. Six weeks after he had returned to Toronto, believing he had convinced the Attorneys General, Ryerson was informed privately that G.E. Taché had introduced a different separate school bill in the Legislative Council one week before. Ryerson advised Macdonald that only the High Anglicans would benefit since the bill permitted anyone subscribing even a nominal amount to a private school to avoid all taxes. Macdonald took the cue and restricted its terms to Roman Catholics.

The session was old before the bill came into the Assembly. The *Globe* of 22 May announced it as a crisis in the rule of Canada—"Romish Priests" versus enlightened principles. What had Taché to do with the schools of Canada West? Opposition to the bill cut across party lines, but the bill passed on the day before adjournment by a majority composed almost exclusively of Lower Canadians in a House reduced to one third. The votes had placed on the statute books the first Separate School Act of Canada West.

The new Act permitted five Roman Catholic heads of families to establish a separate school regardless of the religion of the common school teacher, assured separate schools of a share of the legislative grant proportional to school attendance, and in theory at least left Roman Catholics a choice of which system they would support. The Act fell short of the demands of de Charbonnel, but in later years Ryerson could point out that the bishops' grievances were of their own making since they had drafted Taché's Act.

De Charbonnel had given his approval and thanked the Government for this measure of justice to his church. Scarcely had he arrived back in Toronto, however, before he discovered that he had been duped again by the amendments made after his departure. "He has got a new light," Macdonald warned Ryerson, "and now he says the Bill won't do."[27] The Chief Superintendent was advised to play the peacemaker by stressing the Act's innocuous effects on the Common School System ("this for the people at large," wrote Macdonald) and its beneficence for Roman Catholics, "this to keep them in good humour." But Macdonald feared that de Charbonnel might renew the "unwholesome agitation."

The unwholesome agitation did not reappear until the new year, 1856, and then it originated with an outraged Protestantism. Robert Corrigan, an Irish Roman Catholic convert to Protestantism, was literally kicked and beaten to death at a fair in St. Sylvester, a small town south of Quebec City. The acquittal of the killers by a Roman Catholic judge and jury seemed a travesty of justice, and the government seemed incapable or unwilling to interfere in the matter. The horrible murder of Corrigan shocked Canadian Protestants, uniting Tory and Radical in a cry for the abolition of separate schools in Canada West as partial payment of the debt demanded by Corrigan's blood. Protestant unrest was further increased by de Charbonnel's pronouncement in his Lenten Pastoral that Roman Catholics who did not employ their franchise in the separate school cause were guilty of mortal sin. Even moderate newspapers spoke "against a despotism that would crush liberty of conscience and freedom of thought, a despotism unknown to members of Protestant communions."[28]

When the legislature met in February 1856, it was greeted by a flood of petitions demanding outright repeal of separate school legislation and only one petition in their defence. Despite the unmistakable display of Upper Canadian opinion through mass meetings and petitions, the Upper Canadian Roman Catholic Bishops applied to the Government for an amendment to the Separate School Act. Macdonald and his colleagues were too sensitive to the Protestant temper to venture any ministerial measure thereon. Within two weeks of Parliament's opening, however, J.G. Bowes introduced a private bill to exempt separate school supporters from paying common school rates simply by producing a receipt for taxes paid to the separate school. The bill never reached second reading—in any case it was less than the Roman Catholic bishops desired. But it did revive Bishop Strachan's interest in obtaining Anglican schools. "Surely our claim is as good as that of the Roman Catholics," he wrote John Hillyard Cameron.[29]

The legislature had not heard the last of the separate school question. When George Brown moved for repeal of all separate school legislation, W.L. Felton countered with de Charbonnel's favourite amendment—the same rights for Roman Catholics in Canada West as for dissidents in Canada East. After a night-long debate and twelve fruitless divisions, the debate was postponed. When resumed, five weeks later,

Felton's amendment was voted down. The Roman Catholic hierarchy felt that the Government had broken its pledge and de Charbonnel denounced four Roman Catholic cabinet members in a letter read from every pulpit in his diocese.

De Charbonnel's actions disturbed Protestants more than they did Roman Catholics. The press charged that popish ascendancy was interfering with private judgement and parliamentary responsibility. The Bishop was accused of "filtering British liberty through the will and pleasure of the Roman Catholic Church."[30] Thus the separate school question was cutting across established religious and political party lines, even those of the Orangemen. For the first time Protestant churches other than the Church of England entered the controversy when the Free Church and Wesleyan Methodists officially supported the common school system. Within the Church of England, however, the issue caused an open rupture when Strachan once more attacked the common schools at his visitation to the Clergy, and the Low Church elements gathered strength rapidly in opposition to the separatist tendencies of the High Church faction.

For six years after Bowes' bill touched off that memorable debate in the Assembly, the separate school question provided a recurrent theme for editorials, but no major alterations were made in the existing law. De Charbonnel retired to a French monastery and his polemical duties were assumed by J.M. Bruyère, rector of St. Michael's Cathedral, who, with the assistance of Bishop Pinsonnault of London, carried on a war of words against Ryerson. A river of ink was spilled either for or against separate schools. Thomas D'Arcy McGee split and confused Roman Catholics by insisting that the existing separate school law was useless and Brown seriously compromised the radical Reform position by adopting McGee's ideal of the Irish school system for the four-day ministry of 1858.

Not until 1860 was the burning issue reopened in earnest. Ryerson was in Quebec when Richard W. Scott, member for Ottawa, introduced a new separate school bill which would permit the establishment of separate schools in villages and towns (an omission by oversight in the Taché Act) and eliminate the annual notice required of separate school supporters. Both were reasonable proposals, but they were also a sharp spur to the "high Protestant" horse ridden by George Brown and the bill did not even get a second reading. The following year the persistent Mr. Scott introduced his bill again, but it got even less attention. In 1862, however, the Roman Catholic *Canadian Freeman* demanded that the Ministry redeem pledges which, the *Freeman* of 24 January 1862 said, had been given at the 1861 election in exchange for Roman Catholic votes. Ryerson offered Bishop Lynch of Toronto a bill based on Scott's, but Bishop Horan of Kingston held out for some more final measure to settle the long-vexed question.

Here the problem stood in April 1862, when Scott once more introduced a separate school bill. This latest bill, however, was radically different from its two predecessors, for it smacked of the rankest ultramontanism. Priests were to be *ex officio* trustees, the Church was to control all rules and curricula in separate schools, and the schools themselves were to be exempt from observance of common school holidays and free to set their own. At the second reading Scott announced that the bill had Ryerson's approval. In fact, Ryerson was ill and had not even seen the bill. When he did see it, he advised Macdonald that "it ought by all means to be rejected."[31] After two days' debate the bill was given a vote of government approval at two in the morning. Macdonald explained to Ryerson that Dick Scott was "a very good fellow although no Solon," and assured Ryerson that the bill would be changed in Committee.[32]

Before the bill came back from the select Committee, however, the John A. Macdonald-Cartier Government had been replaced by the John S. Macdonald-Sicotte Government. Purged of its ultramontane clause by the combined efforts of the Committee and Ryerson, the bill was accepted by two Roman Catholic Vicars General only to be shelved for the session by a new cabinet. When it was reintroduced in 1863 the popular excitement it created surpassed any caused by earlier agitation. Opposition amendments were ineffective, yet on the final vote the Upper Canadians opposed the bill thirty-one to twenty-one. Upper Canadian opinion was in a ferment against the measure. Despite McGee's promise of finality, the *Globe* sceptically recalled the warning of the Roman Catholic *Freeman* that the concessions were only an instalment, and the *Freeman* itself soon confirmed the *Globe's* fears.[33] In the general elections which followed, separate schools and "No Popery" were made touchstones for candidates, and the results in at least a dozen constituencies were affected. Numbered among the fallen was Dick Scott.

As Canada turned to consideration of Confederation in 1864 the separate schools agitation subsided. The Quebec resolutions vested educational matters in the local legislatures, but accepted McGee's rider to protect minority rights by freezing the separate school systems in each section of Canada whenever Confederation went into action. This gave the separate school advocates one last chance to assimilate the school systems of Upper and Lower Canada. The *Freeman* of 5 January 1865, called for "a grand and final struggle" to obtain the same privileges as Lower Canadian Protestants, the burden of the campaign to be borne by the Roman Catholic laity to disprove their opponents' claim that they were indifferent to their educational rights.

Apparently the laity still required some prodding or guidance, for more than half of the thirty-three petitions favouring assimilation of the laws which reached the Assembly in 1865 were forwarded by clerics. Ryerson hastened to the defence of the existing system, averring that the concession of 1863 had been accepted as final. The whole excuse for reopening the question was the attempt of some Montreal Protestants to obtain a completely separate school system in Lower Canada. McGee, who had accepted publicly the finality of the Act of 1863, now insisted that if any changes were made in Lower Canada he would demand equal advantages for his co-religionists in the upper province. The Government refused to divulge its plans, announcing that the final educational settlement must await Imperial approval. Despite the opposition on both flanks, the Quebec resolutions were successfully pushed through without altering the educational clause.

When the United Parliament met in its last session in 1866, Confederation was almost a *fait accompli*. Scott's Separate School Act of 1863 had been accepted for better or worse, and the popular reaction to the recent attempt to upset it indicated that the legislation promised for this session was predestined to failure. Finance Minister Galt, the reluctant spokesman for the Lower Canadian Protestants, introduced the expected bill. The answer of the Roman Catholics was a separate school bill introduced by Robert Bell, an undisguised *quid pro quo* which had the support of nine Roman Catholic bishops. The net result of this manoeuvre was the withdrawal of both bills, the resignation of Galt, and great excitement in the Protestant press of Canada West. The newspapers heralded the demise of Bell's bill as "THE LATEST PAPAL IMPER-TINENCE" and "THE BISHOPS FOILED."[34] The only residue was a heritage of bitterness shared by both parties to the separate school question.

Thus Scott's Act of 1863 set the pattern of elementary education for Ontario which remains practically unaltered. If at the moment of passing it seemed a victory for separatism and a defeat for nationalism, it has on the longer view proved itself an acceptable compromise.

XI

Canadian Religious Historiography—an Overview

This paper was read before the annual conference of the American Theological Library Association meeting at the Toronto School of Theology, University of Toronto, in 1991, and was printed with an eight-page bibliography in the Summary of Proceedings, Forty-fifth Annual Conference of the American Theological Library Association *(1991), 97-119.*

It is axiomatic that religion has played a major role in the history of the United States and Canada, both in the shaping of each nation and in the formation of its own particular national character. The American church historian, Robert Handy, has written in his comparative historical study of the churches in the United States and Canada, "Despite many important similarities and continuing relationships, the religious life of (Canada and the United States) developed in somewhat distinctive ways, especially during recurring periods of strain between them."[1] The common experience of Canadians and Americans sharing the same continent has indeed masked very striking differences in their historical experiences, including their religious institutions and outlooks.

To begin, Canada is the second largest country in the world, some 25 per cent bigger in area than the United States and all its dependencies. The Canadian population, however, only approximates that of California, or about ten per cent of the total for the United States. Obviously, such a small population scattered in pockets over half a vast continent and separated by the natural barriers of the Laurentian Shield and the Rocky Mountains, has faced different problems of communication and transportation. Equally important, Canada's history has been shaped by two different demographic and philosophical events.

First, during its first century and a half of settlement, before the British Conquest in 1763, Canada's population was exclusively, by law, French-speaking and Roman Catholic. Even today Quebec's population is 88% Roman Catholic and almost 85% French-speaking. Second, the American Revolution left Canada as the sole remnant of empire on the continent, dependent militarily, economically and politically on Britain, and faced from the south by the hostility of America's self-proclaimed manifest destiny. The fact that Canada was invaded twice by the United States in the space of thirty-seven years served to emphasize historically the counter-revolutionary outlook shared by both French and English-speaking Canadians. Aside from the linguistic division but including narrowly defined religious affiliations, the relative homogeneity of Canadians may be seen as a double defence—against the challenges of nature and against the constant threat of American cultural and political absorption.

The result of the counter-revolutionary tradition combined with a prolonged controversy over the nature of church-state relations in Canada has been to produce in Canada what Robert Handy calls "churchliness"—a national habit of supporting only a few major denominations and an avoidance of religious pluralism as it is known in the United States. The Canadian census lists some one hundred denominations in the country, almost 90% of that population belongs to only six churches.

Of those six denominations, half may be called the "Big Three"—the Roman Catholic with nearly 50% of the population, and the United Church and the Anglican (Episcopalian) with nearly 20% each. The "Little Three"—Lutheran, Baptist and Presbyterian—each claim about 3%. The country's official adoption of the ideals of multiculturalism and religious pluralism cannot hide evidence of that tendency towards majority religious conformity so well described as "churchly."

In terms of Canadian religious history the counter-revolutionary tradition was part of the justification for the attempts to establish a state religion in the remaining colonies, a state religion that also recognized by law the presence of the large Roman Catholic population in a constitutionally Protestant empire. By the middle of the nineteenth century that plan for an established church was abandoned in the face of a North American trend towards separation of church and state, although only one Canadian statute, from 1854, actually uses the "S" word, "separation," and then only incidentally to the purpose of the statute.

The religious historiography of French and French-Canadian Catholicism became well established in the first half of the nineteenth century. Lives of bishops and other religious persons followed the earlier publication of catechisms, missionary accounts of life in New France, and other collections of official documents, including that unique and voluminous hoard of religious and anthropological information, the Jesuit Relations, published in the 1850s by the government of the old Province of Canada in English and French to promote Canadianism. By contrast, until the second half of the century English-speaking churches published little of their histories—even the number of pious Victorian biographies was quantitatively limited.

One pioneer publishing venture, however, held long-term historiographic implications. In 1829 the Canadian Methodist Conference, as part of its defence against charges of being American, founded a denominational journal, the *Christian Guardian*, that was soon hailed as the most reliable newspaper in the Province of Canada. The *Guardian* presses, when converted to steam in the 1850s, began to produce a flood of histories and biographies, and, under the name Ryerson Press, filled this function for a century.[2] Such religious biographies, larded with selected sermons and prayers by the deceased, were little more than denominational hagiographies. Nevertheless, they created more public awareness of Methodism's dynamic and formative influence on Canada than any other Protestant denomination has received.

In many ways developments in Canadian religious historiography have parallelled those in Canadian secular historiography. From the middle of the nineteenth century, the writing of Canadian secular history was also largely unscholarly, popular, even propagandistic, and very general in content. Biographies, the most popular genre, consisted largely of political hagiographies of Canada's past prime ministers. In the first decade of this century, however, three multi-volume historical series were launched—*Canada and its Provinces*, the *Chronicles of Canada*, and the *Makers of Canada*. None of these paid more than lip service to the role of religion in Canadian history. The collective biographies of the *Makers of Canada*, the least satisfactory and the shortest lived series, included only one religious leader among its thirty-one biographees.

World War I, however, caused the first Canadian historiographic revolution. As dominion status and the structure of the British Commonwealth evolved from the crucible of armed conflict, Canadian secular historians became preoccupied for a full generation with attempts to trace the political origins of Canadian nationality and the Commonwealth. Theologically there was an obvious shift from providential history towards a humanistic philosophy, most evident in Canada's first religious academic serial, *The Canadian Journal of Religious Thought*. In the interwar decades, however, the publication of religious historical monographs became thinner than ever—two scholarly volumes, two documentaries inspired by the church union of 1925, and two regional denominational histories. This short list is completed by the first history of Canada's Quakers and by E.H. Oliver's *Winning of the Frontier* (1933), the first attempted overview of the Canadian religious experience.

It took a second World War to start the process of broadening Canadian historical perspectives to the present recognition and inclusion of a wide variety of "special interest" historical fields, eventually even including religion. Perhaps inevitably, that broadening process also began more than two generations of historical reductionism and balkanization. Since 1945 there has been a proliferation of such particularist approaches to the Canadian experience—new associations to investigate urban, social, family, women's, labour, technological, scientific, military, and intellectual history, and perhaps in honesty we should include religious history. Slashing away at our own particular historical tree, we lost sight of the historical woods. The end time of Canadian historiographical analysis should soon, one hopes, give way to a synthesis that will attempt to assess our achievements in specialized studies and to reconstruct a more comprehensive and meaningful picture of Canada's past.

Where has the study of Canadian religious history stood in relation to these other historical interests? Our national religious experience has been subject to most of the same forces as our secular experience—nationalism, regionalism, linguistic separation and secularism—but because religion is a universal or international experience the writing of Canadian religious history has also been subject to external forces largely unknown in secular history, and not confined or confinable to national dimensions. Modernism, fundamentalism, ecumenism, liberalism, electronic evangelism are the most obvious of those forces or developments that created elements in our religious history that do not parallel our secular experience.

Over the years Canadian religious history has been written in several forms—biographies of the faithful and saintly, congregational histories, regional histories, and much more rarely national denominational histories, and finally, in recent years, specialized studies of issues or movements such as church-state relations or social teachings. Of these several types, biographies, and congregational and regional denominational histories are by far the earliest, most numerous, and least scholarly. The specialized studies, dating from the 1950s, are usually the work of professionals and academics, which guarantees their books a certain immortality—but not necessarily popularity. For Canada the new wave of secular biography, embodying the "warts and all" philosophy of history, dates only from the interwar period, and its religious counterpart began just as World War II was approaching. Religious biography still, however, seems almost inevitably constrained by the maxim *nil nisi bonum* (speak nothing but good of the dead).

Canadian religious history in the forms other than biography also seems to suffer from the same distortion. Denominationalism when projected into history gave the impression that the only Christians—perhaps the only humans—inhabiting Canada were members of "Denomination X." Further, Victorian providentialism was expressed as denominational triumphalism, a Christianized "manifest destiny." In the case of French Canada, Catholic triumphalism was first politicized within the Roman Catholic Church by the *nationaliste* school of Abbé Lionel Groulx in the interwar period, and in a secularized form this became the new French Canadian nationalism espoused in Quebec's Quiet Revolution of the 1960s.

Like those Victorian denominational histories and biographies written in a contextual vacuum, the modern specialized and interpretive works in Canadian religious history too frequently fail to provide a comprehensive picture of the role of religion in the total social, intellectual and cultural life of Canada. Canada needs solid general histories of the denominations, but even more it needs an equivalent to the late Sydney Ahlstrom's religious history of the American people to serve as an inspiration, foundation and yardstick for such general histories. Probably the very size of Canada and the decentralized condition of its archival resources has encouraged a regional approach to its religious history.[3] Of the mainline denominations only the Presbyterian Church possesses a modern, comprehensive and national history written by an academic. Because Canadian Presbyterians are numerically insignificant, however, that monograph history fits the Canadian pattern of proportionately greater historical production by the numerically smaller denominations.

Canadian secular history has usually been written as a dichotomy of conflict—every issue has been examined and reported in terms of competition between anglophone and francophone. For Canadian religious history there has been a similar dichotomous typology by which all Canadian religious history could be written in terms of Protestant vs. Roman Catholic.[4] Regardless of their denominational affiliation, however, Canadian church historians have worked exclusively within a philosophical framework based on accepted orthodox Christian doctrine. Canadian religious historians have, like their secular counterparts, tended to avoid philosophizing about their craft, and in the British historiographic tradition have talked more about the "nuts and bolts" of their calling rather than philosophical assumptions.

Past attempts by Canadian historians (all of them Protestant and anglophone) to write a "church" history of Canada have been few and generally unsuccessful. Despite its title, Oliver's *Winning of the Frontier* never tried to impose F.J. Turner's dubious frontier thesis on the facts of Canadian religious history. Almost a quarter-century later, H.H. Walsh produced *The Christian Church in Canada* (1956) under the mentorship of Lorne Pierce, editor-in-chief of Ryerson Press from 1920 to 1960. Walsh's volume fell between two stools— on one side the criticism of secular historians who claimed the work told them nothing they did not already know, and on the other the indisputable fact that no author could single-handedly fill the great lack of solid research into Canada's religious past on which a single-volume synthesis depended.

One attempted solution to this dilemma was a compromise project for a multi-author survey. Walsh and Lorne Pierce planned a three-volume Canadian church history—not *"religious"* history—to mark the centenary of Canadian Confederation. This project, finally completed in 1972, by Walsh,

John Moir and John Webster Grant, also had its inherent problems. Each volume was restricted to 200 pages, and the historiography was institutional rather than social (or people) history. Finally, one author (Moir) was a secular historian, not theologically trained. The result was a work already partly obsolescent at publication, but also partly prophetic because of the new historiographic revolution that was sweeping through the discipline.

That second revolution was the result of many factors, not only internally in the writing and teaching of religious history, but also externally in terms of changes in religious outlook and in the academic world. The methodological shift from traditional historical emphasis on documentation and literary style to social-scientific techniques was obvious, but philosophically liberal humanism was joined rather than replaced by the new emphasis on the social "history" of religion. In Canada, history has always been classed as a humane discipline, closely allied to literature. Never had it been social science, yet now it faced the intrusion of social science methodology and new historiographic assumptions about the scientific study of religion.

Both internal and external factors, however, interacted to their mutual and lasting benefit. First came the changes of Vatican II. Next came a broadening approach to religious studies, embodied in the new university departments of religion that absorbed much from the domain of theological colleges. In Canada a third element was the academic influence of the University of Toronto's renowned historian Donald Creighton who, from the early 1950s, promoted graduate research on Canadian religious topics. As Pierce used his position to disseminate and popularize Canadian religious history in print, Creighton's involvement at the university level did much to legitimate such investigations in the eyes of secular historians.

By the 1960s the Canadian religious history scene was already entering this revolutionary phase, again close on the heels of the parallel developments in secular historiography. This time, however, the changes were even more striking than those that had separated the periods immediately before and after World War I. Now laymen trained in secular history were entering the field of religious history and gaining recognition from the seminary professors who previously had virtually monopolized the teaching and writing of church history. The development of interdenominational consortia of theological colleges (the first and largest being the Toronto School of Theology) produced an academic cross-fertilization as these colleges made wider use of secular historians with special interests in religious history.

As a result of this meeting of disciplines, academic standards in the theological colleges, particularly at the graduate or advanced degree level, were visibly improved. The quality of historical research and writing was markedly enhanced, producing near-equality of doctoral standards in history between secular and theological institutions. At the same time the softening of denominational boundaries and the increased academic interest in religious history has meant the opening of religious archival resources on a totally unprecedented scale to scholars, even from outside the particular denomination. Researchers previously barred or closely controlled in their use of denominational source material are now welcomed as responsible scholars. This development has overcome much of the earlier defensiveness, at least among the larger denominations.

When religious history gained wider acceptance as a further and legitimate area of research *within* the broad spectrum of historical studies, secular institutions responded by giving more curricular attention to the religious elements in Canada's history. Both undergraduate and graduate courses on Canadian religious history were now offered at several universities. This was possible because of the increasing availability of new publications—articles in scholarly journals, religious studies textbooks for undergraduates, and specialized monographs, all by historians of recognized stature in their profession. The great expansion of interest in the 1960s and 1970s led to the founding of several new denominational historical societies that published in some form the papers given at their meetings, and for the writing of still more histories of smaller denominations.

By the 1960s the *Canadian Journal of Theology*, begun in 1955, had become a major vehicle for publication of scholarly research in the historical field. Also, a substantial number of monographs, often based on graduate theses, began appearing in print. By 1960 the Canadian Society of Church History (its name reflecting an older institutional approach) was in existence and hoping to become a scholarly, bilingual, non-denominational organization. Those hopes were not fully realized; instead the past two decades witnessed the founding of several denominational historical societies, including a society for Canadian Jewish history.

Secularly trained Canadian historians, unlike their theological colleagues, continued to view religious history from the vantage point of theological liberalism of the 1920s and 1930s. Only in recent years has the secular historiographic pendulum begun to swing slightly away from liberalism and ecumenism. This fact has perpetuated a certain tension about which forms of religious history should have priority of attention. Denominational histories were still produced despite complaints by the secular historians that this was too narrow an approach. Nevertheless, denominational studies do provide the building stones that make possible comparative research on a trans- or interdenominational level, and for most religious historians their emphasis continues to be denominational.

In this second revolution Canadian religious history seemed to be coming of age. Awakened public and scholarly interest in the field promised greater things to come, but one generation later the rate of progress is obviously slower than expected. The "Current Bibliography of Canadian Church History," published annually by the Canadian Catholic Historical Association since 1964, doubled in size by 1973 and tripled by 1978. Since 1978, however, its size shrank back to that of 1975, suggesting a decline in the publication of Canadian religious history.

In terms of monograph and multi-volume series, however, several developments deserve mention, the most striking being the explosion of interest in Baptist heritage. In the past decade a series of eight volumes of documents and analysis have appeared about Baptists in the Atlantic provinces.[5] A second, but less prominent trend, has been the examination of the impact of the Social Gospel. In turn-of-the-century Canada that vaguely defined movement was seminal in forming national character at all levels, and its pervasive influence reached far beyond the institutional church. The middle period of the Social Gospel in Canada is analysed in Richard Allen's *The Social Passion*, and two valuable investigations of the movement's impact on the Anglican and Presbyterian churches in Canada have been published. These books have, however, barely scratched the surface in examining the Social Gospel's formative influence on Canadian life and attitudes.

In terms of issues and personalities, the historiography of the Social Gospel is still in its infancy. A major theme just now being examined is the export of Social Gospel ideas through the medium of widespread Canadian mission fields and activities—in the Orient, Latin America and Africa. Canadian missionaries imbued with the Social Gospel philosophy had tremendous impact on those countries—the role of Dr. Norman Bethune in the Chinese communist revolution is but one example. At the same time a feedback into Canadian foreign policy (often formulated by mission-related personnel) came from these mission activities.

An analysis of forty-four major monographs on Canadian religious history published in the 35 years between the end of World War II and 1980 reveals some interesting trends. Only three titles come from the 1940s and five from the 1950s, but 19 in the 1960s and 17 in the 1970s make a total of 36 or 81% for those two decades alone. Of the total of 44 volumes, 20 dealt with denominational history (6 of those were regional), 7 each were on social issues and church-state relations, and 5 on education. The remaining 6 were divided equally as biographies or collected works. Significantly, only one book, a collection of essays, tried to assess the relationship of religion and Canadian nationalism.

Increasingly since the 1960s Canadian scholarly journals have given space to articles on religious or religion-related topics. The *Canadian Historical Review* and *Social History/ Histoire sociale* have carried occasional articles of this genre, but *Studies in Religion/Etudes religieuses*, created in 1970 as a successful rival for the older *Canadian Journal of Theology* and as the organ of the discipline of religious studies, has largely failed to promote or attract articles on religious history. Such journals have, however, provided virtually the only outlet for work on the religious aspect of women's history.

Among the larger denominations, Anglicans, Baptists and Presbyterians have received considerable attention from historians, but Lutheran history in Canada continues to be virtually ignored. Most active have been Roman Catholic historians, writing extensively on the question of church-state relations, particularly where this involves denominational schools. Three Roman Catholic orders—the Oblates of Mary Immaculate, the Jesuits, and the Redemptorists—have large-scale historical projects. Until the legal and financial demands of the residential schools question closed the Western Oblate History Project, it produced almost one volume a year in a bilingual series of books. The English Province of Canadian Jesuits has initiated a history project and a volume of biographies has been published. In 1986, the Redemptorists planned several volumes about their world-wide activities, including studies on their order in Canada. To date, three books (two in French and one in English) about Canadian Redemptorists have been issued.

Smaller Canadian religious groups have been better served by the historical fraternity. Reliable volumes have appeared on Jehovah's Witnesses, the Salvation Army, Unitarians, Mennonites, Free Methodists, Doukhobors, Amish, Hutterites and Jews. To these may be added monographs on such varied themes as religion and ethnicity, economic and social policy, the rapidly expanding field of missiological history, and especially studies of natives and Asians. Remarkable by their absence have been researches into theological history and the relationship of religion to Canadian nationalism, but a recent development is a series of specialized religious historical studies of excellent scholarship within the publication programme of McGill-Queen's University Press.

Two major projects in the field of secular Canadian history, both begun in the early 1960s, provide some indication of the role of Canadian religious history within the total national perspective. To celebrate the one hundredth birthday of Canadian confederation in 1967, a definitive multi-author, nineteen-volume history, "The Canadian Centenary Series," was begun. The first volume appeared in 1963, the last exactly twenty-five years later. Volumes 3 to 6, dealing with the settlement period of New France and the immediate post-Conquest decades, gave extensive attention to the role of religion in the colony to the end of the eighteenth century. In the remaining thirteen volumes, on the nineteenth and twentieth centuries, coverage of religion displays wide variations.

From this latter group—the baker's dozen for 1790 to 1967—religious references in four are adequate, two offer incidental references, and four are totally silent on the subject. By contrast, three volumes give extensive attention to religion. Two volumes by the same author, on the development of the north and northwest, are exemplary, and the third, by Donald Creighton, the instigator of much academic interest in religion, shares with one of the earliest volumes the honour of using "religion" as an index entry. Taken as a whole, however, on religion the "Centenary" series confines itself almost exclusively to the question of state-church relations.

The second multi-volume and multi-author project from the 1960s is the *Dictionary of Canadian Biography*, with twelve volumes completed to date in a quarter-century, providing over 6,500 biographies. For the six most recent volumes it is possible to categorize the biographees, and religious figures constitute over 17% of the entries. This is certainly a respectable proportion of historical attention, considering that the *Dictionary* recognizes for organizational purposes twenty other categories of subjects in addition to "Religious." The wide discrepancy between the coverage on religion provided by the *Dictionary of Canadian Biography* and the "Centenary" history series perhaps says more about the focus of interest of most academic secular historians than about the state of Canadian religious historiography *per se*.

Thus far this paper has dealt almost exclusively with the historiography of denominations and religious movements that worked or work primarily in the English language. For the first century and a half of Canadian history however, until the Conquest of 1763, the sources are exclusively in French, and although today several Protestant denominations do operate in French on a limited scale, a large part of the Roman Catholic Church in Canada—in all the provinces but especially in Quebec—is francophone. Historians who would understand francophone Catholicism in Canada and its nationalistic messianism are dependent on documentation which is almost exclusively in French. English sources may offer commentaries on religious events and developments in francophone Canada, but very little of its history has been recorded or analysed in the English language.

Students interested in this rich and rapidly expanding field of French-Canadian history could well start by consulting the relevant "Bibliographic Essay" by Robert Choquette in the *Encyclopedia of Religion in America*. W.J. Eccles's *France in America* (1972) provides an introduction to the period and a broad background to its religious history. The religious history of New France itself is the subject of H.H. Walsh's volume in the Walsh-Moir-Grant trilogy, while the volumes by Moir and Grant deal with the subject as part of the religious pluralism of the past two centuries. Particularly useful as an introduction is

Cornelius J. Jaenen's small volume, *The Role of the Church in New France* (1976).[6] No adequate and modern examination of Catholic-Protestant relations in Canada is available, although several articles on specialized aspects of this theme have appeared.

On a regional basis, the history of the French Catholic church is also short on scholarly studies. Catholicism in Acadia is the subject of Jean Daigle's essay, "L'Acadie, 1604-1763," in Jean Daigle, ed., *Les Acadiens des Maritimes: études thématiques* (1980). Robert Choquette has, over the past decade and a half, produced three volumes, one in English and two in French, on the troubled relations of French and English Catholics in Ontario — *Language and Religion* (1975), *L'Eglise catholique dans l'Ontario français du dix-neuvième siècle* (1984), and *La Foi gardienne de la Langue en Ontario 1900-1950* (1987).[7]

Today the state of Canadian religious historiography shows little change from a decade ago. Religious historical societies include the Canadian Catholic Historical Association (begun in 1932), the Canadian Church Historical Society (Anglican or Episcopalian, begun 1957), Methodist (begun 1975) and two without direct denominational affiliation—the Canadian Society of Church History (1960) and the Canadian Society of Presbyterian History (1975). Each of these produces annual or at least periodical publications of papers, and the substantial Roman Catholic annual volume includes the comprehensive and well-organized current bibliography mentioned above. Smaller publication programmes are carried on by Mennonite, Quaker, and Jewish historical societies. An attempt to co-ordinate the work of these religious historical societies has not achieved much visible success, and the recurrent suggestion to merge these publications in a single journal, along the lines of *Church History,* has not been pursued.

There are still, however, as noted, huge gaps in the denominational history of religion in Canada, and until these are filled by scholarly monographs no general assessments of religious issues in Canadian history will be possible. In 1955 John Webster Grant, the dean of Canadian religious historians, identified four problem areas for future research in Canadian religious history—the influence of religious issues on the Canadian political tradition, church-state relations, Canadian attitudes to denominations, and distinctive features of Canadian religious life.[8] Certainly in the 1960s and '70s denominational history and church-state relations received a great deal of attention from Canadian religious historians—the distinctiveness of Canadian religious life and its impact on national politics have been largely ignored.

Looking back on Canadian religious historiography thirty-five years later, a younger historian wrote in 1990,

> Of all the scholars approaching the study of reli-
> gion in Canada, historians have been, perhaps, the
> most eclectic and often the most reluctant to flee
> the cloister, thereby abandoning certain theologi-
> cal presuppositions and some traditional historical
> methods. The scholarship of the 1980s sustains im-
> pressions that religious historiography in Canada
> has been a virtual Babel of methods, questions and
> interpretations, varying from the overtly pious to
> the quasi-sociological. Equally as disparate are the
> recent publications in Canadian religious history,
> produced in a variety of forms.[9]

The same comments, except regarding methodologies, might be applied to the last century and a half of Canadian religious historiography. From providential to humanist and sociological history, the writing of Canadian religious history has developed no discernible schools and few identifiable trends. As with Canadian secular history, regionalism has been one dominant focus,[10] and size is a second. Smaller denominations, religious orders and interest groups have captured attention at the expense of national themes. The major achievement seems to have been the acceptance of religious history as a legitimate scholarly pursuit in the groves of academe. Now, perhaps, the discipline will begin to move from chaos and fragmentation to some order that can accommodate a variety of religious and historiographic traditions.

Turning from the retrospective to the prospective, at this moment the future of Canadian religious history appears bleak. The mood of enforced intellectual conformity—to the ephemeral political correctness of the day—now threatening Canada's literary world (our version of Communist China's cultural revolution) is a serious discouragement to scholarly publication in this country.[11] The deep economic recession, the tilted field of free trade with the United States, and the current Canadian government's imposition of a value-added tax on books, including the Bible, are wreaking havoc on the Canadian publishing industry. Few doctoral theses will be published, but cannibalized versions, chapter by chapter, may find readier publication in scholarly periodicals. Probably the same fate awaits work by established scholarly historians, for whom there will be little incentive to devote years of research to some project that will only gather dust until discarded posthumously by heirs and/or the cleaning staff. The silver lining of all this may, however, prove to be a more manageable work-load for the harried Acquisitions Librarian!

XII

Towards the Americanization of Religion in Canada

While the paper was written in 1980 and never published, the theme—the definition of and impact of secularism—continues to fascinate historians of religion in Canada. Have the prophetic suggestions come true?

In recent years observers have frequently commented that religion in Canada was in decline—today the evidence seems to point more to a basic change of direction rather than to a decline, and any explanation of that change of direction must begin ironically with a re-evaluation of the American religious experience.

In the history of the United States the American Revolution itself is a central fact and formative influence in creating the American character—that much is self-evident. That the Revolution was also a religious event is almost as self-evident. From the very formation of the American republic the force of religion has contributed to a sense of community among the American people. George Washington said that America's "blessed religion" was necessary for national happiness. Andrew Jackson, after his victory over the British at New Orleans, admonished his troops, "Let us be grateful to the God of battles." This religion, this God of battles, is not however denominational—he, she or it was and is a national or tribal god. Indeed, this God could not be denominational, given the religious tensions preceding the American Revolution when the church and the state of England were viewed as opposite sides of a single repressive coin.

The new religion of the Revolution was the religion of the Enlightenment, the deistic faith in natural rights, common sense and humanism. Interestingly, when the American constitution was written in 1789 only ten per cent of Americans were church members. In Canada at Confederation only the unconverted natives were reported as non-church members. Deism could fit very well into the spiritual needs of God's newly chosen American people on whom rested the future destiny of the world. Deism bypassed that denominationalism so feared by the revolutionary fathers and denounced in our time by Reinhold Niebuhr as divisive and anti-American. Deism made any state-church connection unnecessary and impossible in the new republic. Article VI of the Constitution abolished religious tests for public office, implying religious equality, and the First Amendment completed the Constitution's intention by creating the famous "wall of separation." That Amendment, as scholars have reminded us, was enacted, not invented—it was but the end-product of a long search, under several guises, for religious freedom.

The traditional American self-view of the nation and of the Constitution as being peculiarly connected with the Almighty has persisted through two hundred years. From Washington, Benjamin Franklin, John Quincy Adams, Abraham Lincoln (each a theologian in his own way), one can come to more recent statements of the faith. During the Spanish-American War one senator called his country "God's chosen race to prevent barbarism in the modern world," such being "the divine mission of America." Then he added, "We are trustees of the world's progress, guardians of its righteous peace. The judgement of the Master is upon us, the United States, for the Master has said, 'I will make you ruler over many things.'"

Such imperialism, of course, carries with it a divine obligation, whether it is called the white man's burden or *mission civilisatrice*. In America, that obligation was expressed in Woodrow Wilson's comment, "The world must be made safe for democracy, and America must make the world safe—God helping her she can do no other." This kind of rhetoric can be expected from politicians, but here is a recent quote from Louis Pfeffer, acknowledged expert in American church-state relations: "The First Amendment is the greatest contribution made by the United States to democracy and human progress." Nor is that revolutionary fervour for saving "lesser breeds without the law" dead today, in spite of the experiences of 1812-1814 and Vietnam.

For instance, in February 1978 *Church & State*, the monthly magazine of "Americans United for Separation of Church and State," carried an editorial in February 1978 entitled, "Oh Canada," suggesting that if Quebec separates, the rest of Canada may wish to join the United States. "The dazzling

possibility of doubling the size of the United States and quad-
rupling its resources should not be allowed to blind Congress to
the importance of maintaining a strict church-state separation
in every square inch of territory under the jurisdiction of our
Constitution. We believe, too, that most Canadians would
welcome a departure from the British traditions which have
restricted religious liberty and fostered interfaith divisiveness."

From its very inception, then, the American identity has
been a religious matter. The secular political symbols that
express that sense of identity have been sacralized, that is to
say, have been invested with religious or at least quasi-religious connotations in the eyes of the believers. The American
flag is venerated in a way not known in British practice, where
the Union Jack can without offence be used to decorate
clothing, shopping bags and playing cards. Similar to the ven-
eration of the Stars and Stripes, the American presidency has
acquired certain attributes of a folk religion, for there is now
a divinity that doth hedge a president of all the people. The
presidency is invested with much of the aura of the Germanic
kingship of early Anglo-Saxon times. A president is seen by
many as in some peculiar way being the living embodiment of
the folk or nation—he is a folk kin, elected from an extended
family that is identified by achievement and potential rather
than by inherited blood lineage.

An Anglo-Saxon king was the "folc" or nation incarnated.
So, while crimes against individuals, including murder, could be
satisfied by the payment of compensation, the folk king was
above price—no compensation was great enough to satisfy a
nation deprived of its head. At a time when two murders per
day were occurring in Detroit alone, the killing of the folk-king
John F. Kennedy was horrifying because he embodied the folk,
the American nation, and the act of assassination was quasi-
religious. The killing could also be viewed in another religious
light by some who saw it as an attempt to purge and purify the
chosen people who had broken their covenant with God. In
their eyes John F. Kennedy became the scapegoat—the sacri-
fice to atone for the evils and transgressions in American life—
and the quasi-religious reactions of Americans at that time
comes readily to mind.

Why has no Canadian prime minister been assassinated?
Is it because we have no covenant with God, because we are
not a chosen people and hence blood sacrifices are useless? Is

it because our political leaders have been examples of virtue (even Sir John A. Macdonald insisted that he was an outside pillar of the church), such paragons of clean living (and clean speaking?) that no prime minister has deserved such a dreadful fate, even in the mind of the most unbalanced Canadian? Or, conversely, is it because no prime minister has ever been deemed worthy of the crown of martyrdom? Perhaps Canadians are just too conservative, too law-abiding, too apathetic to bother with the ultimate political violence?

We have not followed that violent route because that collection of elemental, quasi-religious feelings in our own tradition-minded society is attached not to the political leader but to that legal abstraction of our heritage, the Crown. The Canadian government has not become the focus of a civil religion because of this separation of the head of state from the head of government. If that panoply of quasi-religious concepts is attached to a person it is more likely to be attached to the apolitical monarchy or viceroy (our governor general) than to any temporary head of government.

The shock of the assassination of John F. Kennedy led Robert Bellah to analyse, codify and popularize the philosophy of the American civil religion—the religion of the Republic, the religion of national sovereignty, that joint inheritance from both the Enlightenment and the Revolution. Soon after Kennedy's death the United States descended into a vortex of violence—more assassinations, more riots in the streets, and more riots on the campuses. The self-evidence of America's destiny seemed in doubt. More recent events further shook America's religious self-confidence: the defeat in Vietnam and the Watergate scandal. What lay behind these un-American developments? Had God deserted his chosen people, or was God testing and purifying the nation to remind the people of their revolutionary covenant? Watergate itself had occurred in the very heart of the New Jerusalem, where the capitol building corresponds to the Dome of the Rock and the Treasury Department to the Wailing Wall. Americans felt betrayed by human agents who had destroyed that righteousness that exalts a nation.

In retrospect the sequel to Watergate shows that the soul-baring investigations had a purifying, even nullifying effect, for few other countries would dare to wash such dirty linens in public. The inevitable reaction began to appear in the form of a swing to the right—politically, socially, religiously. In terms of religion, the move to the right has strengthened the American tradition of pluralism, has increased growth in smaller and more sectarian groups with an other-worldly orientation, and has fostered militant evangelicalism among those Protestants whom Robert Handy described as the self-seen mainstream of the nation. Evangelical crusades such as those organized by the electronic churches, Anita Bryant's fight against homosexual equal rights legislation, the court decision blocking parochial and in favour of non-secular schools—all are evidence that America is returning to that role as the bearer of righteousness, the role that inspired its foundation. The separation of church and state has become an obsession with God's chosen people, and finds its most vocal supporters among those religious minorities unhampered by any churchly tradition.

Unlike Americans, however, Canadians have never (or hardly ever) had a sense of destiny as overriding, as all-en-compassing as that possessed by the sons and daughters of the American Revolution. We have never really been assured that we are God's chosen people, unless of course we are still in our own particular Mosaic age (pertaining to Moses, not to the cultural diversity promoted by governments hungry for tourist dollars), wandering through the desert of unending Canadian winters. In the mid-1950s Dwight D. Eisenhower proclaimed, "Our (national) government makes no sense unless it is founded in a deeply-felt religious faith, and I don't care what (that faith) is." This affirmation of the American way is not the kind of statement made by a Canadian prime minister, past or present, simply because it is not relevant to the Canadian historical experience. It is a little known but true fact that Richard Nixon was hailed as "an archangel" by the Moonies or Unification Church, and that the Moonies organized a campaign to prevent Nixon's impeachment. No Canadian religious group has as yet come to the aid of any beleaguered Canadian government.

The most obvious difference between Canadians and Americans is our respective views of church-state relations. The defence of the Amendment's sanctity has been carried to remarkable lengths. The Buffalo school board prevented a student bible study group from meeting in the public schools. The United States Supreme Court prevented New Hampshire from flying flags at half-mast on Good Friday—what would that

Supreme Court have thought if it had seen Canadian flags at half-mast to mark the death of two popes? In Tennessee the Department of Transport required a farmer to remove a scripture passage painted on his barn because it could be read from a nearby highway. Complaints have recently been levelled against the United States postal service, not for slow delivery but for a cancellation stamp reading, "Help the St. Vincent de Paul Society help the needy." In Iowa a parks and recreation class in yoga was suspended until authorities were satisfied that Hinduism was not being taught, and in California a judge was charged with violating the American Constitution because he offered defendants the choice of going to church or going to jail.

Canada has no revolutionary tradition. Indeed, the possibility of a viable tradition of protest has been historically squelched by such events as the abortive rebellions of 1837, the crushed Riel rebellion of 1885, the Winnipeg General Strike of 1919 and the 1970 October crisis in Quebec. Canada was basically uninfluenced by the Enlightenment, and unlike the United States has had no sense of divine destiny. Nor have we ever developed any genuine concept of the separation of church and state. In the words of Goldwyn French, there is no overarching myth to explain Canada. These are marked differences from the American experience and each factor has deep implications for our religious development. But there is one other factor central to the explanation of the differences in our respective religious developments—the United States is religiously pluralistic, and Canada is not.

Religious pluralism in the United States is not merely a statistical fact, it is an encouraged principle of the Constitution, whereas in Canada, at least statistically, the great majority of the population is nominally connected with a very few Christian denominations. The 1991 census shows that over eighty percent of the population declares itself Christian. Of these Christians, over eighty percent (or sixty-five percent of the total population) belong to three denominations: Roman Catholic, United Church and Anglican—another ten percent belong to the Lutherans, Presbyterians and Baptists. In other words, two out three Canadians belong to the three largest Christian churches. Three out of four Canadians belong to only six denominations, and the remaining Christians belong to a large number of religious organizations, all minuscule in membership as a proportion of the Canadian population.

Several conclusions flow from this, Canada's own central fact of religious life. First and foremost is a certain widely shared outlook, a churchly attitude rather than sectarian.

In his history of the churches in the United States and Canada, Robert Handy writes, "While Americans, whatever their church affiliation or lack of it, customarily invested certain religious feelings in the nation, increasing its dynamism, optimism, sense of destiny and buoyant self-confidence, Canadian religious feeling was contained much more within church boundaries." Institutionally the churches have identified with Canada in a possessive way that Americans cannot emulate because of the existence of a civil religion and because of the wall of separation. We have, in effect, accepted a sort of extra-legal multiple establishment, but the Canadian churches have tended to follow the lead given by the political state. Thus, the late Victorian movement for Protestant church unions in Canada must be viewed as a result, not a cause, of Canadian confederation.

True, the Canadian churches have viewed themselves as the conscience of the state, but not as its guardian. Perhaps with the sole exception of the Social Gospel movement before the First World War and prohibition immediately after, the Canadian churches have been content to admonish their political leaders without applying overt pressure through the electorate. And if the story of prohibition in Canada is any guide, it would seem that the churches have been unable to organize their membership for political ends during any sustained campaign. They have instead been forced to offer alternatives and have been effectively barred from sharing in civil power because the comprehensiveness inherent in their churchliness makes it impossible to produce any denominational consensus.

The churchliness of Canadians has, however, produced some interesting political consequences of its own. Because any confederation is an admission of inability to produce a unitary political state, Canadian confederation is an obvious proof that we have not overcome regionalism in this, the world's second largest country. As "distinct societies," the parts of Canada are as vocal and self-aware as the whole, if not more so. Regional identities are more viable within Canada than a national identity, and the churches have provided Canadians with surrogate transcontinental identity in two ways. First, it is more meaningful to say "I am an Anglican" or "I am a Baptist" than to say "I am a Canadian." A Nova Scotian may feel strange in British Columbia, but as a Roman Catholic that same person will find the same expression of religion in a Vancouver church as at home. Secondly, religion has sacralized the group or minority rather than the nation as a whole—the Hutterites are an example for today, the Doukhobors for yesterday. Multiculturalism is, ironically, more representative of American religious pluralism than of the historical Canadian religious churchly development.

For two generations after Confederation Canadians had their own dreams of what Canada might become (I deliberately use "become," because the American dream concerns primarily what America is). Like Americans of the pre-Civil War era, Canadians dreamed of "His dominion," to be realized in Canada. Protestant and Roman Catholic in parallel but not identical ways envisaged a Christian commonwealth in northern America. The new Canadians would be integrated—assimilated—to the Canadian way of life through the efforts of the church, not of the state. But this was not to be. If the French-Canadian dream of a Quebec in the West was engulfed by a tidal wave of Protestant Anglo-Saxons, the WASPish ideal of "His Dominion of Canada" was overwhelmed by immigration, materialism, secularism, industrialism, urbanization and finally by Armageddon in the form of the First World War.

The churches have, in a word, fallen prey to technology. The modern technocrat state does not listen, does not need to listen, to the voice of its self-appointed conscience, and it tells the churches so. Church leaders who upbraid a prime minister regarding semi-blasphemous or even vulgar statements are told to mind their own business, which is religion. Religion is simply not useful to a modern technological state. Nor have the churches much support among Canadians at large. It is not merely that church membership has declined, is declining, and probably will continue to decline, but that a technological society has usurped many of the traditional functions of the church. No longer is the curé/minister a reliable resource person, a walking encyclopedia of knowledge regarding agriculture, family relations, child rearing, technology, social etiquette, and home nursing, for a few examples. Instead, today's minister or priest faces a congregation of rival experts possessing more accumulated knowledge than he could hope to acquire in one lifetime. The church also faces the undeniable fact that in North America the state has taken over most of the traditional social and charitable functions of religion.

Behind all these developments, however, is the horrible truth of alienation. Since Victorian times the churches have been aware of the alienation of the working class—that alienation has now spread to the ubiquitous Canadian middle class. Grant Maxwell, in his seminal study *Feedback*, comments:

> Canadians in all walks of life are calling out for help, for evidence that 'somebody cares' in an increasingly mechanized and depersonalized society. Isolation and alienation are caused, at least partially, by social systems, policies and procedures which separate people from one another . . . managing their days and their lives: deciding what they should do and whom they should see.

Such alienated individuals may find an identity or at least support in the small, closed-family atmosphere of the religious sect when both the church and the state leave people feeling like nobodies. It is tragic evidence for the truth of Maxwell's statement that boys hoping to play in a minor hockey league must have a social security number (not a name, just a number of their own).

Just how far the clergy are out of touch with the *vox populi* was reflected in a United Church survey, reported in the *United Church Observer* under the title "Who's Following the Leaders?" When the opinion of church members was compared to that of the clergy on specific issues the gap became a chasm. Only nineteen per cent of the laity agreed with their church's position on abolition of the death penalty, only ten per cent agreed with their church's support of an open immigration policy, and only ten per cent favour the official United Church position on acceptance of Quebec separatism. Although the United Church has not spoken definitively on the question of civil rights versus police powers, only eighteen per cent of those polled saw police powers as a threat to civil liberties. On each of these as well as other issues queried in the poll, by a wide margin the laity of the United Church were more conservative than the clergy—on the death penalty the ratio was three to one, on immigration two to one and on Canadian unity eleven to two in conflict with their church's official position.

Apparently, Canadians are more conservative than formerly, and the laity more conservative than their supposed clerical leadership. At the heart of this discrepancy is the definition of the church. Does the Church speak for the church? No, reply the majority; the organization is NOT equal to the believers. An item in the *Presbyterian Record* underlines this point. A feature article by an ordained minister gives support to the Department of National Revenue's circular of February 1975 regarding the possible decertification of tax-exempt charitable foundations, including churches, if they meddle in politics. The author views the government's statement not as intimidation but as a well-deserved political rap on the clerical knuckles. The church, the writer asserts, has no business making political statements and cannot justify its lobbying and pressuring of large corporations in the name of social justice. The church is out of order and out of character when it speaks on native land claims, environmental pollution, third world issues, etc. How does the author know this? The government's information circular tells him so.

Canada's future religious choice will probably be between a sort of sectarian alienation based on supposed separation of church and state or a traditional church-like accommodation to the present and future order of society. If we follow the American example the present relative decline in membership among main line churches will continue, and the smaller, more evangelical groups and sectarian movements and bodies quite outside the Judeo-Christian tradition will continue to increase in strength, in visibility, in vocalization and in influence. Many of these groups with their greater stress on individual salvation share that lack of enthusiasm for contemporary social and political issues evidenced in the past by evangelical leaders.

This other-worldly emphasis fits comfortably into the American scene where separation of church and state provides a shield and an excuse for reciprocal noninterference, and where a religious consensus (call it the civil religion of the Republic) has traditionally sacralized the national identity. The same trend towards conservatism and withdrawal in Canada was expressed in the popular reception of Anita Bryant, and in the pressure to censor school books. An Ontario sociologist writing for Americans United for the Separation of Church and State pointed to the distribution of bibles among school children by the Gideon Society as an infringement of the

Helsinki Agreement on Human Rights which, he suggested, the United States government should bring to the attention of the Canadian government.

If I am correct in foreseeing a move towards greater religious pluralism and increased separation in Canada between the realm of Caesar and the realm of God, then an obvious void is appearing which may foreshadow further internal troubles. That void of course involves identity. The Canadian churches have provided alternate identities for Canadians in the absence of any strong and sacralized political nationalism, but if indeed the churches have lost or are losing their former position, if they are becoming denominations on the American model, if we are abandoning a church mentality and if the rising forces of pluralism and separatism are committed to non-identity and desacralization, what will fill that identity void? The process of, or drift towards, the americanization of Canadian religious life is already under way and its repercussions will probably add to our national instability. The attacks will come not from atheists but from devout religious persons who hold a diametrically opposed view of the role of religion in Canadian life. In 1968, William Kilbourn wrote, "The special qualities of Canadian religious history have both symbolized and helped make possible a separate Canadian identity." Only a few years later religious life in Canada, like so many other aspects of our national life and culture, seems to be more and more approximating that of the United States.

John Sargent Moir:
A Bibliography

The following bibliography is a work in progress since Professor Moir continues to publish at a rapid rate. Besides the works to come, older publications are still to be discovered in journals and encyclopedias that never sent an offprint to the author for inclusion in his publication list. Moreover, the following does not include John Moir's book reviews, which are legion.

ARTICLES

"Early Methodism in the Niagara Peninsula," *Ontario History* XLIII:2 (1951) 51-8.

"Methodism and higher education 1843-1949, a qualification," *Ontario History* XLIV:3 (1952) 109-28.

"Fitzgibbon's secret visitor," *Ontario History* XLVIII (1956) 108-110.

"The Settlement of the Clergy Reserves, 1840-1855," *Canadian Historical Review* XXXVII:1 (1956) 46-62.

"An early town meeting," *Ontario History* XLIX (1957) 198-212.

"The Correspondence of Bishop Strachan and John Henry Newman," *Canadian Journal of Theology* III:4 (1957) 219-25.

"The Origins of the Separate School Question in Ontario," *Canadian Journal of Theology* V:2 (1959) 105-18.

"A Circuit Rider on the River Thames: The Diary of William Case, 20 June - 26 August 1809," *Western Ontario Historical Nuggets*, No. 25, University of Western Ontario (1958).

"An early record of Laura Secord's walk," *Ontario History* LI (1959) 105-8.

"Laura Secord Again," *Ontario History* LIV (1962) 190.

"Mr. Mackenzie's Secret Reporter," *Ontario History* LV:4 (1963) 205-13.

"Four poems on the Rebellion of 1837, by Susanna Moodie," *Ontario History* LVII:1 (1965) 47-51.

"The Canadianization of the Protestant Churches," Canadian Historical Association, *Annual Report 1966*, 56-69.

"American Influences on the Canadian Protestant Churches before Confederation," *Church History* XXXVI:4 (1967) 440-55.

"The Roots of Disestablishment in Upper Canada," *Ontario History* LX:3 (1968) 247-58.

"The Problem of a Double Minority: Some Reflections on the Development of the English-Speaking Catholic Church in Canada in the 19th Century," *Histoire Sociale/Social History* 7 (April 1971) 53-67.

"Church History: has it a future in Canada?" *Canadian Journal of Theology* XVI (1970) 1-2; reprinted in *The Journal of Canadian Church History* XIII:1 (1971) 2-3.

"Confrontation at Queen's: a Prelude to the Disruption in Canada," *Presbyterian History* XV:1 (1971).

"The Quay of Greenock: Jurisdiction and Nationality in the Canadian Presbyterian Disruption of 1844," *Scottish Tradition* (1975) 38-53.

"Scottish Influences on Canadian Presbyterianism," *Scotia: American-Canadian Journal of Scottish Studies* II:1 (1978) 38-42.

"Robert McDowall and the Dutch Reformed Church Mission to Canada, 1790-1819," *de Halve Maen* LIII:2 (1978) 3-4, 14-16.

"Twenty Years Retrospect: the Canadian Society of Church History," Canadian Society of Church History *Papers, 1979*, 76-98.

"Robert McDowall, Pioneer Dutch Reformed Church Missionary in Upper Canada," *Presbyterian History* XXIII (1979), XXIV:1 (May 1980).

"'Loyalty and Respectability': The Campaign for Co-Establishment of the Church of Scotland in Canada," *Scottish Tradition* IX/X (1979-80) 64-82.

"James Frederick McCurdy: Christian Humanist," Canadian Society of Presbyterian History *Papers, 1981*, 1-20.

"Canadian Protestant Reaction to the *Ne Temere* Decree," *Study Sessions*, Canadian Catholic Historical Association, Ottawa (1981) 79-90.

"The Founding of the Canadian Society of Biblical Studies," *Studies in Religion* XI:1 (1982) 9-12.

"'Mildewed with Discretion': Toronto's higher critics and public opinion in the 1920s," *Studies in Religion* XI:2 (1982) 173-9.

"Coming of Age, but Slowly: Aspects of Canadian religious historiography since Confederation," *Study Sessions*, Canadian Catholic Historical Association, Ottawa (1983) I:89-98.

"Notes of Discord, Strains of Harmony: The separation and reunion of the Canadian and British Wesleyan Methodists, 1840-1847," Canadian Methodist Historical Society *Papers, 1984*, IV, no pag.

"A Vision Shared? The Catholic Register and Canadian Identity before World War I," in *Canadian Issues, VII, Religion and Culture: Comparative Canadian Studies* (1985) 356-66.

"'On the King's Business': The Rise and Fall of the Layman's Missionary Movement in Canada," *Bibliothèque de la Revue d'Histoire Ecclésiastique*, Fascicule 71, *Miscellanea Historiae Ecclesiasticae* VII (1985) 321-33.

"Through Missionary Eyes: The Glasgow Colonial Society Papers as a Source of Social History," Canadian Society of Presbyterian History *Papers, 1986*, 51-64.

"The Stool of Repentance: The Disciplinary Role of the Presbyterian Courts of Session in Victorian Canada," Canadian Society of Presbyterian History *Papers, 1986*, 51-64.

"Competition or Co-operation? Aspects of Presbyterian-Methodist Relations in Canada's Atlantic Region," (abstract) Canadian Society of Presbyterian History *Papers, 1997*, 47-8.

"John Strachan's Sermon on the Death of Bishop Mountain: A Question of Motives," *Journal of the Canadian Church Historical Society* XXX:1 (1998) 179-87.

"John Strachan and Presbyterianism," Canadian Society of Presbyterian History *Papers, 1999*, 5-16.

"John Strachan's Journal of a Tour of Upper Canada, 1828," *Journal of the Canadian Church Historical Society* XLII (2000) 59-79, 111-24.

MONOGRAPHS

Church and State in Canada West: Three studies in the relation of denominationalism and nationalism, 1841-1867. Toronto: University of Toronto, 1959.

Two Democracies. Toronto: Ryerson, 1963. Co-author.

Changing Perspectives in Canadian History. Toronto: Dent, 1967. Co-author.

The Canadian Experience. Toronto: Ryerson, 1969. Co-author.

Northern Destiny. Toronto: Dent, 1970. Co-author.

The Church in the British Era (vol. 2 of *The Christian Church in Canada*). Toronto: McGraw-Hill, Ryerson, 1972.

Enduring Witness: A History of the Presbyterian Church in Canada. Toronto: Presbyterian Publications, 1974.

For the Record: A brief introduction to definitions, policies and practices for the records of the Presbyterian Church in Canada. Toronto: Presbyterian Church in Canada, 1979.

A History of Biblical Studies in Canada: A Sense of Proportion. Chico, California: Scholars Press, 1982.

Enduring Witness: A History of the Presbyterian Church in Canada, 2nd ed. enl. and rev. Toronto: Committee on History, Presbyterian Church in Canada, 1987.

Sowing the Good Seed: A History of St. Paul's Church and Two Centuries of Presbyterianism in the Simcoe Area, 1793-1993. Simcoe, Ontario: St. Paul's Presbyterian Church, 1993.

The Labour Not in Vain: A History of Alexandra Presbyterian Church, Brantford, Ontario, 1845-1995. Brantford, Ontario: Alexandra Presbyterian Church, 1994.

A Handbook for Canadian Presbyterians. North York, Ontario: Record Books, 1996.

A History of Norfolk Lodge No. 10, A.F. & A.M., G.R.C., and Freemasonry in Norfolk County, 1998.

CONTRIBUTED CHAPTERS AND SHORT ARTICLES

"Sectarian Tradition in Canada." *The Churches and the Canadian Experience.* Toronto: Ryerson, 1963.

"Kirke, Sir David," "Kirke, Sir Lewis," "Kirke, Thomas." *Dictionary of Canadian Biography,* I. Toronto: University of Toronto, 1966.

"Religion," and "Communications" (co-author). *The Canadians.* Toronto: Macmillan, 1967.

"Ontario." *Canada.* Toronto: Ryerson, 1967.

"The Upper Canadian Religious Tradition." *Profiles of a Province.* Toronto: Ontario Historical Society, 1967.

"Donald Grant Creighton." *Character and Circumstance.* Toronto: Macmillan, 1970.

"Bayne, John." "Green, Anson." "Willson, Hugh Bowlby." Dictionary of Canadian Biography, X. Toronto: University of Toronto, 1972.

"Religion." *Handbook Canada.* Ottawa: Government of Canada, 1975.

"Relations between Church and State in Canada West, 1841 to 1867." In S. Crysdale and L. Wheatcroft, eds. *Religion in Canadian Society.* Toronto: Macmillan, 1976.

"Reassessing Presbyterian Record Sources." *Readings in Ontario Genealogical Sources.* Compiled by Don Wilson. Conference on Ontario Genealogical Sources. N.P., 1979.

"George Brown, Christian Stateman." In W.S. Reid, ed. *Called to Witness: Profiles of Canadian Presbyterians* II (1980) 39-46.

"*The Canadian Baptist* and the Social Gospel Movement, 1879-1914." In J.K. Zeman, ed. *Baptists in Canada: Search for Identity Amidst Diversity.* Wolfville, Nova Scotia: Acadia University, 1980.

"Canada and the Huguenot Connection, 1577-1627." *Proceedings of the Huguenot Heritage Conference held at Trinity College, University of Toronto, 27 April 1985,* 65-78.

"Calvinism." "Grant, John Webster." "Goforth, Jonathan." "Jogues, Isaac." "Macdonnell, Daniel James." "McDowall, Robert." "McGregor, James." "Mackay, George Leslie." "McLeod, Norman." "McPherson, Aimee Semple." "Presbyterian and Reformed Churches." "Robertson, James." "Scott, Robert Balgarnie Young." "Shearer, John George." "Strachan, John." *The Canadian Encyclopedia.* Edmonton: Hurtig, 1985.

"A Biographical Sketch of John Webster Grant, with a List of His Major Writings." In Moir and McIntire, eds. *Canadian Protestant and Catholic Missions 1820s-1960s: Historical Essays in Honour of John Webster Grant.* New York: Peter Lang, 1988.

"De Charbonnel, Armand-François-Marie." (In collaboration with M.W. Nicholson.) "Dadson, Ebenezer William." "Jenkins, John." "Macdonnell, Daniel James." *Dictionary of Canadian Biography,* XII. Toronto: University of Toronto, 1990.

"James Frederick McCurdy: Father of Biblical Studies in Canada." In *Called to Witness: Profiles of Canadian Presbyterians,* vol. 3. Hamilton, Ontario: Committee on History, The Presbyterian Church in Canada, 1991, 45-54.

"Canadian Religious Historiography—an Overview." *Summary of Proceedings, Forty-fifth Annual Conference of the American Theological Library Association.* 1991, 97-119.

"Shearer, John George." *Dictionary of Hamilton Biography* III. Hamilton, 1992, 266-90.

"Frank, Scientific Discussion." In Mark G. McGowan and David B. Marshall, eds. *Prophets and Prodigals: Readings in Canadian Religious History, 1608 to Present.* Toronto: McGraw-Hill Ryerson, 1992, 266-90.

"Through Missionary Eyes: The Glasgow Colonial Society and the Immigrant Experience in British North America." In Catherine Kerrigan, ed. *The Immigrant Experience: Proceedings of a Conference held at the University of Guelph 8-11 June 1989.* Guelph: University of Guelph, 1992, 95-109.

"Toronto's Protestants and Their Perception of Their Roman Catholic Neighbours." In McGowan and Clarke, ed. *Catholics at the Gathering Place.* Toronto: The Canadian Catholic Historical Association, 1993, 313-27.

"Defining Sacred Space," Plate 53, *Historical Atlas of Canada, II, The Land Transformed.* Toronto: University of Toronto Press, 1993. (Co-author)

"MacVicar, Donald Harvey." "Snodgrass, William." "Warden, Robert Harvey." *Dictionary of Canadian Biography,* XIII. Toronto: University of Toronto, 1994.

"'Who pays the Piper...,: Canadian Presbyterianism and Church-State Relations." In William Klempa, ed. *The Burning Bush and a Few Acres of Snow.* Carleton Library Series #100. Ottawa: Carleton University Press, 1994.

"From Sectarian Rivalry to National Vision: The Con-tribution of Maritime Presbyterianism to Canada." In Charles H.H. Scobie, ed. *The Contribution of Presbyterianism to the Maritime Provinces of Canada.* Montreal and Kingston: McGill-Queen's University Press, 1997.

"John Strachan (1778-1867): Faith and Loyalty United." In Michael Clarke, ed. *Canada: Portraits of Faith.* Chilliwack, B.C.: Reel to Reel, 1998, 40-41.

"Petitot, Emile." *Dictionary of Canadian Biography*, XIV. Toronto: University of Toronto, 1998.

"Coughlin, Charles Edward." *Dictionary of Hamilton Biography*, IV. Hamilton 1999, 54-57.

EDITED BOOKS

History of the Royal Canadian Corps of Signals, 1903-1961. Ottawa: R.C.C.S., 1962.

Rhymes of Rebellion. Toronto: Ryerson, 1965.

The Cross in Canada. Toronto: Ryerson, 1966.

Church and State in Canada, 1627-1867: Basic Documents. Toronto: McClelland & Stewart, 1967.

Readings in Canadian Civics. Toronto: Ryerson, 1968. (Co-editor)

Character and Circumstance: Essays in Honour of Donald Grant Creighton. Toronto: Macmillan, 1970.

The Tide of Time: Historical Essays by the late Allan L. Farris. Toronto: Presbyterian Church in Canada, 1978.

Canadian Protestant and Catholic Missions, 1820-1939: Historical Essays in Honour of John Webster Grant. New York: Peter Lang, 1988. (Co-editor)

Church and Society: Documents on the Religious and Social History of the Roman Catholic Archdiocese of Toronto. Toronto: The Archdiocese of Toronto, 1991.

Selected Correspondence of the Glasgow Colonial Society, 1825-1840. Toronto: The Champlain Society, 1994. (Co-editor)

Called to Witness: Profiles of Canadian Presbyterians. A Supplement to Enduring Witness. Hamilton: Committee on History, Presbyterian Church in Canada, Vol.3, 1991; Vol.4, 1999.

Gifts & Graces: Profiles of Canadian Presbyterian Women. Hamilton: Committee on History, Presbyterian Church in Canada, 1999.

Endnotes

Foreword

1. John S. Moir, "The Political Ideas of the *Christian Guardian*, 1829-1849" (Unpublished Master's Thesis, University of Toronto, 1949).

2. John S. Moir, *Rhymes of the Rebellion: Being a Selection of Contemporary Verses about the Recent Unpleasantness in Upper Canada, 1837* (Toronto: Ryerson Press, 1965).

3. John S. Moir, "The Relations of Church and State in Canada West, 1849-1867" (Unpublished Ph.D. Dissertation, University of Toronto, 1954).

4. Thomas Millman, *"Church and State in Canada West..."* Reviewed in *Canadian Historical Review* XLI (March 1960), 79.

5. John S. Moir, *Enduring Witness: A History of the Presbyterian Church in Canada* (Don Mills: Presbyterian Publications, 1974), xi.

6. John S. Moir, "'On the King's Business': The Rise and Fall of the Laymen's Missionary Movement in Canada," *Miscellanea Historiae Ecclesiasticae,* VII (Brussels, 1985).

7. Besides the articles in this collection, see John S. Moir, "A Vision Shared? The *Catholic Register* and Canadian Identity Before World War I," in *Canadian Issues/Thèmes canadiens*, vol. 7, William Westfall and Louis Rousseau, eds. (Ottawa: The Association of Canadian Studies, 1985), 356-66.

8. Goldwyn French, *"Enduring Witness,"* Reviewed in *Canadian Historical Review* LVIII (September 1977), 313.

9. John S. Moir, ed., *Called to Witness: Profiles of Canadian Presbyterians* (Toronto: Presbyterian Publications, 1975).

10. John S. Moir, ed., *The Tide of Time: Historical Essays by the late Allan L. Farris, Professor of Church History and Principal of Knox College, Toronto* (Toronto: Knox College, 1978).

11. Letter from Jacqueline Moir to the author, 20 January 2001.

12. John S. Moir, "Toronto's Protestants and Their Perceptions of Their Roman Catholic Neighbours," in Mark G. McGowan and Brian P. Clarke, eds., *Catholics at the Gathering Place: Historical Essays on the Archdiocese of Toronto, 1841-1991* (Toronto: Canadian Catholic Historical Association & Dundurn Press, 1993), 313-27.

13. John S. Moir, *Two Democracies* (Toronto: Ryerson Press, 1963); *The Canadian Experience* (Toronto: Ryerson Press, 1969); T. T. Ferris, G.A. Onn, and J.S. Moir, *Readings in Canadian Civics* (Toronto: Ryerson, 1968); *Northern Destiny* (Toronto: Dent, 1970; *The Cross in Canada* (Toronto: Ryerson Press, 1966); and *Church and State in Canada, 1627-1867; Basic Documents*, Carleton Library Series, No. 33 (Toronto: McClelland and Stewart, 1967).

14. K.A. MacKirdy, J.S. Moir, and Y.F. Zoltvany, eds., *Changing Perspectives in Canadian History: Selected Problems*, revised edition (Don Mills: J.M. Dent & Sons, 1971), xi.

15. John S. Moir and Thomas McIntire, eds., *Canadian Protestant and Catholic Missions, 1820-1939: Historical Essays in Honour of John Webster Grant* (New York: Peter Lang, 1988) and John S. Moir, ed., *Character and Circumstance* (Toronto: Macmillan, 1970)

16. John S. Moir, *Sowing the Good Seed: A History of St. Paul's Church and Two Centuries of Presbyterianism in the Simcoe Area, 1793-1993* (Simcoe: St. Paul's Presbyterian Church, 1993); *The Labour Not in Vain: A History of Alexandra Presbyterian Church, Brantford, Ontario, 1845-1995* (Brantford: Alexandra Presbyterian Church, 1994); *A History of Norfolk Lodge No. 10, A.F. & A.M., G.R.C., and Freemasonry in Norfolk County* (n.p., 1998).

The Sectarian Tradition in Canada

1. The term "denomination," used in the United States specifically to describe a church-structured organization within a political state where no form of establishment exists, has in Canada a much looser but more literal usage, being applied to any autonomous religious body, whether church- or sect-structured, which can be distinguished by name.

2. *The Social Sources of Denominationalism* (New York, 1957), 19.

3. E.T. Clark, *The Small Sects in America* (Nashville, 1927), 26-9.

4. *Works of the Rev. John Wesley*, 3rd American edition (New York: Carlton and Porter, 1856), VII, 317.

5. A.E. Ryerson, *Canadian Methodism: Its Epochs and Characteristics* (Toronto, 1882), 140-60.

6. T.R. Millman, *The Life of the Right Reverend, the Honourable Charles James Stewart* (London, Ontario: Huron College, 1953), 72-3.

7. J.G. Hodgins, ed., *Documentary History of Education in Upper Canada* (Toronto: Ontario Department of Education, 1894-1910) V. 27.

8. Isaac Buchanan to Willam Morris, 5 July 1844, Morris Papers, Queen's University Archives.

9. T.L. Smith, *Called Unto Holiness: The Story of the Nazarenes: The formative years* (Kansas City: Nazarene Publishing House, [1962], 29.

10. G.W. Brown, *Building the Canadian Nation* (Toronto: Dent, 1922), II, 375.

11. "Church History," *Encyclopedia Canadiana* (Ottawa: Canadian Co., 1957-8), 162.

12. S.D. Clark, "The Religious Sect in Canadian Economic Development," in B.R. Blishen *et al.*, *Canadian Society: Sociological Perspectives* (Toronto, 1961), 386.

Canadianization of the Protestant Churches

1. N.G. Smith, "Nationalism in the Canadian Churches," *Canadian Journal of Theology* IX (2), April 1963, 112-25.

2. Egerton Ryerson, *Canadian Methodism: Its Epochs and Characteristics* (Toronto 1882), 154-55.

3. George Spragge, ed., *The John Strachan Letter Book: 1812-1834* (Toronto: Ontario Historical Society, 1946), 74.

4. A.N. Bethune, *Memoir of the Right Reverend John Strachan, D.D., LL.D., First Bishop of Toronto* (Toronto, 1870), 249-50.

5. *The Minutes of the Annual Conferences of the Wesleyan-Methodist Church in Canada from 1824 to 1845 . . .* (Toronto, 1846), 65.

6. *Christian Guardian*, 25 June 1834.

7. *Colonial Advocate*, 30 October 1833.

8. *Minutes of the Annual Conferences . . .*, 251.

9. Paul Knaplund, ed., *Letters from Lord Sydenham, Governor-General of Canada 1839-1841, to Lord John Russell* (London: G. Allen & Unwin, 1931), 95.

10. William Gregg, *Short History of the Presbyterian Church in the Dominion of Canada,* 3rd ed. rev. (Toronto: Poole Publishing, 1900), 23.

11. *Draft of an Answer to the Dissent and Protest of Certain Ministers and Elders who have seceded . . .* (Kingston, 1844).

12. *Minutes of the Synod of the Presbyterian Church in Canada in Connection with the Church of Scotland* (Toronto, 1844), XV, 33-34.

13. *Ecclesiastical and Missionary Record*, May 1847, December 1849.

14. J.S. Moir, *Church and State in Canada West* (Toronto, 1959), 4.

15. Ibid., 54.

16. Bethune, 249-50.

17. Ibid., 250-52.

18. A.W. Mountain, *A Memoir of G.J. Mountain, D.D., D.C.L., Late Bishop of Quebec* (Montreal, 1866), 292-99.

19. Strachan to Canterbury, 7 June 1851, Parliamentary papers, 1852, (355), II, 9, Public Archives of Ontario. From England Bethune wrote in 1852 and 1853 of the SPG's incompetence to manage the Canadian Church: A.N. Bethune to Strachan, 18 November 1852, 11 March 1853, Strachan Papers, Public Archives of Ontario.

20. Bethune, 265.

21. Strachan to Bishop Skinner, 5 July 1856, Letter Book 1854-62, 141, Strachan Papers, Public Archives of Ontario.

22. A.N. Bethune, *A Charge Delivered at the Visitation of the Clergy and Churchwardens of the Archdeaconry of York . . ., 1852,* (Toronto, 19. Six years later Strachan believed the voluntary system had failed: Strachan to S. Biggs, 18 March 1858, Strachan Letter Book 1854-62, 245, Public Archives of Ontario.

23. Memorial of Whitaker *et al.* and reply of J. Strachan, 9 September 1864, Strachan Papers.

24. H.C. Cooper, *The United Church of England and Ireland in Canada: A Sermon, preached before the Synod of the Diocese of Toronto . . .* (Toronto, 1865).

25. *Journals of the Proceedings of the Provincial Synod of the United Church of England and Ireland in Canada. Third Session* (Montreal, 1865), 12.

26. Ibid., 34.

27. *The Presbyterian*, May 1860.

28. William Proudfoot to David Anderson, 13 July 1846, Proudfoot Papers, Presbyterian Church Archives.

29. *Canadian Presbyter*, February 1857.

30. Ibid., July, August 1957.

31. Ibid., April 1858.

32. Ibid.

33. *Census of Canada*, 1871, IV.

34. *A Historical and Statistical Report of the Presbyterian Church in Canada, in connection with the Church of Scotland, for the Year 1866* (Montreal, 1867), 137-38.

35. Ibid., 147.

36. Ibid., 155, 165-72.

37. *The Minutes of the Twelve Annual Conferences of the Wesleyan Methodist Church in Canada, from 1846 to 1857 . . .* (Toronto, 1863), 159.

38. *Christian Guardian*, 2 July 1851.

39. C.B. Sissons, *Egerton Ryerson, His Life and Letters* (Toronto: Clarke Irwin, 1937, 1947), II, 295.

40. *Minutes of the Twelve Annual Conferences . . .* , 269.

41. Ibid., 307.

42. *Canadian Independent*, June 1859.

43. W.I. Grant and F. Hamilton, *George Monro Grant* (Toronto, 1905), 155-56.

44. F.A. Walker, "Protestant Reaction in Upper Canada to the Popish Threat," *Canadian Catholic Historical Association Report*, 1951, 107.

American Influences on Canadian Protestant Churches

1. I.F. Mackinnon, *Settlement and Churches in Nova Scotia*, 1742-1776 (Montreal, 1930), 29-31.

2. Juw fon Wearinga, "The First Protestant Ordination in Canada," *The Bulletin*, Archives Committee of the United Church of Canada, No.11 (1958), 19ff.

3. Mackinnon, 96.

4. Minutes of Council 23 December 1776, 5 January 1777, Nova Scotia B, vol. 17: 87, 90-91, National Archives of Canada (NAC).

5. M.W. Armstrong, *The Great Awakening in Nova Scotia* (Hartford: American Society of Church History, 1948), 61-87.

6. *Canadian Independent*, November 1862.

7. Ibid., May 1867.

8. G.E. Levy, *The Baptists of the Maritime Provinces, 1753-1946* (Saint John: Barnes Hopkins, 1946), 103.

9. G.H. Lee, *An Historical Sketch of the First Fifty Years of the Church of England in the Province of New Brunswick (1783-1833)* (Saint John, 1880), 135; A.W. Eaton, *The Church of England in Nova Scotia and the Tory Clergy of the Revolution* (New York, 1892), 155-57.

10. Carleton to Lord North, 26 August 1783, Nova Scotia A, vol. 103: 158-61, NAC.

11. J. Parr to Lord Shelburne, 9 October 1789, Shelburne Papers, vol. 88: 124, NAC.

12. Charles Inglis and 17 other clergymen to Guy Carleton, New York, 24 March 1783, Nova Scotia A, vol. 103: 33-40, NAC.

13. Eaton, *The Church of England . . .*, 115-6. Nine of the Petitioners subsequently joined the Loyalist exodus to Nova Scotia.

14. R.V. Harris, *Charles Inglis, Missionary, Loyalist, Bishop (1734-1816)* (Toronto, 1937), 59, 72.

15. T.R. Millman, *The Life of the Right Reverend, the Honourable Charles James Stewart, D.D. Oxon., Second Anglican Bishop of Quebec* (London, Ontario: 1953), 62, 67.

16. 26 George III, cap. 84, amended by 3 & 4 Victoria, cap. 33.

17. M. Richey, *A Memoir of the Late Rev. William Black, Wesleyan Minister* (Halifax, 1839), 127.

18. Nathan Bangs, *Life of the Rev. Freeborn Garretson* (New York, 1829), 178.

19. T.W. Smith, *History of the Methodist Church within . . . Eastern British America*, 2 vols. (Halifax, 1877), I, 208.

20. William Bennett to Duncan McColl, Granville, 20 March 1817, McColl Papers (microfilm), Archives of the United Church of Canada.

21. Smith, I, 356.

22. H. Esson to the Moderator of Glasgow Presbytery, 17 June 1826, Church of Scotland Synod Papers, Queen's University Archives.

23. A. Ivison and F. Rosser, *The Baptists in Upper and Lower Canada before 1820* (Toronto: University of Toronto Press, 1956), chap. X.

24. Ibid., chap. VIII.

25. E.R. Fitch, ed., *The Baptists of Canada: A history of their progress and achievements* (Toronto: Standard Publishing Co., 1911), 109-10; *The Gospel Tribune*, July 1854.

26. W. Gregg, *History of the Presbyterian Church in the Dominion of Canada, from the earliest times to 1834* . . . (Toronto, 1885), 182-3.

27. Ibid., 167ff.

28. A.K. Buell to A. Peters, 11 April 1831, Correspondence of the American Home Missionary Society relating to Canada, United Church Archives.

29. John Banks, "American Presbyterians in the Niagara Peninsula, 1800-1840," *Ontario History* LVII (September 1965), 135-40.

30. *The Presbyterian*, 27 November 1839, quoting from *Home Missionary*, October 1838.

31. A.H. Young, "More Langhorn Letters," *Papers and Records of the Ontario Historical Society* XXIX (1933), 51.

32. G. French, *Parsons & Politics: The Role of the Wesleyan Methodists in Upper Canada and the Maritimes from 1780 to 1855* (Toronto: Ryerson Press, 1962), 42.

33. G.F. Playter, *The History of Methodism in Canada* (Toronto, 1862), 105.

34. Ibid.

35. E.A. Cruikshank, ed., *The Correspondence of Lieut. Governor John Graves Simcoe, with allied documents relating to his administration of the government of Upper Canada,* 5 vols. (Toronto: Ontario Historical Society, 1923-31), V, 247; I, 43.

36. Playter, 138.

37. Ibid., 144.

38. Ibid., 147.

39. Ibid., 166, 168.

40. "Minutes of several conversations of the British Methodist Missionaries in the Provinces of Upper and Lower Canada . . .," United Church Archives.

41. Playter, 178.

42. Ibid., quoted 235.

43. Ibid., quoted 241.

44. "A recently rescued letter of Egerton Ryerson," *The Bulletin,* Archives Committee of the United Church of Canada, No. 16 (1963), 32.

45. *The Minutes of the Annual Conferences of the Wesleyan Methodist Church in Canada from 1824 to 1845* (Toronto, 1846), 2-3, 18-20, 46-9.

46. John Strachan, *A Sermon preached at York, Upper Canada, Third of July, 1825, on the Death of the Late Lord Bishop of Quebec* (Kingston, 1826), 26; Colborne to Murray, private, 19 August 1824, "Dr. Strachan's letter and Chart produced more excitement than any part of the discussion that took place on the subject" (Q 352: 28, 35, NAC).

47. Colborne to Lord Goderich, 3 September 1832, Q 374: 851-2, NAC.

48. R. Watson to Lord Goderich, 22 November 1832, Q 254: 496, NAC.

49. "Copy of a letter from the Bishop of Toronto to the Duke of Newcastle," Parliamentary Papers (1853), (141), 14, Public Archives of Ontario.

50. Cf. J.S. Moir, "The Correspondence of Bishop Strachan and John Henry Newman," *Canadian Journal of Theology* III (October 1957), 220.

51. A.N. Bethune to John Strachan, 25 January 1836, Strachan Papers, Public Archives of Ontario; A.N. Bethune, *Memoir of the Right Reverend John Strachan, D.D., LL.D., First Bishop of Toronto* (Toronto, 1870), 249ff.

52. Archbishop of Canterbury to John Strachan, 20 December 1851, copy, Strachan Papers, Public Archives of Ontario.

53. J.S. Moir, *Church and State in Canada West: Three Studies in the Relation of Denominationalism and Nationalism, 1841-1867* (Toronto: University of Toronto Press, 1959), 25.

54. Ibid.

55. *First Annual Report of the Canadian Foreign Missionary Society, 1853* (Montreal, 1853).

56. For a contemporary poetical reference see "A Sympathetic Ode" in J.S. Moir, ed., *Rhymes of Rebellion: Being a Selection of Contemporary Verses about the "Recent Unpleasantness" in Upper Canada, 1837* (Toronto: Ryerson Press, 1963), 70.

57. *Canadian Presbyterian Magazine*, February, 1855, on the Madiai case; or *The Ecclesiastical and Missionary Record*, October 1849, on the Achilli case.

58. Fred Landon, "When Uncle Tom's Cabin Came to Canada," *Ontario History* XLIV (January 1952), 1-5.

59. A.F. Kemp, *Digest of the Minutes of the Synod of the Presbyterian Church of Canada* (Montreal 1861) 347-55.

60. Alex Murray, "American Slavery as a Disruptive Factor in Canadian-American Church Relations," unpublished paper delivered to the Canadian Historical Association at Montreal, 9 June 1961.

61. J.K. Lewis, "Religious Nature of Early Negro Immigration to Canada and the Amherst Baptist Association," *Ontario History* LVIII (June 1965), 117-32; W.H and J.H. Pease, "Uncle Tom and Clayton: Fact, Fiction and Mystery," *Ontario History* L (1958), 61-73; Fred Landon, "The Work of the American Missionary Association among Negro Refugees in Canada West, 1845-1864," *Papers and Records of the Ontario Historical Society* XXI (1924), 198-205.

62. Murray, op. cit.

The Christian Guardian and Upper Canadian Politics

1. Paul Knaplund, ed., *Letters from Lord Sydenham, Governor General of Canada, 1839-1841, to Lord John Russell* (London, 1931), 54.

2. W.H. Kesterton, *A History of Journalism in Canada* (Toronto, 1967), 11.

3. *Christian Guardian* (hereafter *C.G.*), 2 October 1830.

4. *C.G.*, 7 December 1831.

5. *C.G.*, 21 December 1831.

6. *C.G.*, 28 December 1831.

7. *C.G.*, 25 April 1832.

8. For analyses of the controversial union, and the subsequent disunion, of the Canadian and British Wesleyan conferences, see C.B. Sissons, *Egerton Ryerson, His Life and Letters*, vol. I (Toronto, 1937), 152 et seq.; Goldwyn French, *Parsons & Politics* (Toronto, [1962]), 135-255, and John S. Moir, "Notes of Discord, Strains of Harmony: The Separation and Reunion of the Canadian and British Wesleyan Methodists, 1840-1867," *Canadian Methodist Historical Society Papers* 4 (1984), 1-7.

9. *C.G.*, 27 March, 24 April 1833.

10. *C.G.*, 13 November 1833. See also Sissons, *Ryerson*, I, 198-99.

11. *C.G.*, 13 November 1833.

12. *C.G.*, 20 November 1833.

13. *C.G.*, 4, 11 December 1833, 8 January 1834.

14. *C.G.*, 4 June 1834.

15. *C.G.*, 21 January 1835.

16. *C.G.*, 27 April 1836.

17. *C.G.*, 4 May 1836.

18. See Sissons, *Ryerson*, I, 315ff.

19. *C.G.*, 24 January 1838.

20. *C.G.*, 7 February 1838.

21. *C.G.*, 25 April 1838.

22. *C.G.*, 21 March 1838.

23. *C.G.*, 18 April 1838.

24. *C.G.*, 6 June 1838.

25. *C.G.*, 11 July 1838.

26. *C.G.*, 6 April 1839.

27. *C.G.*, 11 July 1838.

28. *C.G.*, 6 April 1839.

29. *C.G.*, 8 May 1839.

30. *C.G.*, 5 September 1838.

31. Joseph Stinson to Robert Alder ("entre nous"), 23 May 1839, File 159, Box 23, Wesleyan Methodist Missionary Society Papers, United Church Archives, (hereafter WMMS).

32. Alder to Stinson, 8 October 1839, File 158, Box 23, WMMS.

33. *Minutes of the Annual Conferences of the Wesleyan Methodist Church in Canada, 1824 to 1846 . . .* (Toronto, 1846), 234.

The Canadian Baptist and the Social Gospel

1. The major Canadian work is Richard Allen, *The Social Passion: Religion and Social Reform in Canada 1914-28* (Toronto, 1971). Among the significant articles are W.H. Magney, "The Methodist Church and the National Gospel," *The Bulletin (The United Church Archives)* 20 (1968); G.N. Emery, "The Origin of Canadian Methodist Involvement in the Social Gospel Movement 1890-1914," *The Bulletin* 26 (1977); Richard Allen, "The Social Gospel as the Religion of Agrarian Revolt," in Ramsay Cook and Carl Berger, eds., *The West and the Nation* (Toronto, 1976).

2. See, for instance, Brian Fraser, "Theology and the Social Gospel among Canadian Presbyterians: A Case Study," *Studies in Religion* VIII:1 (1979), 35-46; and W.W. Judd, "The Vision and the Dream," *The Journal of the Canadian Church History Society* VII:4 (December 1965).

3. Charles M. Johnston, *McMaster University, Volume One: The Toronto Years* (Toronto, 1976); W.G. Carder, "Controversy in the Baptist Convention of Ontario and Quebec 1908-1928," *Foundations* 16 (1975), 355-76; W.E. Ellis, "Gilboa to Ichabod: Social and Religious Factors in the Fundamentalist-Modernist Schisms Among Canadian Baptists, 1895-1934," *Foundations* 20 (1975); Fundamentalist," *Ontario History* LXX:4 (December 1978), 263-80. See also Jones H. Farmer, ed., *E.W. Dadson: The Man and His Message* (Toronto, 1902), Part I, Chap. VI and Part II, Chap. VII, for an old, brief and uncritical account of Dadson's editorial writings.

4. C.H. Hopkins, *The Rise of the Social Gospel in American Protestantism, 1865-1915* (New Haven, 1940), especially Part I.

5. H.U. Trinier. *A Century of Service* (Toronto: Baptist Convention of Ontario and Quebec, 1954), 70.

6. See *The Canadian Baptist* (hereafter cited as *CB*), 6 March 1879, 22 May 1879, 17 April 1879, 6 January 1881, 18 December 1879, 8 December 1881, and 6 April 1882.

7. *CB*, 4 December 1879.

8. *CB*, 31 January, 11 September 1884.

9. *CB*, 24 November 1887.

10. *CB*, 18 September 1884.

11. *CB*, 26 February, 29 January, 19 February 1885.

12. *CB*, 2 October 1884.

13. *CB*, 12 March 1885.

14. *CB*, 14 May 1885.

15. *CB*, 20 August 1885.

16. *CB*, 11 February 1886, 10 March 1887 *et passim*.

17. *CB*, 25 February 1886.

18. *CB*, 18 March 1886.

19. *CB*, 25 March 1886.

20. *CB*, 8 July 1886.

21. *CB*, 8 July, 5 August, 7 October 1886.

22. *CB*, 18 June, 16 February 1888.

23. *CB*, 13 January 1887.

24. *CB*, 4 September 1890.

25. *CB*, 21 January 1892.

26. *CB*, 14 July 1892.

27. *CB*, 18 August 1892.

28. *CB*, 3 May 1894.

29. *CB*, 12 July 1894.

30. *CB*, 4 March 1897.

31. *CB*, 21 December 1893.

32. *CB*, 8 March 1894.

33. *CB*, 3 September 1896.

34. *CB*, 14 January 1897.

35. Trinier, 82.

36. Ibid., 85.

37. *CB*, 7 June, 23 October 1902.

38. *CB*, 20 November 1902.

39. *CB*, 11 December 1902, 1 January, 5 February, 12 February 1903.

40. *CB*, 28 January 1904.

41. *CB*, 4 February 1904.

42. *CB*, 28 April 1904. See also Trinier, 88, regarding the possible desire to have a theologically trained editor.

43. Trinier, 93.

44. *CB*, 15 December 1904.

45. *CB*, 28 February 1905.

46. *CB*, 25 November 1909.

47. *CB*, 10 January 1910.

48. *CB*, 14 February 1910.

49. *CB*, 24 February, 21 April 1910.

50. *CB*, See C.M. Johnston, 110.

51. *CB*, 8 May 1913.

52. *CB*, 5 March 1914.

53. *CB*, 2 July 1914.

54. *CB*, 30 July 1914.

Problem of a Double Minority

1. For an account of Canadian Roman Catholic historiographic development that came in the next dozen years see my "Coming of Age, but Slowly: Aspects of Canadian religious historiography since Confederation," *Canadian Catholic Historical Association Study Sessions* (1983), I: 89-98., and the annual bibliography published by the Canadian Catholic Historical Association.

2. *Census of Canada*, 1871, Vol. 4.

3. Based on *Census of Canada*, 1911, and F.J. Audet, *Canadian Historical Dates and Events* (Ottawa, 1917).

4. This territorial devolution was completed when Macdonell was made bishop of Regiopolis in 1826 and MacEachern of Charlottetown in 1820. Kingston was thus the first Roman Catholic diocese established in the British Empire since the Reformation, and its erection came a quarter-century before the "Papal Aggression" controversy was sparked by a similar development in Great Britain.

5. This analysis is based on Audet, 166-70. In Prince Edward Island, 52 priests of Scottish origin were appointed, of whom 30 belonged to the Clan Macdonald. Of the 52, 28 were trained at the Quebec seminary and 10 at Montreal. See *Memorial Volume 1772-1922. The Arrival of the First Scottish Catholic Emigrants in Prince Edward Island and After* (Summerside, 1922), 109-27.

6. "Legion," ASSOCIATION OF IRISH GENTLEMEN, *A brief View of the State of the Catholic Church in Upper Canada, Shewing the Evil Results of an Undue Predominance of the French Foreign Element in the Administration of Ecclesiastical Affairs, and of the Advisableness of Petitioning the Sovereign Pontiff for a more Just Proportion of Bishops and Priests from the Old Country* (Toronto, 4 December 1858).

7. *Memorial Volume 1772-1922*, 72.

8. H.J. Somers, *The Life and Times of the Hon. and Rt. Rev. Alexander Macdonell, D.D., First Bishop of Upper Canada, 1762-1840* (Washington: Catholic University of America, 1931), 42. Mrs.

Joseph Greene, "St. Vincent de Paul's Church," *Niagara Historical Society Publications No.13*, (1906), 26, comments on the numerical prominence of Irish among early Roman Catholic settlers.

9. See, e.g., Bro. Alfred Dooner, *Catholic Pioneers in Upper Canada* (Toronto: Macmillan, 1947), 20-21, n. 40 *et passim*.

10. J.R. Teefy, ed., *The Archdiocese of Toronto and Archbishop Walsh: Jubilee Volume 1842-1892* (Toronto: G.T. Dixon, 1892), 64, "The Irish Catholics . . . came in such numbers as soon to constitute the bone and sinew of the Church in this country."

11. W.J. Macdonell, *Reminiscences of the Late Hon. and Right Rev. Alexander Macdonell . . .* (Toronto, 1888), 6 *et passim*. Between 1824 and 1835, Macdonell received at least £3,550 and 1,600 acres from the government.

12. Macdonell to J.J. Lartigue, 2 April 1821, "There are some Irish families . . . not being accustomed to pay tythes to Catholic clergymen in their own country do not consider themselves obligated to do so now." Macdonell Papers, I, 79-80, Public Archives of Ontario.

13. Unlike the French-Canadian bishops, the English-speaking bishops were chronically short of funds until the post-Confederation years, a fact which several congregations exploited by opposing church building projects. As James Baby reported of St. Paul's parish, Toronto, in 1824, "None, hardly of the people . . . have paid their subscription money." Edward Kelly, *The Story of St. Paul's Parish, Toronto* (Toronto, 1922), 44. As late as 1891, that particular congregation was paying $3,650 interest annually on the church debt (ibid., 137-9).

14. Macdonell to Cardinal Weld, 6 May 1827, complaining that Irish priests bring their "politics and party feelings" to Canada: Macdonell Papers, III, 268-9, Public Archives of Ontario; Macdonell to Major Hillier, 23 March 1823, has dismissed 4 Irish priests and others are "roaming through the country to the no small injury of religion and of the people over whom they wish to acquire influence." Ibid., II, 198; Macdonell to the Rev. Angus Macdonald, 20 August 1832, "Some of my Irish clergy taking advantage of the reduced state of my mind have done and are still doing all they can to weaken and oppose my authority." Ibid., VIII, 1063-6.

15. Of 48 priests ordained in the London diocese between 1857 and 1884, at least 25 bore Irish surnames. See J.F. Coffey, *The City and Diocese of London, Ontario, Canada. An Historical Sketch* (London, 1885), 61-2.

16. The "Papal Aggression" controversy prevented the emergence of a Catholic-Protestant. Reform alliance as surely as the grow ing Irish influence in the Church destroyed the earlier conservative alliance between Macdonell and the Orange Order. In the latter connection, it must have been common and unpleasant knowledge among Irish Catholics that their bishop owed much of his prestige with the Imperial and colonial governments to his role as chaplain of the Scottish Catholic troops who had helped to crush the Irish rebellion of 1798.

17. Arthur Monahan, "A Politico-Religious Incident in the Career of Thomas D'Arcy McGee," Canadian Catholic Historical Association, *Report 1957*, 39-51.

18. J.A. Gallagher, "The Irish Emigration of 1847 and its Canadian Consequences," Canadian Catholic Historical Association, *Report 1935-6*, 43-57; G.R.C. Kerr, "The Irish Adjustment in Montreal," *Canadian Historical Review* XXXI (1), March 1956, 39-46; W.P. Bull, *From Macdonell to McGuigan* (Toronto, 1939), 134.

19. J.J. Curran, ed., *Golden Jubilee of St. Patrick's Orphan Asylum*, (Montreal, 1902), 25ff.

20. Macdonell to Cardinal Weld, 6 May 1827. Macdonell Papers, III, 268-9.

21. L.K. Shook, "St. Michael's College: The Formative Years, 1850-53," Canadian Catholic Historical Association, *Report 1950*, 43. When de Charbonnel's ambitious plans for a Little Seminary failed to develop for lack of money, teachers and pupils, educational energies were channelled into the classical college that became St. Michael's.

22. F.A. O'Brien, *Most Reverend Dennis O'Connor, D.D., C.S.B., Archbishop of Toronto, Ontario: Life and Work of a Saintly Prelate* (Kalamazoo: Augustinian Print, 1914), unpaged.

23. F.J. O'Sullivan, *The Chronicles of Crofton* (Toronto: Hunter-Rose, 1926), 174.

24. C.B. Sissons, ed., *My Dearest Sophie: Letters from Egerton Ryerson to his Daughter* (Toronto: Ryerson Press, 1955), 55.

25. P.F. Cronin, "Early Catholic Journalism in Canada," Canadian Catholic Historical Association, *Report 1935-6*, 31-42; Agnes Coffey, "*The True Witness and Catholic Chronicle*: Sixty Years of Catholic Journalistic Action," Canadian Catholic Historical Association, *Report 1937-8*, 33-46. On the role of the *Mélanges Religieux*, see Jacques Monet, "French Canadian Nationalism and the Challenge of Ultramontanism," Canadian Historical Association, *Historical Papers 1966*, 41-55.

26. See Sister Maura, *The Sisters of Charity, Halifax* (Toronto: Ryerson Press, 1956), 2, 6-7; Anon., *The Life and Letters of Rev. Mother Theresa Dease, Foundress and Superior General of the Institute of the Blessed Virgin Mary* (Toronto, 1916), 11: Mary Hoskin, *History of St. Basil's Parish* (Toronto, 1912), 52 *et passim*; Marion Bell, "The History of the Catholic Welfare Bureau," (unpublished M.S.W. thesis, University of Toronto, 1949), 14 *et passim*.

27. Theobald Spetz, *The Catholic Church in Waterloo County* (Kingston: Catholic Register, 1916), 226-38.

28. J.A. Lenhard, "German Catholics in Ontario," Canadian Catholic Historical Association, *Report 1936-7*, 41-5.

29. *Anno Domini MDCCCCI*, 2 vols. (Toronto, 1902), I, 81.

30. Spetz, 130-261.

31. In "Catholicism and Secular Culture: Australia and Canada Compared" (*Culture* XXX, No. 2 [juin 1969], 93-113), Timothy Suttor points to several historical factors which have blunted the "racial memory" of English Canadian Catholicism.

32. See e.g. Shook, 45.

33. Richard J. Dobell, *Fifty Golden Years 1913-1961, St. Augustine's Seminary* (Scarborough, Ontario: The Seminary, 1963), 1; Bro. Alfred Dooner, 212, 215-6.

34. George Boyle, *Pioneer in Purple, the Life and Work of Archbishop Neil McNeil* (Montreal: Palm Publishers, 1951), 33, 70.

35. Toronto *Globe*, 29 January 1876.

36. H.C. McKeown, *The Life and Labors of Most Rev. John Joseph Lynch, D.D., Cong. Miss., First Archbishop of Toronto* (Montreal, 1886), 308-9.

37. D.A. O'Sullivan, *Essays on the Church in Canada* (Toronto, 1890), 17, "Every Catholic is . . . an ultramontane Catholic, and . . . whoever is not ultramontane is no Catholic."

38. J.C. Dent, *Canadian Portrait Gallery*, 4 vols. (Toronto, 1880), I, 145.

39. E.J. Legal, *Short Sketches of the History of the Catholic Churches in Central Alberta*, (Winnipeg: West Canada Publishing Company, 1914) 27.

40. Legal, 104-13.

Origin of the Separate Schools Question

1. J.G. Hodgins, ed., *Documentary History of Education in Upper Canada*, 28 vols. (Toronto, 1894-1910), III, 124. Hereafter cited as *DHE*.

2. Ibid., IV, 4.

3. Ibid., 32.

4. Ibid., 15.

5. Ibid., 232, 236-43, 249-62.

6. J.G. Hodgins, *Legislation and History of Separate Schools in Upper Canada, 1841-1876* (Toronto, 1897), 30.

7. E. Ryerson to W.H. Draper, 29 March 1847, Hodgins Papers, Public Archives of Ontario.

8. *DHE*, VIII, 142.

9. Ibid., IX, 11.

10. Twelve resident heads of Roman Catholic families were now required instead of ten, as formerly, to establish a separate school where the common school teacher was a Protestant.

11. *Globe*, 9 July 1850.

12. Ibid.

13. *DHE*, IX, 208.

14. Ibid., 240; X, 88. Some 34,000 destitute Irish settled in Toronto in 1847 alone.

15. Ibid., X, 91-2.

16. *Globe*, 24 June 1851.

17. *DHE*, IX, 237 *et seq.*

18. *Copies of Correspondence between the Roman Catholic Bishop of Toronto and the Chief Superintendent of Schools on the Subject of Separate Common Schools in Upper Canada . . .* Toronto, 1853), 7 *et seq.*

19. *DHE*, X, 163.

20. Adam Townley, *Seven Letters on the Non-Religious Common School System of Canada and the United States* (Toronto, 1853), 51.

21. *Globe*, 2 and 5 April 1853; cf. Francis Hincks, *Reminiscences of his Public Life* (Montreal, 1884), 312.

22. *DHE*, X, 295-302.

23. Ibid., XI, 109.

24. *Dr. Ryerson's Letters in reply to the Attacks of the Hon. George Brown, M.P.P.* (Toronto, 1859), 32.

25. *DHE*, XII, 8.

26. H.C. McKeown, *The Life and Labors of Most Rev. John Joseph Lynch, D.D., Cong. Miss., First Archbishop of Toronto* (Montreal, 1886), 296, n.; *DHE*, XII, 16-19.

27. *DHE*, XII, 40.

28. *News of the Week*, 2 February 1856.

29. J. Strachan to J.H. Cameron, 10 March 1856, Letter Book 1854-1862, p.124, Strachan Papers, Public Archives of Ontario.

30. *News of the Week*, 11 July 1856.

31. *DHE*, XVII, 214; ibid., 198-213.

32. C.B. Sissons, *Life and Letters of Egerton Ryerson*, 2 vols. (Toronto, 1937, 1947), II, 446.

33. *Globe*, 20 March 1863; *Canadian Freeman*, 19 March 1863.

34. Bowmanville *Statesman*, 9 August 1866; St. Catherines *Constitutional*, 9 August 1866.

Canadian Religious Historiography

1. Robert T. Handy, *A History of the Churches in the United States and Canada* (New York, 1977), vii.

2. See W.S. Wallace, ed., *The Ryerson Imprint* (Toronto, 1954) and Lorne Pierce, *The House of Ryerson 1829-1954* (Toronto, 1954).

3. In his perceptive article, "The Religious History of Atlantic Canada: The State of the Art," *Acadiensis* 15:1 (1985), 152-74, Terence Murphy suggests that the qualitative impact of the postwar religious historiographic revolution appeared in the Atlantic region only in the 1970s.

4. N.K. Clifford, "Religion and the Development of Canadian Society: An Historiographic Analysis," *Church History* 38 (December 1969), 506-23.

5. Baptists in other regions have produced a few monographs but nothing comparable to production in the Atlantic region.

6. An abbreviated version of this volume was also published as "Historical Booklet No. 40" by the Canadian Historical Association in 1985.

7. The ethnic nature of the Catholic Church in western Canada is a major theme in several diocesan histories from that region, but the only general history of that vast area, A.G. Morice's two-volume *History of the Catholic Church in Western Canada* (Toronto, 1910) is now of limited value.

8. John Webster Grant, "Asking Questions of the Canadian Past," *Canadian Journal of Theology* 1:2 (July 1955), 102-3.

9. Mark G. McGowan, "Coming Out of the Cloister: Some Reflections on Developments in the Study of Religion in Canada, 1980-1990," *International Journal of Canadian Studies/Revue internationale d'études canadiennnes* 1-2 (Spring-Fall/Printemps-automne 1990): 177. See also Guy Laperièrre, "L'histoire religieuse du Québec: Principaux courants, 1979-1988," and Paul Laverdure, "Tendences dominantes de l'historiographie religieuse au Canada anglais," *Revue d'histoire de l'Amérique française 42:4* (Printemps 1989), 363-87.

10. Symptomatic of this tendency, a regional society, the British Columbia Church History Group, has recently been established.

11. See "The Silencers," "A War of Words," and "Saying 'No' to the Old Ways," *Maclean's*, 27 May 1991, 40-43, 44-56, 48-50.

Other Publications
by Paul Laverdure

Redemption and Renewal:
The Redemptorists of English Canada, 1834-1994
(Toronto: 1996). Hard cover, illus., index, bibliographic notes,
6 x 10, xvii+380 p. Originally $34.95.
Including shipping, handling and all taxes,
Now $24.95.

Murder in the Monastery:
Catholic and Orthodox in Yorkton, 1934
(Yorkton: 2001). Issue 15, Redemptorist North American
Historical Bulletin. Soft cover, illus., 8 1/2 x 11, 20 p.
Includes taxes, shipping and handling,
$4.00.

Twelve Lays of Christmas:
Carols, Hymns, Prayers and Poems
by the Redemptorists of English Canada
(Yorkton: 2001). Soft cover, illus., 4 x 5, viii+24 p.
Includes taxes, shipping and handling,
$3.00.

Brother Reginald:
A Poet in Moose Jaw
(Yorkton: 2002). Soft cover, illus.,
5 1/2 x 8 1/2. Forthcoming.
Includes taxes, shipping and handling,
$7.50.

Send cheque payable to:

Laverdure & Associates
Box 246,
Gravelbourg, Sask.
SOH 1XO Canada.

prices subject to change without notice